BRA

LATE
VICTORIAN
WORLD

edited by Matthew Gibson and
Sabine Lenore Müller

BRAM STOKER
and the LATE VICTORIAN WORLD

edited by Matthew Gibson and
Sabine Lenore Müller

CLEMSON
UNIVERSITY
PRESS

First Edition, 2018
Paperback Edition, 2022

ISBN: 978-1-942954-64-4 (print)
ISBN: 978-1-80207-031-6 (paperback)
eISBN: 978-1-942954-65-1 (eISBN)

Published by Clemson University Press
in association with Liverpool University Press

For information about Clemson University Press,
please visit our website at www.clemson.edu/press.

Library of Congress Cataloging-in-Publication Data
Names: Gibson, Matthew, 1967- editor. | Müller, Sabine Lenore, editor.
Title: Bram Stoker and the late Victorian world / edited by Matthew
Gibson and Sabine Lenore Müller. Description: First edition. | Clemson,
South Carolina : Clemson University Press in association with Liverpool
University Press, 2018. | Includes bibliographical references and index.
Identifiers: LCCN 2018029857 (print) | LCCN 2018048825 (ebook) |
ISBN 9781942954651 (e-book) | ISBN 9781942954644 |
Subjects: LCSH: Stoker, Bram, 1847-1912--Criticism and interpretation.
Classification: LCC PR6037.T617 (ebook) | LCC PR6037.T617 Z576
2018 (print) | DDC 823/.914--dc23
LC record available at https://lccn.loc.gov/2018029857

Typeset in Minion Pro by Carnegie Book Production.
Printed and bound by CPI Group (UK) Ltd, Croydon CR0 4YY

Contents

Section II: Science, Technology, and Ideas

Section III: Politics and Society

Illustrations

Acknowledgments

Matthew Gibson would like to express his gratitude to Serena Thirkell and Toby Crick for allowing him to reproduce an unpublished letter from Edward Burne-Jones to Bram Stoker dated May 2, 1895. He would also like to express his thanks to Harvard Art Museums for allowing him to reproduce D. G. Rossetti's *The Blessed Damozel*, and to Bridgeman Images of London for permitting him to reproduce Charles Rossiter's *Children in a Church Yard*. He would further like to thank the staff at the Brotherton Library, University of Leeds, for their courtesy and help. Finally, he would also like to acknowledge the generosity of the Metropolitan Museum of New York in allowing the free reproduction of digital images, which enabled him to reproduce Velazquez's *Juan de Pareja* in his chapter.

Rebecca E. May would like to thank the staff of the University of Pittsburgh Archives Services Center and Jessy Horkey, Director of Microfilm, Mahoning County Commissioners Office, Youngstown, Ohio.

Matthew Gibson and William Hughes would like to thank Princeton University Library for providing them with a copy of Bram Stoker's letter of November 14, 1884 to Laurence Hutton. © Noel Dobbs & Robin MacCaw 2018. Published courtesy of the Bram Stoker Estate Collection.

Abbreviations

D	*Dracula*, ed. Roger Luckhurst (Oxford: Oxford University Press, 2011)
GoL	*The Gates of Life* (New York: Cupples and Leon Co., 1908)*
JSS	*The Jewel of Seven Stars*, ed. Kate Hebblethwaite (Oxford: Oxford University Press, 2008)
LA	*Lady Athlyne: an Annotated Edition*, ed. Carol Senf (Westcliff-on-Sea: Desert Island Books, 2007)
LWW	*The Lair of the White Worm and The Lady of the Shroud*, with an introduction by David Stuart Davies (Ware: Wordsworth Editions, 2010)
SnB	*Snowbound: the Record of a Theatrical Touring Party*, ed. Bruce Wightman (Westcliff-on Sea: Desert Island Books, 2000)
SoS	*The Shoulder of Shasta*, ed. Alan Johnson (Westcliff-on-Sea: Desert Island Books, 2000)
SP	*The Snake's Pass* (Dingle: Brandon, 1990)
TLS	*The Lady of the Shroud*, introduced by Ruth Robbins (Stroud: Alan Sutton Publishing, 1997)
TMS	*The Mystery of the Sea*, ed. Carol A. Senf (Kansas: Valancourt Books, 2007)

* *The Gates of Life* is the American edition of Stoker's novel *The Man* (1905), and contains subtle differences from the earlier version. For this reason, while Matthew Gibson and Damian Shaw have used this one, Carol Senf refers to the earlier edition in her own piece and so uses a separate set of citations.

Contributors

Jimmie E. Cain is currently Professor of English at Middle Tennessee University, having earlier served in the U.S. Army from 1973 to 1976 as a crew chief on a UH-IH "Huey" helicopter, and having studied for a Ph.D. in Victorian Literature at Georgia State University. His publications include "*Women*: The Siren Calls of Boredom," *The Review of Contemporary Fiction* (1985) (*Women* is a novel by Charles Bukowski); "'Writing in his musical key': Terence Malick's Vision of *The Thin Red Line*," *Film Criticism* (2000); "War Comes to Cicely," *Critical Studies in Television* (2006); *Bram Stoker and Russophobia: Evidence of the British Fear of Russia in* Dracula *and* The Lady of the Shroud, McFarland & Co., Inc. (2006); and "The Combat Veteran as a Monstrous Other," *Vergemeinschaftung in Zeiten der Zombie-Apokalypse* (2015).

Anne DeLong is an Associate Professor of English at Kutztown University of Pennsylvania, where she teaches courses in nineteenth-century British literature and women's studies. She received her Ph.D. in English from Lehigh University. DeLong is the author of *Mesmerism, Medusa, and the Muse: The Romantic Discourse of Spontaneous Creativity* (2012) and *Classic Horror: A Historical Exploration of Literature* and *The Victorian World: A Historical Exploration of Literature* (both forthcoming). She is currently working on a research monograph tentatively titled *Haunted Narratives: The Subversive Supernatural in Ghost Stories by Victorian Women Writers.*

She has also published a critical edition of Marie Corelli's first novel, *A Romance of Two Worlds* (2011). DeLong is co-editor of *The Journal of Dracula Studies* and President of the Transylvanian Society of Dracula.

Rui Carvalho Homem is Professor of English at the University of Oporto, Portugal. He is the author of *Shakespeare and the Drama of Alterity* (in Portuguese; 2003) and *Poetry and Translation in Northern Ireland: Dislocations in Contemporary Writing* (2009), and the editor of several collections on Irish writing, early modern English drama, translation, and intermediality. As a literary translator he has published annotated versions of Shakespeare, Christopher Marlowe, Seamus Heaney, and Philip Larkin. He is currently the Chair of ESRA, the European Shakespeare Research Association.

Matthew Gibson is Associate Professor of English Literature at the University of Macau. He is the author of *Yeats, Coleridge and the Romantic Sage* (2000), *Dracula and the Eastern Question: British and French Vampire Narratives of the Nineteenth Century Near East* (2006), and *The Fantastic and European Gothic: History, Literature and the French Revolution* (2013). He is currently collaborating with William Hughes on a *Selected Correspondence of Bram Stoker*.

Terry Hale has worked for most of his academic career in the fields of translation studies, nineteenth-century French literature, and the Gothic, although originally trained as a solicitor (Nottingham Law School), and taught law for a number of years at Paris Nanterre University. His various publications include editions of J.-K. Huysmans's *Là-bas* (as *The Damned*), Robert Desnos's early Surrealist classic *Liberty or Love!* (1993), and *The Dedalus Book of French Horror: the 19th Century* (1998). In 1998 he was invested Chevalier de l'Ordre des Arts et des Lettres by the French Government.

William Hughes is Professor of Medical Humanities and Gothic Literature at Bath Spa University, England. He is the author, editor or co-editor of nineteen books, including *Beyond Dracula: Bram Stoker's Fiction and* *its Cultural Context* (2000), *The Historical Dictionary of Gothic Fiction* (2013), *That Devil's Trick: Hypnotism and the Victorian Popular Imagination* (2015) and *Key Concepts in the Gothic* (2018). He is a past President of the International Gothic Association and was editor of the journal *Gothic Studies* from its first volume in 1999 to its twentieth in 2018.

Rebecca E. May is a Teaching Assistant Professor at Duquesne University, where she teaches classes in writing, literature, and the medical humanities. Her research in Gothic literature and experimental medicine has appeared in *Nineteenth-Century Contexts* and Julie Peakman's *Sexual Perversions 1670–1890*.

Sabine Lenore Müller currently works as an Associate Professor of English Studies at Zhejiang International Studies University. She has presented papers, published articles, and organized conferences focused on Irish Studies topics, comparative literature, and environmental philosophy. In 2014 she worked as a post-doctoral research fellow at the University of Macau. Under the supervision of Prof. Matthew Ian Gibson she collaborated in a project focusing on the edition of Bram Stoker's manuscripts and correspondences. In 2015 she co-organized and contributed to an international symposium on Bram Stoker and his Victorian connections held in Macau.

Carol Senf, Professor at Georgia Tech, specializes in Gothic Studies, focusing on Bram Stoker. She has written three books and a number of articles on Stoker, as well as one book and a number of articles on *Dracula*, and annotated two of his novels to make them accessible to readers. She has also written on film adaptations of Stoker novels and on Stephen King, Joseph Sheridan LeFanu, Mary Shelley, and Montague Summers, as well as on mainstream nineteenth-century writers, including the Brontes, Dickens, Eliot, Hardy, and Sarah Grand. Her most recent book (co-authored with Sherri Brown and Ellen Stockstill) is *A Research Guide to Gothic Literature in English* (2018). After raising two sons, she and her husband Jay live in Atlanta with their dog Mickey and two cats, Frida and Whitby.

Damian Shaw joined the University of Macau in 2008 and holds an assistant professorship. He has also lectured in South Africa (1997–2002) and Quanzhou (2002–08) in English Literature. He was a language researcher and specialist music editor for the Cambridge International Dictionary of English. Damian's research interests relate to colonial writing of the Romantic and Victorian eras, including poetry, travel writing, and anti-slavery literature, as well as the Gothic. He is particularly interested in representations of China and Africa during this period.

Preface

The almost spectral image of the unsmiling Stoker, staring from the few old photographs which remain of him, are perhaps not quite as iconographic as the various film stills of the actors who played his most famous creation, Dracula, but in recent years they have become increasingly visible. Since Harry Ludlam wrote his first biography in the 1960s, and brought back to attention the initial novel that had spawned such a cultural phenomenon, further interest in the Gothic genre has propelled *Dracula* to the position of a classic, studied in many major English literature degree courses across the world. Likewise the rising interest in the Victorian theater, promoted by the likes of Jacky Bratton, has also led to an increased interest in Stoker's working milieu, the Victorian stage, in which he played a prominent if somewhat arduous role as Acting Manager to Henry Irving at the Lyceum. The success of recent bestselling biographies by the likes of Paul Murray (2004) and David Skal (2017), placing him firmly in the context of the Fin-de-Siècle and his Irish background, have demonstrated the growing fascination with the man and the rest of his world outside *Dracula*.

Interest in the fiction that he wrote besides *Dracula* has been steadily increasing over time. William Hughes's seminal *Beyond Dracula* (Palgrave, 2000), a work which opened up Stoker's other sixteen books to the general public, is perhaps the first tome of this kind, and was of immeasurable value in drawing attention to Stoker's other fictional works. Carol Senf's first monograph on Stoker, *Science and Social Science in Bram Stoker's Fiction* (Greenwood, 2002), also went "beyond Dracula" in observing the effect of the contemporary episteme on Stoker's work. Lisa Hopkins's study of 2007 also analyzed Stoker's wider fiction, although under particular themes rather than as a "text-by-text" analysis.[1] In 2010 Carol Senf's second monograph on Stoker, *Bram Stoker* (University of Wales Press), explored the larger contribution made by the author to developing the Gothic as a genre. Catherine Wynne has provided the only monograph to date that actually places Stoker's fiction in the context of his life and experience as a theater manager in her book *Bram Stoker, Dracula, and the Victorian Gothic Stage* (Palgrave Macmillan, 2013).

In relation to collections of essays on Stoker's fiction, so far only three of any great note have been published. The first was William Hughes and Andrew Smith's *Bram Stoker: History, Psychoanalysis, and the Gothic* (Palgrave, 1998), and two more recent ones: in 2014 Four Courts Press published *Bram Stoker: Centenary Essays*, edited by Jarlath Killeen, to celebrate the Stoker centenary in 2012; and Catherine Wynne edited a collection of essays entitled *Bram Stoker and the Gothic: Formations to Transformations* (Palgrave Macmillan, 2013), in which the contributors examined the wider significance of the Gothic genre on Stoker's other fictional works.

Where this collection is different from the aforementioned ones is its context and emphases. Unlike in the editions edited by Hughes, Smith, and Wynne, few of the pieces in this volume are particularly theoretical or concerned with issues such as gender, post-colonialism, or psychoanalytical study. That is not to say that the importance of imperialism, Stoker's Irish identity, or attitudes to women are not explored. Rather, the aim has been to ground the study of Stoker's fictional and nonfictional work empirically against the background of the late Victorian world, drawing upon manuscripts and archives, such as Stoker's correspondence, and his own enthusiasms and interests, and in particular against the background of his metropolitan life. The result is a volume of essays that attempts to restore the historical realities of both Stoker's late Victorian and early Edwardian context, and in doing so to provide a window onto that milieu through his life, work, and fiction.

The essays are divided into three sections: Professions; Science, Technology and Ideas; and Politics and Society. The first section begins with an essay entitled "Bram Stoker, *Dracula* and the English Common Law," by Terry Hale, which observes Stoker's work as a clerk of petty sessions in Ireland, his late training as a barrister, and the impact of the famous "Regina vs. Dudley and Stephens Case" (1884), and how these experiences played a part in shaping first *The Snake's Pass* and then *Dracula*. This is followed by Rui Carvalho Homem's investigation of Stoker's role as theater manager and reviewer, his relationship with Sir Henry Irving, how these impacted his portrayal of Irving in his memoirs, and the extent to which Stoker was attempting to fashion his own and Irving's image in the public eye. In the third chapter, Matthew Gibson expatiates on Stoker's relationship, again as reviewer and theater manager, with scene-painting, portrait-painting, and the profession of the painter, and how these elements influence and are portrayed in his novels, in particular *The Mystery of the Sea* (1903), *The Shoulder of Shasta* (1895), and *The Gates of Life* (1908).

The second section, Science, Technology and Ideas, approaches Stoker's fiction from the perspective of both technology and beliefs during the epoch. Sabine Lenore Müller's piece explores Stoker's attitudes to evolutionary theory and ideas of community against the backdrop of his close friendship with the socialist novelist Hall Caine. In the fifth chapter, Anne DeLong's "Communication Technologies in Bram Stoker's *Dracula*: Utopian or Dystopian?" observes principally the portrayal of "cutting-edge" technology, balancing the dystopian uses of technology like shorthand and type-writing against their more Utopian uses. The last piece in this section, by Rebecca E. May, observes the practices of the coroner in the nineteenth century, with particular emphasis on the rise of medical expertise, to argue that *Dracula* as a novel can be understood as a failed autopsy.

The third section, Politics and Society, begins with Jimmie E. Cain's examination of Bram Stoker's attitude to international politics and the British Empire, first through his life and secondly through his writings. In chapter eight, Damian Shaw looks at Stoker's ambiguous portrayal of the aristocracy in his novels, to conclude that, in works such as *The Jewel of Seven Stars*, Stoker condones a new type of aristocrat, which involves a eugenic blending with other races. In chapter nine Carol Senf examines the portrayal of the American "frontiersman" in novels such as *Dracula* (1897), *The Man* (1905) (rewritten as *The Gates of Life* (1908)), and *The Shoulder of Shasta* (1895), and outlines Stoker's ambivalent attitude to a figure that was already disappearing as a result of urbanization. Finally, there is a short coda: an edited letter from Stoker to Laurence Hutton, the theater critic and travel writer to whom he sent some of his most interesting correspondence.

What emerges in all of these essays is the extent to which Stoker was a man whose personality and beliefs were beset by contradictions. He was an Irish Home-ruler who also held high esteem for the British Empire as a bulwark against Russia; an advocate of the Anglo-Saxon people who was prepared to scorn and ridicule the English aristocrat against his Celtic counterparts in *The Lady of the Shroud*; a devotee of American culture who both praised and denigrated the American frontiersman in his novels; a man who analyzed the temperament of the artist in terms of both its advantages and disadvantages, as well as its various schools; a man who both praised and satirized the aristocracy in equal measure.

Looming large in Stoker's life and work is the "Guv'nor:" his boss, Sir Henry Irving, who afforded him the opportunity to embrace the metropolitan life in London as Acting Manager of the Lyceum, the exact nature of whose relationship with Stoker still divides critics and biographers. Both David Skal and Paul Murray question the degree to which the portrayal of firm friendship and partnership which Stoker promotes in *Personal Reminiscences of Henry Irving* is in fact correct,[2] with Murray noting the somewhat spiteful way in which Irving encouraged one of Stoker's enemies, Louis Frederick Austin, who worked for the company on their American tours as an informal secretary, to satirize him publicly,[3] and Skal noting that it was H. J. Loveday, the stage manager, and not Stoker, who shared a key from the office to the backstage.[4] Irving's immense importance for shaping Stoker's career—and even the personalities of some of his fictional creations—is undeniable. However, as this volume shows, relations with other notables and dignitaries of the era, such as Edward Burne-Jones, Edward Dowden, Hall Caine, Rudyard Kipling, and Genevieve Ward all made their impact upon his life and his writing. The Lyceum provided Stoker with a radiant network of eminent friends and associates that was of enormous importance in molding his fiction and ideas, and these very biographical influences are amongst the themes discussed in the following volume.

Just as important, however, is the climate of ideas and practices in this era. Indeed, the late Victorian and early Edwardian world, a time of growing technology, high imperialism, mutating political alliances, continuing progress in evolutionary theory, changing artistic trends, changing relations between men and women, and aristocratic decline, was an era not only different from the earlier part of the nineteenth century but one in which the actual pace of change had accelerated, and was accelerating even further. This pace of change, and with it an ominous sense of destruction, is perhaps recorded in Stoker's penultimate novel, *The Lady of the Shroud* (1909), but almost all Stoker's novels are capable of reflecting the topical zeitgeist, whether the mania for Egyptology in *The Jewel of Seven Stars* (1903) or the passion for the new world and frontiersman-ship in *The Gates of Life* (1908) and *The Shoulder of Shasta* (1905). These ideas and more find their imprint in Stoker's novels owing to the immense thirst for knowledge possessed by the author.

This volume grew from an original seminar held at the University of Macau over March 26–28, 2015, based on the ongoing project by Matthew Gibson and William Hughes to collect Bram Stoker's correspondence with a view to publishing a selected edition. It is a great pleasure to be able to bring several of the original pieces, together with some additions, to the attention of Stoker scholars and students, and to contribute to the ongoing promotion of Stoker's fiction and non-fictional writing.

SECTION I

Professions

CHAPTER ONE

Bram Stoker, *Dracula*, and the English Common Law

Terry Hale

Introduction

Over the course of the last two decades or so there has been a wide range of biographical and critical responses to Bram Stoker and his literary *oeuvre*: Bram Stoker in relation to Henry Irving; Bram Stoker in relation to nineteenth-century Ireland; Bram Stoker and homosocial desire; Bram Stoker in relation to the homosexual subcultures of the period; Bram Stoker and the concept of modernity; Bram Stoker in relation to the Victorian stage, particularly the Lyceum; Bram Stoker as Victorian and Edwardian man of letters; and, of course, Bram Stoker as the author of *Dracula*. In many cases these approaches, and there are others, tend to overlap.

One issue that has received scant attention, however, has been Stoker's legal career.[1] This is all the more surprising as it is generally accepted that those writers who have occupied the lawyer's stool for however short a period, and no matter how unwillingly, tend to develop a kind of legal imagination which informs all their subsequent work. This is certainly the case with Balzac, Dickens, and Wilkie Collins, to name but three.

In many cases, only a minimal formal training—indeed, in some cases (Trollope provides a good example), no formal training of any kind—is necessary to develop this legal imagination. Balzac spent only two-and-a-half years in the mid-1820s as a junior legal clerk, learning how to draw up contracts, learning how to get out of them, and, more importantly, learning that there is no defense against the legal profession. Not surprisingly, the experience marked him for life. "It is difficult for a young man to remain pure"—Balzac later wrote with characteristic pessimism about a legal education—"he will have seen the oily wheels of every fortune, the hideous wrangling of heirs over corpses not yet cold, the human heart grappling with the Penal Code."[2] Not surprisingly, Balzac is often seen as the pre-eminent nineteenth-century French author with regard to matters of legal chicanery and unhappy marriages.

Dickens's hated legal career was even more short-lived. But his stint, aged fifteen, as a junior clerk at the premises of Ellis and Blackmore in Holborn had a similar level of impact on his future development as a writer. Even Wilkie Collins, perhaps the primary architect of British sensation fiction, occupied the lawyer's stool for only five years—his formal training taking the same shape, despite the disparity in their ages, as that of Stoker forty years later at the Inner Temple, of a pupillage at Lincoln's Inn. Collins qualified for the Bar in 1851, never practiced law, but wrote incessantly about legal matters, mainly of a criminal nature, until his death thirty-eight years later.

Stoker's practical and academic involvement with the law was not a short-term matter as it was with Balzac, Dickens, or even Collins. In one way or another, he spent the best part of sixteen years learning the law: twelve years as a Civil Servant in and around Dublin, starting at the age of nineteen; and four years in London reading for the Bar at the Inner Temple in the second half of the 1880s, qualifying as a barrister in 1890, at the relatively advanced age of forty-three.

In addition to these sixteen years of direct contact with the law, however, Stoker also worked for some twenty-seven years (including the four years of his pupillage) in a largely legal-commercial capacity as Sir Henry Irving's business manager both at the Lyceum and on tour in the United States and elsewhere. The legal aspects of such a position should not be minimized. Stoker's duties, which were entirely unrelated to the artistic direction of the theater, would have focused primarily on five areas where a knowledge of the law was either useful or essential: firstly, contractual and commercial issues related to the Lyceum's vast army of actors, designers, playwrights, musicians, and composers, together with stage-hands, technicians (carpenters, lighting crews, scene-painters, seamstresses, dressers, etc.), front and back of house staff, and outside contractors and suppliers; secondly, copyright issues, some of an extremely complex nature; thirdly, issues related to Irving's lease of the theater, including responsibility for building work, maintenance of the property, general finance, contracts of insurance, and even ticket fraud;[3] fourthly, the hiring of venues for the Lyceum's touring company at home and abroad; and, finally, the legal and logistical issues of transporting and lodging large traveling companies, together with their costumes and sets, vast distances.

Some idea of the legal complexities with which a theater manager might be confronted is given by Stoker's "A Moon-Light Effect" (1908)[4]—a story dealing with the bankruptcy of a theater, the seizure of its assets by the Receiver, and the legal situation regarding goods belonging to an independent scene-painter renting space in the theater's workshop. Indeed, the entire story hinges on the nature of the lease that the scene-painter's wily solicitor had insisted he signed with the lessee of the theater.

The range, nature, and scale of the legal problems likely to arise when a company was on tour abroad must have been staggering. The Lyceum's first tour of America and Canada in 1883–84, for example, involved a company of several hundred performers and technicians, not forgetting the three wigmakers required to tend the cast's eleven hundred wigs, together with the transportation of the spectacular sets and costumes for twelve plays. During the course of the next twenty years, and a further seven tours, the Lyceum company, together with their enormous loads of scenery and costumes, traversed more than 50,000 miles by train, braving storms, floods, and blizzards in order to perform in locations as far afield as San Francisco, New Orleans, and Montreal.[5] Not only was Stoker the administrative genius behind all this activity, but he was also responsible for every legal and quasi-legal aspect of these tours, from negotiating contracts with theaters, transportation companies, and hotels to chasing claims for lost property along the way.

This article is about the impact of Stoker's legal education on his fiction, particularly with regard to *Dracula*. More precisely, I hope to demonstrate that *Dracula* is not only a novel written by a barrister but a novel that *only* a barrister *could* have written. Indeed, every major incident in the work, and many of the minor ones as well, seem charged with legal implications, even if many of those implications may not be immediately visible to the non-lawyer. Indeed, it could be argued that these legal issues drive the narrative in much the same way as they drive the narrative of the author's first novel, *The Snake's Pass*.

Consequently, in the first section we shall examine *The Snake's Pass* in relation to Stoker's early legal experiences in Ireland. Though published in 1889, by which time Stoker was already reading for the Bar, the novel's gestation was a long one, the main plot structure occurring to the author in 1881, three years after he left the Irish Civil Service to work for Irving in London but five years before he began reading for the Bar. Much of the actual composition of the novel, clearly a very piecemeal process, doubtlessly occurred during his August vacations or while touring, both at home and abroad, with the Lyceum.[6] More precisely, the date of the novel's publication in serial form would seem to suggest that the final stint of writing probably occurred during the Lyceum's third tour of the United States in 1887–88.

The result is a novel which is not only profoundly rooted in Stoker's own experience of rural Ireland but also culminates in a spectacular theatrical denouement inspired by the author's access to other London theaters besides the Lyceum, particularly those offering visually extravagant melodrama. *The Snake's Pass*, however, is also a novel largely grounded in Stoker's interest in and experience of a vast range of legal issues. As we shall see, Stoker's thinking about all these issues is still relatively unsophisticated, especially in comparison with *Dracula*, published eight years later, but the work undoubtedly qualifies as a "legal novel" as defined by John Henry Wigmore in his seminal 1908 statement on the subject as "a novel in which [...] a lawyer ought to be interested, because the principle or the profession of the law forms a main part of the author's theme."[7]

In the second section, we shall examine the reasons behind Stoker's decision to read for the Bar, examining the nature of his legal training in the second-half of the 1880s and looking at the changing socio-demographic composition of the legal profession at the time.

Just as *The Snake's Pass* was the product of a long period of gestation, so was *Dracula*—a period of gestation, in fact, that included his four years of study for the Bar. On this basis, it is hardly surprising that *Dracula* can almost be read as a novel framing complex hypothetical questions about the application of the law, especially but not only as it relates to serious criminal offenses such as murder and manslaughter: the types of question, in short, with which law students to this day are confronted in degree-level examination papers or those set by the Law Society or the Bar Council as a requirement for entry into the legal profession as solicitor or barrister.

This is the subject of the third section of this paper, and as we shall see, some of these issues are so hypothetical and, in a narrow legal sense, controversial, given that the English Common Law is a system that is always in a slow but continual state of flux and change, mainly, in the nineteenth century, because of the process of judicial decision-making rather than the passage of new legislation, that it seems at times as if Stoker is leading us into a nihilistic legal impasse in *Dracula*. This nihilistic impasse is particularly marked by the manner in which Van Helsing and the Crew of Light routinely flout every aspect of English law, openly committing burglary, perjury, homicide, and other felonies, including the most serious charge of all, conspiracy to commit murder (English law has always judged conspiracy a particularly heinous offense), with the same impunity with which Dracula stalks his victims.

Finally, we shall conclude with a discussion of one particularly notorious Victorian murder case, *Regina v. Dudley and Stephens* (1884), that Stoker cannot but have discussed in considerable detail during his pupillage at the Inner Temple. This case not only involves acts of cannibalism and vampirism on the high seas, a clear link to Stoker's favorite watering-hole of Whitby, but also offers not only Dracula a potential line of defense to multiple charges of murder but also Van Helsing with regard to his highly unusual, controversial, and, indeed, arguably fatal treatment of Lucy Westenra.

Stoker's Irish Legal Career: *The Snake's Pass*

Stoker's twelve years in the Irish Civil Service between 1866 and 1878 have been well documented by biographers, especially Paul Murray.[8] Perhaps the key event in these years was his promotion in 1876 to the post of Inspector of Petty Sessions (what we would call today the Magistrates' Court), which not only allowed him to travel around the Irish countryside but would also have provided him with considerable insight into rural crime and local sources of conflict, particularly with regard to unpaid rents, tax evasion, and disputes among farmers—notably, with regard to property transactions and, more notably still, bargains made when one or both of the parties was intoxicated.

Staffed by lay magistrates assisted by clerks in the role of advisors, the Petty Sessions marked Stoker's first real contact with the law. In *The Man* (1905), Stoker referred to the work dismissively, as "low people speaking of low crimes."[9] Nonetheless, he was ambitious enough to compile a 248-page manual, *The Duties of Clerks of Petty Sessions in Ireland* (1879), providing guidance on how to deal with the everyday cases that came before the courts, including how to handle such undesirables as peddlers, paupers, lunatics, deserters, and mutineers or resolve disputes involving pawnbrokers or stray cattle, not to mention the issuing of dog licenses and the procedures for dealing with lost postage stamps. A legal career is not always a glamorous one.

Though McGillivray describes these clerks who advised the lay magistrates as solicitors, the administrative reforms then taking place in Ireland, of which Stoker himself was an early beneficiary, would have taken decades to work their way through the system.[10] The majority of clerks would have had at best a patchy knowledge of the relevant law, usually gained piecemeal in an attorney's office; hence the need for Stoker's manual. Not surprisingly, Stoker's exposition of the laws applied in the Petty Sessions would seem to have proved a useful and popular work of reference for some years to come.

In *The Snake's Pass*, Arthur Severn, a wealthy Englishman buying property in the west of Ireland, has little good to say about the local legal profession, and imports legal advisors from England to transact his business, a clear indication of the author's attitude to his fellow countrymen, Protestant or Catholic. Stoker must also have heard many stories about the grasping and unscrupulous behavior of peasant farmers such as Black Murdock, the Gombeen Man of *The Snake's Pass*, who uses his position as a local money-lender to manipulate the warm-hearted but credulous Phelim Joyce into an unfavorable part-exchange of the lease on his farm and lands in order to search for the treasure he believes is buried there.

But the legal issues—both civil and criminal—implicit in Stoker's first novel extend much further than this, including Murdock's harassment of Joyce by means of diverting a watercourse, the subsequent flooding of the latter's land as a result of the ill-judged excavation of a bog in search of buried treasure, the issuing of slanderous allegations concerning the morals of Joyce's daughter, the threat of her being subjected at some time in the future to a serious sexual assault, and, ultimately, Murdock's attempted murder of his associate Bat Moynahan by getting him so drunk that he will lose his way and perish in a bog (*SP* 190–224).

Doubtless, many of these incidents were standard rural hazards at the time. As such, Stoker would certainly have been familiar with the legal position regarding treasure trove and diverted watercourses, the latter the subject of numerous cases of trespass and nuisance under common law. He would also have known that Murdock's threat to rape Norah Joyce was not an offense either at common law or under the Offences Against the Person Act 1861, it being a clear legal principal since the seventeenth century that mere words cannot constitute an assault unless accompanied by a physical act. Stoker shows off his legal knowledge here by further placing the threatened assault in the future. This was the situation in *Stephens v. Myers* (1830), in which it was specifically ruled that a threat to inflict harm at some point in the future does not constitute an assault either.

Stoker would also have been aware that, though far beyond their means, some of the remedies available to Joyce or his daughter were only available in expensive civil actions in the fields of tort or defamation. Indeed, Stoker can hardly have been unaware of the landmark case of *Rylands v. Fletcher* (1868), which also concerned the flooding of the plaintiff's land with resulting damage. The ruling in this case gave rise to a new doctrine of strict liability. More generally, as is often the case with Stoker's legal dilemmas, *The Snake's Pass* not only depends on recent case law but also anticipates future legal developments. Some sixty or so years later the decision in *Rylands v. Fletcher* was further extended in *Donoghue v. Stevenson* (1932), thereby largely inventing the modern concept of negligence by defining the duty of care owed by one party to another when loss is involved.

Perhaps the most interesting legal nicety that Stoker raises in the novel, however, concerns the question of homicide. If Moynahan had perished in the bog as Murdock intended, would the latter's actions and intentions be sufficient to secure a conviction for murder? For a lawyer, this is an issue of causation—the question being whether Moynahan's death could be viewed as a natural or foreseeable consequence of Murdock's action of getting him drunk. In 1946 the distinguished American academic lawyer R. M. Perkins argued that if a man was assaulted in a building but died as a result of an earthquake before he recovered consciousness, it would not be murder because the defendant could not have foreseen such an outcome; if the same assault occurred on a seashore, however, and the assailant had left his victim in imminent peril of an incoming tide by which he drowned, the reverse would be true.[11] This line of argument was followed in *Hallett* (1969), an Australian case in which an injured man was left slumped in the back of a car on a beach following a fight. Even without the element of deliberate malice involved in Murdock's decision to get Moynahan drunk, always a difficult matter to prove, it is not unlikely that a court would indeed decide that death was a foreseeable consequence of the act of supplying the victim with alcohol.

The Snake's Pass represents a trial run for *Dracula*. The narrator, like Jonathan Harker in the later novel, is engaged in a voyage of discovery that brings him face to face with a land of stagnation, superstition, and an apparent lack of legality. Tellingly, Arthur Severn's innate sense of legality comes to the rescue in a minor subplot concerning his imagined rivalry with Dick Sutherland with regard to Norah Joyce's hand, though the two men do not realize at this stage that they are both in love with the same woman. When confronted by a distraught Sutherland, Severn is able to show him the title deed to some land he had bought earlier on his friend's behalf in anticipation of the latter's own marriage to Norah (*SP* 135–36).

Finally, with regard to Stoker's representation of Victorian Ireland, one other tale—"The Man from Shorrox" (1894)[12]—requires mention, since it hinges on a traveler's rights in common law to accommodation at an inn. Indeed, there is case law dating back to the fifteenth century suggesting that the only restrictions to this principle relate to the traveler's good behavior and the availability of accommodation. A sixteenth-century decision, *White's case* (1558), is still cited to this day in similar disputes. Later cases deal with such issues as how far a traveler has to travel to be considered a traveler (a matter explicitly avoided in Stoker's story by the information that that traveler has come a considerable distance, possibly from Manchester), and the landlord's responsibility for the loss of valuables.

In Stoker's story a bumptious English commercial traveler demands accommodation in the best room in an Irish rural inn only to discover in the middle of the night that he is sharing a bed with the corpse of a friendless old local attorney who is awaiting burial the following day. Written while Stoker was already at work on *Dracula*, one cannot wonder whether this common law right to accommodation does not underlie the Count's insistence that he is invited into the home of his victims rather than simply forcing an entrance.[13] Certainly, such a condition does not seem to feature to any great extent in earlier vampire tales, though Stoker's use of such a trope may also be influenced by his knowledge of Gaelic folklore regarding first-footing: that is, that the first person to enter a house or household on New Year's Day is a harbinger of good fortune. In the folklore of other countries, notably Greece, the first person to cross the threshold may equally be a harbinger of ill-fortune.

Stoker the Barrister

Bram Stoker began his legal training on 3 May, 1886, and was called to the Bar a few days short of four years later on 30 April, 1890. Superficially, at least, this all looks relatively straightforward. There were only two formal entrance requirements at that time: first, candidates had to provide proof of a liberal education; second, they were required to nominate two sponsors (i.e. referees) prepared to vouch for their personal integrity. These requirements were common across all four Inns of Court where such training took place: Lincoln's Inn, Inner Temple, Middle Temple, and Gray's Inn.

The entrant then followed a process of "pupillage"—a form of apprenticeship to an established barrister,[14] to whom they paid a standard fee of 100 guineas,[15] together with the practice of "keeping of terms," i.e. the requirement that the student should dine a certain number of times—three meals per term over twelve terms—with legal colleagues. The purpose of these meals was (and still is) to develop an appropriate professional ethos and *esprit de corps*. Though the identity of the barrister who shared his chambers with Stoker (i.e. with whom Stoker served his pupillage) was not previously known, it is now possible to identify him as Frederick Inderwick, a Bencher of the Inner Temple, who was one of the leading divorce lawyers of the period.[16]

Finally, after 1872, a series of Bar exams—one in English law and one in Roman law—had to be successfully negotiated. Usually, the process of qualification took between three and five years.

Stoker's two degrees in science and mathematics, both awarded by Trinity College, Dublin, in the early 1870s, would have more than satisfied the requirement that candidates needed to provide proof of a liberal education. Likewise, more than a decade of work in the Irish Civil Service, albeit in the lower echelons, would have provided Stoker with a list of possible sponsors prepared to vouch for his good character. After nearly eight years in London, however, it is much more likely that the hospitable Stoker recruited his sponsors, either directly or indirectly, from among his well-connected contacts made through the Lyceum. Frederick Inderwick, for example, was a noted first-nighter and, in particular, a regular patron of the Lyceum.[17] Besides being an established clubman, he had a range of antiquarian interests. Since his clients and acquaintances included Oscar Wilde and James McNeil Whistler, his close social ties with Stoker, Irving, and, indeed, Ellen Terry, are by no means surprising.

Another particularly well-placed contact was the solicitor George Lewis, later Sir George Lewis, a close friend of and legal advisor to Henry Irving. Though Lewis and Lewis was one of the three major practices specializing in criminal law in the capital by the mid-century, from the outset it had always encouraged theatrical clients. George Lewis's father, James Lewis, had represented such celebrities of the early Victorian stage as Charles Matthews, Madame Vestris, and Charles Kean; his uncle, George Hamilton Lewis, a shrewd bankruptcy lawyer, had advised playwrights such as Tom Taylor, Dion Boucicault, and T. W. Robertson, in addition to acting as solicitor to the Dramatic Authors' Society.[18]

By the late 1860s George Lewis was already advising royalty on delicate matters—in particular, the Prince of Wales, who risked being named as co-respondent in a divorce case about to be brought by Sir Charles Mordaunt against his wife, both members of the Marlborough House set.[19] In the decade following his uncle's death in 1879, George Lewis and his wife Elizabeth became celebrities in their own right, not least on account of the parties they held at their home in Portland Place, where the fashionable and theatrical world commingled. Nonetheless, business was business, and one particular issue for which Irving turned to Lewis for professional advice was his troubled marriage.

Irving's marital woes provide a key link between the Lyceum and Stoker's subsequent legal training. Irving had married Florence O'Callaghan, daughter of Daniel O'Callaghan, a surgeon in the Indian Army, in July 1869. It was not a marriage made in heaven. Firstly, Irving had proposed to her only after the death of the actress Nellie Moore, whom he had courted for the previous five years, a few months earlier.[20] Secondly, the social asymmetry between the two families was so great that Irving's family did not even attend his wedding.[21] Though Florence had given birth to their first child in August 1870, by Christmas the same year the couple were living apart. Matters came to a head on the opening night of *The Bells* in November 1871 when, traveling home in a carriage, Florence is reputed to have insulted the actor by asking: "Are you going on making a fool of yourself like this all your life?" Apparently, Irving stepped out the carriage and never saw her again.[22] Nor, however, would she agree to a divorce.

Like Lewis, Stoker must have soon realized that divorce work was a very remunerative branch of the law in the closing decades of the nineteenth century. The cost of the divorce case brought by Sir Colin Campbell against his wife in 1886 amounted to some £4,940 in lawyers' fees alone, effectively bankrupting him.[23] In fact, at the time Stoker started his pupillage with Inderwick, Lewis had been acting for Lady Colin Campbell for some years. More particularly, following an earlier judicial separation that had been largely conducted without public scrutiny, a new divorce petition—in which Lady Colin was defending herself against no less than five accusations of adultery, including one with the duke of Marlborough, while counterclaiming that her husband had committed adultery with a house-maid as well as infecting her (the wife) with venereal disease at the moment her marriage was belatedly consummated—was about to hit the headlines.

The team Lewis assembled on Lady Colin's behalf was a formidable one: it consisted of Sir Charles Russell, Q.C., a barrister widely acclaimed for his powers of oratory and cross-examination; Frederick Inderwick,

Q.C., who, in addition to his expertise in divorce proceedings, was no less accomplished in cross-examination; while the junior member of the team, Charles Matthews, would later become a distinguished criminal lawyer in his own right.[24]

Campbell v. Campbell and Others had been expected to last three or four days. In the event, and much to the delight of the press, the jury did not retire to consider their verdict until the eighteenth day of the trial. The result was a stalemate: Colin was not guilty of adultery with a house-maid; his wife was not guilty of adultery with the duke of Marlborough, nor any of the other co-respondents, despite the insistence of a waiter at the Royal Purfleet Hotel to the contrary.[25] Purfleet, a Victorian leisure destination to the east of London, would later resurface in *Dracula* as the Count's principal lair.

One can only imagine Stoker's delight at being able to follow such a complex case—with regard not only to the legal argumentation involved and the daily drama of cross-examination but also to the vast information-gathering process underlying it, a process dependent on George Lewis's management of the army of private enquiry agents he had at his beck and call. Some of this excitement finds its way into *Dracula*, in which the Crew of Light embark on a similar information-gathering exercise. Nor should it be forgotten that Stoker's working notes make reference to a Police Inspector named Cotford, a character perhaps partly subsumed by Van Helsing in the published version of the novel.[26]

The prestige of the Bar is not based solely on the nature of the barrister's calling, often seen as a route into politics and the high offices of state, but also on the fact that, historically, the profession itself recruited widely among the younger sons of the greater landed gentry and minor aristocracy. Even as late as 1835, some half-century before Stoker began his legal training, some 26 percent of barristers belonged to either the greater gentry or squirearchy.[27] Some further idea of the social exclusivity of the bar can be provided by two other figures. In 1835 27 percent of barristers were educated at Eton, Westminster, or Harrow; while some 52 percent had attended either Oxford or Cambridge.[28]

Thus, some fifty years earlier, Stoker's relatively modest social origins coupled with his father's financial standing would almost certainly have precluded any chance of him reading for the Bar at any of the London inns-of-court. Stoker's father, Abraham Stoker, let us remind ourselves, was still listed as a junior clerk in 1836, twenty years after joining the Irish Civil Service, and would not receive promotion to the position of Senior Clerk until the very eve of his retirement, some seventeen years later in 1853.[29] Men in Bram Stoker's situation, especially in their youth, were simply not in a position to enter into such a high risk speculation as reading for the Bar.

By 1886, however, Stoker's own financial situation was relatively assured, at least as long as Irving's health lasted and provided the two men did not have a serious falling out. But, though spry and active, Irving was by then only two years away from his fiftieth birthday. Who could have guessed then that he would still be treading the boards right until the moment of his death nineteen years later in 1905?

Nor was Irving an easy man to work with, not least, as Barbara Belford notes, because he had an unfortunate tendency to surround himself with parasites.[30] One such member of Irving's personal entourage, at least in Stoker's eyes, was the Irish journalist L. F. Austin, who had been recruited to act as the actor's press secretary in 1882. Indeed, there is some evidence that Irving took a sadistic delight in goading the generally amenable Stoker on Austin's account, matters rising to a head during the Lyceum's second U.S. tour of 1884/85.[31] This rivalry, coupled with Irving's own fickleness, might in itself have provided sufficient motive for Stoker to think about an escape plan of some kind.

Meanwhile, the Bar itself had been slowly changing over the past fifty years in three important respects. Firstly, entry to the Bar was becoming more democratic—or, at least, more middle class—in nature. In statistical terms, the representation of the middle classes rose from 61 percent in 1835 to 73 percent in 1885. Or, to put matters another way, the gentry were slowly abandoning the bar and their places were being filled "by the sons of professionals, businessmen and civil servants."[32] Men, in other words, from the same sort of background—or almost the same sort of background—as Stoker himself. Secondly, this relative democratization of the Bar also had a demographic dimension. As Daniel Duman notes: "Although the shift [in middle class representation] was relatively modest, it may have been sufficient to explain the movement away from the agricultural south and towards the urban north and the cities of Ireland and

Scotland."[33] And, finally, the expansion of university education in the nineteenth century also changed the composition of the Bar to Stoker's advantage. This did not lead to a decline in the representation of Oxford and Cambridge at the Bar, which, in fact, continued to increase. What it did mean, though, was a significant rise in the number of non-Oxbridge graduates entering the Bar. In 1885, the year before Stoker began his legal training, two-thirds of this non-Oxbridge total was furnished by just two U.K. institutions: the University of London, with 36 men; and his old alma mater Trinity College, Dublin, with 26 men.[34]

Stoker's progress through his legal training would seem to have been smooth and unremarkable. True, he took the best part of four years to gain admission rather than the more usual three, but this may be explained by the Lyceum's third and fourth American tours of 1886/87 and 1887/88—Stoker was simply not available in London to fulfil his "terms." Moreover, the Bar examinations, introduced in 1872, not without some controversy, would have provided little challenge for a man whose entire career had revolved in one way or another around legal issues, involving not only the administration of Criminal Law but also contracts, copyright, and leases.

"Secret Things Belong to God": Legal Paradox in *Dracula*

In light of the fact that Stoker himself would seem to have considered his admission to the Bar in 1890 as *the* principal achievement of his life, the dearth of material on the legal dimension of Stoker's literary career is all the more surprising.

Indeed, as Paul Murray notes, in the 1891 census Stoker "listed his occupation as 'Barrister, Theatrical Manager, and Author' in that order."[35] His wife, the former Florence Balcombe, went one step further. According to Belford, during the twenty-five years that his wife outlived him, Florence Stoker only ever referred to her husband in print as a barrister: "never as the author of *Dracula* or the Acting Manager for the late Sir Henry Irving."[36]

In both cases, the implicit suggestion is, of course, that Stoker and his wife were motivated by snobbery. Further evidence for this hypothesis is provided by Stoker's two principal biographers: Murray notes that

Stoker owned a "fine collection of statutes in his library,"[37] the implication being that this was presumably for display purposes or to impress visitors; Belford argues that Stoker "anchors" Dracula's standing by having Jonathan Harker "quip" that Dracula "would have been a wonderful solicitor";[38] and, finally, both authors suggest that Stoker's close personal identification with Van Helsing is evidenced by his description of the latter either as a "lawyer" (Belford) or a "barrister" (Murray).[39]

There are perhaps a number of misconceptions here. Given that in Stoker's day the gentry, let alone the landed aristocracy, would have protested the right of a mere solicitor to be considered a gentlemen, the idea that Dracula's prestige would have been enhanced by such a title is highly suspect. While some barristers might justly lay claim to the status of being gentlemen, that status, unless such a man had achieved considerable eminence in his field, derived from the fact that his family were considered to be members of "society" and that he himself had attended a public school, possibly followed by a suitable university. Solicitors, on the other hand, were viewed by Victorian society as, at best, professional men. There were few solicitors who attained the social rank of George Lewis and in his case one can only wonder how many of the prominent men who attended his gatherings were accompanied by their wives.

Dracula's claim to nobility, on the other hand, is vouchsafed by the fact that he is a *bona fide* count with a lineage dating back to the Middle Ages. What Jonathan Harker finds astonishing—and what Stoker wants us (the reader) to find astonishing—is surely that a client of the stature of Count Dracula would bother himself with the legal minutiae of a straightforward property transaction in a faraway country or concern himself with the details of shipping some unidentified personal effects, which later prove to be nothing more than boxes of earth, to that same country. Nor was Stoker's ownership of law reports and statutes merely for show. His interest, fascination even, with the law underpins every page of both *The Snake's Pass* and *Dracula* (and other more minor works besides). Stoker's ownership of statutes and law reports is a marker of his own private interests and ambitions.

Secondly, Van Helsing's legal status, whether as a lawyer or a barrister, is dubious in the extreme. Though it is quite plausible that he does indeed possess a doctorate of laws in addition to the M.D., D.Phil, and D. Lit. that we are told about elsewhere, presumably all awarded by the University of Antwerp or some other renowned northern European seat of learning, the possession of such a higher degree confers no right to practice law in England or Wales, whether as an attorney, a solicitor, or a barrister. He is, quite simply, what the French would call a *jurist*: a person with an academic knowledge of the law but one who is not an officer of the court and who has no rights of audience—in other words, something of a legal "quack" or imposter. Stoker's 1910 collection of essays *Famous Imposters* would seem to suggest that this was a topic in which he had some interest.

More significantly, it is to say the least ironic that Van Helsing reminds his former pupil Dr. Seward that he is a "lawyer" in relation to issuing a fraudulent death certificate—the second of two such fraudulent death certificates, as Seward has already signed off Mrs. Westenra's death from shock without demur—intended to prevent the local coroner from starting an investigation into Lucy's death (*D* 140, 152, 269). Indeed, by their actions Van Helsing and Seward entirely defeat the purpose of the 1887 Coroner's Act, specifically designed to determine the cause of sudden, violent, and unnatural deaths, and leaving Seward, in particular, open to the charge of fabricating evidence with intent to pervert the course of justice.

Yet, again, however, we see Stoker's legal background informing his fiction. In fact, Stoker may have been mindful of such matters because he was familiar with the case of *R. v. Vreones* (1891), in which a false declaration pertaining to a sample of wheat resulted in a conviction for a similar offense, namely perverting the course of justice. As is often the case with Stoker, this case is still cited in legal textbooks to this day. In fact, by acceding to Van Helsing's request to falsify Lucy's death certificate, Seward is leaving himself open to not only professional disgrace but also imprisonment.[40]

Paradoxically, however, on the basis that the only physical sign of a criminal assault on Lucy takes the form of two small puncture marks on her neck, the most serious charge likely to be entertained by the English courts against Count Dracula is one of actual bodily harm (s.47 of the Offences against the Person Act 1861), potentially punishable by five years' imprisonment, though, in practice, the lesser charge of common assault, potentially punishable by only a year's imprisonment, would generally have been preferred.

If Dracula was not an invited guest but a trespasser—that is, if, in this context, his intrusion into Lucy's room was unlawful, for example, because he was a burglar—the matter would be different, at least prior to the Homicide Act 1957. Before then, under the common law, in a case where a man causes death in furtherance of committing a felony, such as theft or rape, the intention to commit the lesser crime automatically provided the necessary malice aforethought for a conviction for the more serious charge.[41] In other words, in such cases the prosecution had only to prove the defendant's intention to commit burglary, not the intention to commit murder, a much more difficult task.

This is not the case in *Dracula*. The fact that Dracula needs to be invited inside by his host is stressed throughout the novel, thus evading any possibility of the type of legal wrangling over the issue of trespass or burglary providing "constructive malice" for murder. In *Dracula*, at least, the tradition of the vampire seeking permission to enter his victim's home may derive from a legal nicety, but Stoker's insistence on the matter implies that he was aware of the legal significance of such a distinction.[42]

Finally, while we are on the subject of constructive malice, what about the case of Mrs. Westenra, who dies of shock as a result of one of Count Dracula's nocturnal excursions to visit Lucy? At least, here, a layman might imagine, we have a *prima facie* case of murder or at least manslaughter, especially given the previous careful emphasis on Mrs. Westenra's heart condition. Alas, this takes us into the rarefied area of so-called special issues of causation, notably death caused by means of fright or surprise, where the common sense view of law does not necessarily prevail.

The view of early legal writers was that the law could take no cognizance of a killing caused by mere mental suffering, because, in the words of Sir Matthew Hale, writing in the mid-seventeenth century, "no external act of violence was offered, whereof the common law can take notice and secret things belong to God."[43] Needless to say, such an approach has been qualified over the years. Thus, in *R. v. Towers* (1874), the defendant shouted at a girl holding a young child in her hands. The girl's consequent screams so frightened the baby that it suffered from convulsions and died a month later. This case is significant because the defendant was convicted of manslaughter on the grounds that, while strong and violent language in itself would not be enough to secure a conviction for manslaughter were the victim an adult, it did not apply in the case of a child of such tender years.

The ruling in *Towers* was extended to an adult in *R. v. Hayward* (1908), in which a wife suffering from a heart condition was chased into the road by her husband and promptly died of a heart attack. Here we have a very similar situation to that involving the death of Mrs. Westenra. In *Hayward* a conviction for manslaughter was secured on the grounds that, even if a healthy person would not have suffered injury in such circumstances, the defendant must take his victim as he finds him, another solid legal maxim. At last, eleven years after the publication of *Dracula*, the English courts had found a legal formula liable to lead to the conviction of Mrs. Westenra's assailant.[44]

The main point, however, is not that, like Lucy's death, Mrs. Westenra's death from a heart attack is a random event in an unstructured work of fiction but that Stoker's thinking in relation to these matters was informed by his reading of statutes and law reports, his knowledge of legal procedure, and his anticipation of likely developments in case law. *Dracula* may be a work of fantasy, but it is one firmly anchored in the English common law.

Cannibalism on the High Seas: *R. v. Dudley and Stephens* (1884)

One case with which Stoker cannot but have been extremely familiar at the time of his pupillage was that of *R. v. Dudley and Stephens*. Dealing as it does with murder under conditions of supreme provocation, indeed, the very fight for survival, the case attracted worldwide interest in 1884. Although the Queen's Bench Division, to which the proceedings were eventually transferred—one of many bizarre procedural issues that haunted the case from the outset[45]—soundly rejected the defense of the accused at the time, a defense based on the doctrine of necessity (i.e., the notion that, in exceptional circumstances, an individual may break the law to prevent an even greater evil from befalling or on the grounds of self-preservation), *R. v. Dudley and Stephens* has proved to be a case that simply refuses to go away. More than 130 years later it is still the subject of intense legal debate, while students in every common law jurisdiction across the globe are required to scrutinize it as a standard part of their legal training in criminal law. Arguably, it also provides a major interpretive clue to Stoker's *Dracula*.

The facts, though not lacking in gruesome detail, are, at least, reasonably straightforward.[46] On July 5, 1884, the *Mignotte*, an ageing thirty-three-ton yacht *en route* from Falmouth to a new owner in Sydney, foundered in heavy seas in the south Atlantic some 2,000 miles from the South American coastline, the nearest practicable land mass. The captain, Tom Dudley, a man of tremendous integrity and presence of mind, immediately launched the dinghy and evacuated the crew of three: Edwin Stephens (mate), Ned Brooks (able seaman), and Richard Parker (cabin boy). Food and water soon began to run short. By July 13, all four men had begun to drink their own urine, a standard practice in such situations. Some three or four days later the food ran out and the first of several discussions occurred with regard to the drawing of lots to determine who should be sacrificed in order that the others might survive. On or around July 25 a general decision was made by way of nods and signs that Richard Parker, the seventeen-year-old cabin boy—who, having drunk sea-water, was believed to be dying—should be sacrificed. This was possibly accompanied by a sham drawing of lots. Dudley duly accomplished the task by thrusting a penknife into Parker's throat and catching the blood in a chronometer case. Later, in his prison cell, he gave an account of what happened next: "'I can assure you that I shall never forget the sight of my two unfortunate companions over that gastly meal we all was like mad wolfs who should get the most and for men fathers of children to commit such a deed we could not have our right reason."[47] Five days later, Dudley and his two surviving companions were picked up by the *Moctezuma*.

And that should have been that. For although such instances of cannibalism on the high seas were not at all rare in the days of wooden sailing ships (which in the case of those carrying timber from North America could remain afloat for years after being dismasted by high winds and heavy seas, their crews perishing one by one in conditions of the most appalling deprivation), the courts, whether intentionally or unintentionally, rarely, if ever, intervened. When Stoker questioned the fishermen on the seashore in Whitby it was almost certainly in search of such tales of maritime catastrophe, represented graphically in his most famous novel by the account of Dracula's arrival in Whitby on board one such "vampire" ship (*D* Ch. 7) and, symbolically, by the author's fusion of the religious significance of Christ's blood as a sign of the transubstantiation with the sailor's notion of the life-giving quality of blood as the inverse of that harbinger of madness and death, sea-water. Arguably, Stoker's interest in such matters was initially triggered by *R. v. Dudley and Stephens* and only later became the material for a work of fiction.[48]

In 1884, however, following an attempt a decade earlier, officials from the Home Office and other government departments had decided to clamp down on cannibalistic practices at sea.[49] The result of this was that almost immediately after their return to England Dudley and Stephens were arrested and charged with the murder of the cabin boy, Brooks effectively providing Queen's evidence. The intricacies of this trial need not concern us here, although there are many aspects that seem distinctly dubious today, not least the fact that one of the members of the jury would seem to have informed Captain Dudley that the outcome of the case had been decided in advance: namely, that he was to be convicted of murder and, as a consequence, would receive the mandatory death sentence, but that he would subsequently be offered a free pardon as soon as it could be arranged.[50] In the event, this was exactly what happened, except for the fact that both Dudley and Stephens served a sentence of six months' imprisonment before they were released. Tom Dudley subsequently emigrated to Australia, where he would seem to have prospered.

The impact of all this legal chicanery was the very opposite of what the authorities intended. Rather than stifling rumors of cannibalistic practice at sea, discussion of such events reached fever pitch in the popular press. More significantly, the defense of necessity, summarily rejected by Baron Huddleston, who presided over the start of the trial at Exeter Assizes, and at best a nebulous concept in English law until that moment, entered into legal folklore. Over the years, it has resurfaced in different forms in various cases, some very significant, including *R. v. Bourne* (1939), in which necessity was allowed as a defense to a statutory felony of procuring an abortion if the act was done in good faith for the purpose only of preserving the life of the mother;[51] and *Re A (conjoined twins)*

(2001), in which it was allowed as a defense for a surgeon who had been forced to save the life of one congenitally joined twin at the expense of a weaker sibling. By and large, in Britain the defense of necessity has been much more successful in medical cases than in other areas of law, but this is not necessarily the case in other common law jurisdictions.[52]

With regard to *Dracula*, such a defense is open with regard to both the Count, who, it might be argued, needs to kill in order to survive (the very issue facing Captain Dudley and Edwin Stevens), and the Crew of Light, whose various unlawful activities, it might also be argued, are likewise motivated by issues of self-preservation, the preservation of their own species, or, in the case of the treatment of Lucy Westenra, the choice between the lesser of two evils (i.e., a dangerous, as yet untested, and, therefore, presumably unlawful blood transfusion versus the patient's death or transformation into a vampire).

Indeed, is not the paradox at the heart of *Dracula* the fact that Van Helsing and his Crew of Light behave in an increasingly unlawful manner as the novel progresses, arguably committing every conceivable crime, from the falsification of death certificates through to assault, burglary, criminal damage,[53] murder, and conspiracy to commit murder, with the same apparent impunity as Dracula himself? Moreover, is not the legal jeopardy of the Crew of Light of an altogether more serious nature than that of their adversary? As we saw earlier, the most grievous charge that could be brought against the latter amount to little more than a minor assault. But even this would have involved convincing a skeptical jury in an era of scientific progress that the puncture wounds in Lucy Westenra's neck were caused by a four-hundred-year-old foreign nobleman who is capable not only of raising himself from the dead but also of transforming himself at will into other life forms.

Van Helsing's legal situation in this respect is a particularly unenviable one with regard to Lucy Westenra's death. The nineteenth century was a period of increasing professionalism in the medical field, a professionalism greatly encouraged by the British Medical Association. As a medical practitioner, however, his status is no more assured than it is as a lawyer. Indeed, one concomitant of the increased professionalism of the medical profession was an increased intolerance for unlicensed practitioners and "quacks." One such case concerns an Irish-born quack doctor named John St. John Long who was convicted of manslaughter in 1830 after his patient, a previously healthy woman, died following an unnecessary treatment for tuberculosis which involved creating weeping sores.

Stoker may not have known of this case, but he would have been familiar, if only by reputation, with the Irish-born quack Francis Tumblety (c. 1833–1903), later a suspect for the Whitechapel Murders. Stoker's friend Hall Caine, a noted hypochondriac, had met Tumblety in Liverpool in the mid-1870s, presumably becoming a member of the latter's homosexual coterie and later acting as a publicist on his behalf in London.[54] Neither writer was probably aware that as early as 1860 Tumblety had been linked with the deaths of his patients in at least three separate jurisdictions in North America, narrowly escaping prosecution on each occasion. But Stoker, with his trained legal mind, must have had his suspicions about Tumblety's sanity.

Prosecutions for manslaughter even against licensed doctors and surgeons were becoming increasingly common in Britain during the nineteenth century, too, especially in the wake of the Medical Act 1868, which drew a legal distinction between qualified and unqualified practitioners. Such prosecutions tended to be related to mistakes (such as the administration of an overdose of morphia), slips (including the accidental substitution of strychnine for bismuth during the formulation of a medicine), or violations of safe practice (including drunkenness and ineptitude).[55] In all three of the examples mentioned above the result was an acquittal. But such was not the outcome in an 1862 case of a surgeon named Robinson, whose gross want of skill and care resulted in the death of a woman following childbirth.

Given the extremely unusual and untested treatment of Lucy Westenra (which in an era before blood groups were recognized would invariably have resulted in death), not to mention Van Helsing's unlicensed status, the judge's remarks in this case may have an ominous undertone: "Every medical man was of course liable to make a mistake, and he would not be criminally responsible for the consequences if it should appear that he had exercised reasonable skill and caution, and it was only in the case where a medical man [...] was guilty of gross negligence, or evinced a gross want of knowledge of his profession, that he could be held criminally responsible."[56] Robinson was convicted and imprisoned. The defense of necessity notwithstanding, Lucy Westenra's death presents a *prima facie* case of what we would call today medical negligence.

Dracula, like *The Snake's Pass* before it, is a legal novel in the fullest sense of the term—not only a work in which the law plays a key role but, arguably, a work generated by a series of incidents (or what a lawyer would call "fact situations") emerging from the English common law, incidents that, in many cases, seem to predict with considerable accuracy future developments in English case law. Though even the educated lay reader may not be able to identify all these themes, such themes anchor a work of the wildest fantasy in a legally consistent world, and one which, legally speaking, is clearly recognizable today. Finally, although, as noted earlier, it would seem throughout *Dracula* that Stoker was leading the reader into a nihilistic impasse, ultimately this is not the case: over the course of the last 120 years or so the common law, sometimes prompted by legislation, has evolved considerably such that many of the inconsistences or more rebarbative aspects have been thoroughly reformed. It is to Stoker's credit that *Dracula* is not only such an engaging legal novel but also such a visionary one.

CHAPTER TWO

"Receptive Emotion"?
Stoker and Irving—Collaboration, Hagiography, Self-fashioning

Rui Carvalho Homem

In a brief passage from Bram Stoker's *Personal Reminiscences of Henry Irving*, Stoker offers an account of how, in May 1895, Irving was awarded his knighthood. The narrative duly highlights the exceptionality of the moment, "the first time that in any country an actor had been, *quâ* actor, honoured by the State;" and it stresses the overwhelming applause that followed, nationally and internationally, since "the telegrams, letters and cables began to pour in from all parts of the world."[1] However, in the broader economy of a text that extends beyond 500 pages, offering a detailed description of Stoker's experience as business manager for Irving at the Lyceum Theatre in London (1878–1905), a text that centers on the actor's rise to his fame as the quintessential Shakespearian star of the late Victorian and Edwardian stage, and often goes into great detail in order to record and vindicate the traits that arguably defined Irving's superlative merit and greatness—in such a text (otherwise rather garrulous and marked by Stoker's "lifelong weakness for name-dropping"[2]), the events of May 1895 are narrated with comparative concision, and almost in subdued tones.

The brevity with which Stoker reports on that key episode may in itself be rhetorically significant. It suggests that the culmination of Irving's fame and public recognition, hence also a high point in the hagiographic

33

and teleological design of the *Personal Reminiscences*,[3] can only be properly celebrated with a reverence that requires a terse diction—words that will be weightier if they are fewer. The account comes, after all, from the biographer and memorialist who, in the course of dozens of previous chapters, had extolled the development of Irving's artistic identity, theatrical authority, and public prominence. No less tellingly, Stoker's extensive narrative also signaled his own involvement (if not agency) in that momentous process—as Irving's "acting manager" and close friend; so close indeed that "we could almost read a thought of the other," with such complicity as could be observed (Stoker's own phrase) "in a husband and wife who have lived together for long."[4]

This article ponders the professional collaboration between the two men and the memorialization that Stoker offers of such rapport, in light of Stoker's espousal of a poetics of drama and the stage. Such poetics draws on his experience (prior to his association with Irving at the Lyceum) as both theatergoer and reviewer in Dublin. Likewise, it draws on the acknowledged influence of key authors on drama and on Shakespeare—prominent among whom was the Trinity College Dublin professor and Shakespearean scholar Edward Dowden. Stoker's arrogation of a measure of critical authority with regard to drama and the stage will be considered alongside the terms in which, throughout the *Reminiscences*, he claims, discreetly but in no uncertain terms, the role not just of a dutiful assistant and confidant but of a *maker* of Irving's fame. In other words: if Stoker has been credited with an ability to experience "profound admiration for others,"[5] my reading of his memoirs will balance such ability against a wish for self-inclusion in the celebratory design.[6] It is unquestionable that Stoker sustainedly makes the case for his status as a protector and celebrator, a keeper of the sanctuary, a proactive compiler of the scriptural wake of Irving's growth to glory. From someone in Stoker's position, though, his comparative "reticence" (a word that he favors) in his account of Irving's being knighted can be read as the ostentation of a false modesty, that tasteful coyness (apparent in the light of his "husband and wife" analogy) which implicitly challenges readers with a regendering of the proverbial saying that "behind every great man ...," and chimes with the insight (apparently current among their collaborators), that Stoker played a "maternal to Irving's paternal" role at the Lyceum.[7]

In spite of its terseness, Stoker's vignette of the moment when Irving received his knighthood leaves no doubt about its inscription in the imperial designs to the center of which the actor had quickly risen. In both earlier and later years, Irving's theater, the Lyceum—which "dominated Shakespeare on the English stage" from the 1870s to the turn of the century[8]—was regularly visited by dignitaries of the late Victorian and Edwardian establishment in the framework of festivals such as the Jubilees of 1887 and 1897, and Edward VII's coronation. The importance of such institutional distinction would have been all the more apparent at the turn of the century, when the heyday of the Lyceum's *theatrical* fame was already past; in the closing years of Irving's life, that theater had entered a "steady and irrevocable decline."[9] Not that the appertaining anxieties transpire much in the *Reminiscences*—Stoker repeats rather his and Irving's pride in hosting performances and receptions that emphasized their centrality to imperial power and Establishment values: "They were from every part of the world and of every race under the sun. […] Everywhere a sense of the unity and the glory of Empire. […] the heart-beat of that great Empire on which the sun never sets."[10]

Indeed, Irving's and Stoker's understanding of the bonds that the Lyceum, especially through Shakespeare, could help foster seemed to involve language and ethnicity rather than a strict delineation of nationality and politics. Under the motto "Blood is Thicker than Water," the *Reminiscences* include an account of Irving's generosity to American seamen from a visiting warship, whom he invited to the theater, and who offered a memorable salute when Irving, in turn, visited their ship—which prompted the following observation from Stoker:

> there is no such sound in the world as that full-throated Anglo-Saxon cheer which begins at the heart—that inspiring, resolute, intentional cheer which has through the memory of ten thousand victories and endless moments of stress and daring become the heritage of the race.[11]

Making the Lyceum a focus for celebrations of imperial greatness entailed an awareness of security concerns: "It did not do to neglect precautions on such an occasion when the spirit of anarchy stalked abroad."[12] The extent to which the Lyceum endorsed establishment values and became a venue for royal pageantry also allowed Stoker to claim for Irving a sort of surrogate kingship as host of such events: in his words, the moment when the Lyceum became the site of a reception that marked the Coronation of Edward VII in 1902 also "crowned Irving's reign as Master and Host."[13] The role played by Stoker's account of such happenings in his memoirs consolidates a homology between the royal power that they commemorated and the artistic power of the commemorators.

This homology arguably reflects a late Romantic exaltation of artistic talent, combined with the positivistic celebration of great men as the secular pantheon of a nation—a project, arising from Auguste Comte's "religion of humanity" and with well-known English developments,[14] that in late Victorian Britain found memorable eventuations in the world of literature and the arts, with Shakespeare (the national Bard) as its inevitable center.[15] This combination is not devoid of perplexities. Stoker's celebration of Irving and, indeed, his entourage in their rise to fame highlights a fundamental ambivalence in his mindset: a discourse of progress sustained by material and technological development, gauged and charted in historical terms, is balanced in Stoker's narrative against the mystery of genius; and the inexplicability of genius is of one piece with the dynamics of emotional response, justified by the audience's supposed recognition of the glimpses into a higher truth afforded by Irving and his Lyceum productions in the fullness of their theatrical excellence.

As regards the material side of this ambivalent nexus—that which measures and celebrates the "truth to life" (the verisimilitude) of a theater that appears fully committed to naturalistic practices (and indeed deployed "the best special effects which the technology of the day could create"[16])—Stoker is adamant (in a passage from the *Reminiscences*) about the accuracy with which their stagecraft attempts to replicate the empirically validated conditions of the world out there, since "there must be nothing which would show to the student falsity to common knowledge" (248).[17] He supports this with close and repeated observation of Irving's practice, hailing its punctilious commitment to factual accuracy. With regard to the broader cultural contours of any production, he credits Irving with a zest for inquiry into the historical and geographic variety of Shakespeare's representational range, declaring (for example) that "Irving did not think of playing *The Merchant of Venice* until he had been to the Levant"[18]—apparently on the assumption that the Bard would have direct and impeccable knowledge of the elsewheres conjured by his drama. In a similar vein, he confirms Irving's reliance on specialized consultants— hence, "when the church scene of *Much Ado About Nothing* was set for the marriage of Claudio and Hero, he got a Catholic priest to supervise it."[19] Additionally, he stresses again and again the actor–manager's commit- ment to scrupulous literalism in the material design and execution of his productions, relying on the manufacturing prowess of the industrial era to ensure sets and props of the utmost "exactness of detail."[20] This emphasis in the *Reminiscences* is all the more significant for its being at odds with remarks by other observers, pointedly Ellen Terry, who (in a passage in *The Story of My Life*) made the case for a contrast between the "strictly archaeological" rationale of other productions and Irving's supposedly less factual, "very gravely beautiful and effective" and arguably more poetic practice, with regard to theatrical referentiality—as materi- ally realized in sets and props.[21] Terry's observation hints at the possibility that Stoker might in fact be more of a literalist than Irving himself. Irre- spective of such a conjecture, Stoker explicitly theorizes representational literalism as a reflection of context, as when he connects this theater to the proud scientism of his age: His *Reminiscences* abound in remarks such as: "Modern science can record something of the actualities of voice and tone"; "scientific progress can be marked even on the stage;" and "To 'pass a character through your mind' requires a scientific process of some kind."[22] In a passage from the same chapter as the last remark, Stoker also suggests that an ability to understand character (prior to enacting it) through such a "scientific process" would in fact be naturally built into the brain, and morphologically revealed by the presence of "large frontal sinuses—those bony ridges above the eyebrows," credited with "the power to distinguish minute differences," and hence a "knowledge of 'character'," by the dubious but then tantalizing "science" of physiognomy.[23]

Culturally and historically, with an important bearing on the rapport between art and power, it is also significant that Stoker's discourse of prog- ress and science becomes strikingly gendered. In a chapter celebrating Ellen Terry, he claims that the age of empirically grounded intellectual inquiry had brought in a "natural" style of acting: "Ellen Terry belongs to the age of investigation. She is of those who brought in the new school of natural acting. [...] She enlarged the bounds of art from those of convention to those of nature; and in doing so gave fuller scope to natural power."[24] As has been widely documented, Irving tended to deny Terry opportunities for stardom if those could in any way lessen the actor–manager's own salience and centrality.[25] As for Stoker, while he acknowledges and celebrates Terry's greatness, he leaves no doubt in this chapter of the *Reminiscences* that, for his positivistic assessment of a triumphant point of arrival, the point at which art effaces itself in order to yield "nature," the standards (the very terms) are thoroughly male—even if he otherwise raves about Terry's radiant feminine beauty: "In this 'natural' method also individual force counts for its worth and the characteristic notes of sex are marked. [...] She has to the full in her nature whatever quality it is that corresponds to what we call 'virility' in a man."[26]

Key aspects of Stoker's critical attitude to drama and the stage had developed in his pre-London, pre-Lyceum years, when he started writing unpaid reviews for the *Dublin Evening Mail* with a zest that ensured reviews would come out the day after the performance (which had previously not been the case),[27] and saw him soon enjoying a significant immersion "in Dublin theatre life [of] the 1870s," "on friendly terms with visiting actors" and other stage professionals.[28] Indeed, that experience proved decisive to the extent that Stoker then contributed to making Irving "a darling of the Dublin establishment,"[29] following a series of sometimes ecstatic stage successes, and Irving's recognition of this was to lead to Stoker's own position at the Lyceum. In one of those early theater reviews, Stoker had expressed his belief that his day and age had brought to fruition a potential that Shakespeare had contained but not proved able to develop in full because his age had not commanded the right material means. For Stoker, such a perception had to support the notion of a greater responsibility on the part of latter-day actors if they were to do justice to the progress that characterized their own age: "The nineteenth century has so far improved on the sixteenth in dramatic and histrionic art that a greater concentration is necessary."[30]

Stoker's teleological reading of theatrical (and, indeed, general) history thus explicitly includes a correlation of the early modern and late Victorian periods as comparative high points that evince a pattern of progress.

This may have been one of the aspects of Stoker's intellectual makeup that show his debts to Edward Dowden, whom he knew from Trinity and with whom he regularly corresponded.[31] In his *Shakspere: A Critical Study of His Mind and Art* (1875)—which became "the most widely read book on Shakespeare" in this period[32]—Dowden resorted throughout to organic imagery to propose a study of the growth of an artist's oeuvre, but conceded that context was equally key, since "[i]n order that an organism [...] should exist at all, there must be a certain correspondence between the organism and its environment."[33] From such reflections Dowden proceeds to describing Shakespeare's immediate environment in terms that amount to construing Elizabethans as forerunners of the Victorian bourgeoisie. Indeed, for Dowden the age of Shakespeare—and of "Spenser, Raleigh, Jonson, Bacon, Burleigh, Hooker"—was "an age eminently positive and practical."[34] This view also allowed him to make a case for empiricism as the very core of Englishness, with its matrix in the age of Shakespeare and in its drama:

> Can we discover anything possessed in common by the scientific movement, the ecclesiastical movement, and the drama of the period? That which appears to be common to all is *a rich feeling for positive, concrete fact.* The facts with which the drama concerns itself are those of human character in its living play.

And, further vindicating this factuality, this supposed literalness in the artistic apprehension of the real, he concludes: "The Elizabethan drama gives us the stuff of life itself."[35]

Emphatic as it is, Dowden's emphasis on the factual as the enabling referential ground of Shakespeare's work is ultimately mitigated and balanced by a quasi-grudging accommodation of the elements of spirituality and passion. This inflection in his argument appears to reflect the cogency, for Dowden, of notions of synthesis and totality as defining the Bard's uniqueness. Indeed, and despite his assertion that "men's lives in the drama of Shakspere are not disorganised and denaturalised by irruptions of the miraculous," since "[t]he one standing miracle is the world itself,"[36] Dowden acknowledges "that Shakespeare lived and moved in two worlds—one limited, practical, positive; the other a world opening into two infinites, an infinite of thought, and an infinite of passion."[37] And this involves extending the Elizabethan–Victorian nexus from the stress on the empirical and material to the spiritual and ideal—Dowden honoring, in the process, the metaphysical strands in the broader intellectual range of his own century:

> We need to supplement the noble positivism of Shakspere with an element not easy to describe or define, but none the less actual, which the present century has demanded as essential to its spiritual life and well-being, and which its spiritual teachers — Wordsworth, Coleridge, Shelley, Newman, Maurice, Carlyle, Browning, Whitman (a strange and apparently motley assemblage) — have supplied and are still supplying. The scientific movement of the present century is not more unquestionably a fact, than this is a fact.[38]

This accommodation, of crucial importance for an age in which "the tension between religious and scientific worldviews was especially pronounced,"[39] clearly resonates in Stoker's abundant reflections on drama and the theater in essays and reviews and, at much greater length, in the *Reminiscences*. Throughout the volume, Stoker's analysis of the Lyceum's achievements hinges on the convergence of genius (with its measure of inscrutability) and the material expertise that comes from highly professional management. It would be tempting to see the two elements in this nexus embodied respectively in Irving, the physically rather frail theatrical artist, and Stoker, his sturdy "acting manager." However, and in a manner that reveals the self-fashioning[40] dimension to the venture for which the *Reminiscences* provide a textual realization (rather than merely a record), Stoker is at pains to signal that the competences proper to spirit and fact at the Lyceum were not so simply allocated—and that both Irving and himself contributed under both headings (albeit to different extents) to the project's collaborative success.

Read in context, however, Stoker's celebration of Irving's and his own talents is enveloped in uncertainties and counter-narratives. Stoker's position at the Lyceum was hardly as prominent as he came to represent it, since it was balanced against the prerogatives enjoyed by others, notably

Henry Loveday, the stage manager.[41] Contemporary observers (including George Bernard Shaw) also noted that Irving tended to play a number of people around him against one another, while benefiting from their rival efforts to create for him an undeserved intellectual aura, "'an entirely fabulous reputation as a man of profound learning.'"[42] It is against such a contested background that one has to read Stoker's claims for Irving *and himself* as the central figures of the Lyceum, repeatedly emphasizing the skills that vindicate the "manager" element in Irving's distinction as the epitome of the "actor-manager" system;[43] while this is counterpointed, at various key moments in the *Reminiscences*, by Stoker's reminders of his own substantial contributions to the partnership. These included, in Stoker's narrative, his intellectual credentials and artistic sensibility, the perceptual skills derived from his long acquaintance with the theater (before the years of the Lyceum, as compulsive theatergoer and incidental critic), and also the inclusive traits of what a later age might describe as the "emotional intelligence" of this industrious business manager.

One of the arguments pursued in this article is that the conceptual and argumentative core for Stoker's complex vindication of practical and sensitive talents is dramatic in origin; and that, when one considers the relevant historical framework, this involves probing the tension between, on the one hand, interpersonal or relational dimensions, and, on the other, the singularity of individual exploration and revelation. In the heyday of character criticism—that so often addressed Shakespeare's "mode of drawing characters" (as Coleridge had phrased it earlier in the century)[44] as its favorite showcase—it is hardly surprising that character should be the unquestionable centerpiece of Irving's and Stoker's understanding of dramatic representation. This is emphasized, in fact, by a passage of the *Reminiscences* in which "the conception and development of character" becomes of one piece with the fashioning of a "great artist:"

[we were] talking of that phase of Stage Art which deals with the conception and development of character. In the course of our conversation, whilst he was explaining to me the absolute necessity of an actor's understanding the prime qualities of a character in order that he may make it throughout consistent, he said these words:

"*If you do not pass a character through your own mind it can never be sincere!*"

I was much struck with the phrase, coming as it did as the crown of an argument—the explanation of a great artist's method of working out a conceived idea. To me it was the embodiment of an artistic philosophy.[45]

Such emphases are balanced against Stoker's admission that he had never "had the privilege of seeing a play [properly] 'produced'" before he met Irving.[46] Indeed, this alertness to plot and production (the structuring and integrative dimensions of stage art) claims a cumulative rather than adversarial engagement with the poetics of character that unquestioningly grounded both men's views on the theater, developed and consolidated in the course of those decades of collaboration at the Lyceum.

Again and again, combining his account with citation of Irving's own views, Stoker expounds throughout the *Reminiscences* their shared understanding of drama and the theater. Their consensual understanding of it hinges on a commitment—relayed from dramatist to manager (both producer and director) and from them to the actors, and at every stage grounded on individual talent—to enacting semblances of human identity and behavior trusted to yield a revelatory insight into some human essence: "of all workers in imagination, the actor has most need for understanding; for on him is imposed the task of re-creating to external and material form types of character written in abstractions."[47] As quoted by Stoker, Irving was unstintingly essentialistic in his understanding of the bonds between genuine art and what he saw as its enlightening, unmediated, inexplicable effect—with little room for circumstance and contingency: "'truth is supreme and eternal. [...] Sincerity, which is the very touchstone of Art, is instinctively recognised by all.'"[48] Since this rests on an understanding of truth as revealed (rather than construed or constructed), Stoker argues for a necessary bond of congeniality at every level and moment in the crafting of a theatrical production. Further, he praises Irving's perceptiveness in identifying roles that would fit (or not) his specific gifts for representing the human, despite the breadth of his talent as actor, and his ability to adjust them to audience and circumstance:

an actor should be a judge of character; an understander of those differences which discriminate between classes and individuals of the class. [...]
The finer and more evanescent evidences of individuality must to a large extent be momentary. No true artist ever plays the same part alike on different repetitions.[49]

Ethos, in short, always takes priority over *mythos* in such observations—and, in Irving's and Stoker's poetics of the stage, it realizes its revelatory effect through a strong reliance on *pathos*.[50] Stoker's early account of Irving playing *Hamlet* is a case in point: in a segment of the *Reminiscences* headed "Irving's passion," he describes how the actor's "whirlwind of passion at the close of the play scene [...] night after night, stirred the whole audience to frenzied cheers," indeed "exalted by ready sympathy [which] lifted us to unwonted heights."[51] And this is presented as bringing an advancement of learning, as when, for example, "by speech and tone, action and time, he conveyed to his auditory the sense of complex and entangled thought and motive in his wild scene with Ophelia."[52] For Stoker, this transmission of a supposed deeper truth about the character, and indeed about human nature through the character, operates especially through a spiritual and indeed mystical dimension. This is what, in one of his reviews from 1876, Stoker explicitly misses in Salvini's Hamlet—"where is Hamlet the mystic, the man of melancholy, the man of action cramped and warped by the doubts of the dreamer?"[53]– and will explicitly praise as a signal trait of Irving's Hamlet, observed both the same and the following year. In the first instance (1876), Irving is celebrated for understanding that "the great, deep, underlying ideal of Hamlet is that of a mystic."[54] In the second (1877), Stoker acknowledges "an advance" in Irving's performance, since by then "the wild, fitful, irresolute, mystic, melancholy prince that we know in the play [...] [is] given with a sad picturesque gracefulness which is the actor's special gift;" to which he adds: "Mr. Irving's Hamlet is essentially a subjective performance."[55]

The psychological density for which Stoker praises Irving is of one piece with his celebrated transformative powers, as the actor seems to mutate into the character, or allow himself to be possessed by it. This is emphatically noted with regard to another Shakespearean creation that buttressed Irving's fame: "It has often amazed me to see the physiognomy of Shylock gradually emerge from the actor's own generous countenance."[56] And this attribution of transformative *and revelatory* power acquires, as an object of Stoker's prose, a close affinity with his taste for the extraordinary, deepened (as many, including Catherine Wynne, have noted) by "the Gothic climate at the Lyceum," sustained by "Irving's supernatural productions from *Faust* to *Macbeth*."[57]

The latter topic has obtained significant attention in the broader critical processing of Stoker's writing, contexts, and legacy.[58] In the remainder of this chapter, I am interested rather in extending my attention to the link between the twin, mutually balanced components of Stoker and Irving's collaboration, as described by the former: the spiritual or psychological bond, and the empirical or material basis of their joint venture. Probing this duality deeper should provide a more solid footing for my central suggestion that, at every stage, the commemorative and hagiographic design of the *Reminiscences* is as much about Stoker himself as it is about Irving—a project for self-fashioning, the delineation by and for the memorialist of a high-profile authorial and social persona of considerable talents, as much as for the glorification of another. Additionally, it should consolidate my point that the conceptual and argumentative grounds for Stoker's self-fashioning through a narrative about Irving are inherently dramatic and character-centered.

The prevalent doctrine on character at the Lyceum would seem to be expressive rather than constructive, to involve an assimilation of actor and role, rather than the crafting of a fiction. These are matters that, in the internal economy of Stoker's text in the *Reminiscences*, are given significant attention. Such attention is justified both by the avowed wish to offer an account of a genius (Irving) duly buttressed by extensive reflection— Stoker gives him as "secure in his intellectual position with regard to the theory of acting" and dedicates a chapter to "Irving's Philosophy of his Art"[59]—and to establish, rhetorically, the credentials of a memorialist (Stoker), who is himself operating out of an attitude of critical inquiry rather than mere wide-eyed reverence. It is in such a framework that Stoker explains how Irving disagreed with French actor Constant Coquelin's "theory that an actor in portraying a character must in the so doing divest himself of his own identity."[60] In context, Irving's endorsement of the contrary view was to some extent undermined by the skepticism of some of his contemporaries—prominently including Shaw, always dismissive of Irving's stage talent[61]—who apparently thought that he always played himself, rather than "the part" as the playwright had crafted it.[62] Nonetheless, Irving's belief in the need to find a point of convergence between the actor's personality and a dramatically assumed identity—in order to be "*sincere*," you have to "*pass a character through your own mind*"[63]—unequivocally hinged on a sense of the mutual dependence of artistic and personal truth.

Fundamentally for my argument on the dual validation that Stoker seeks with the *Reminiscences*, the moment at which Irving is evoked as sharing (with him, of course) the key, italicized nugget of wisdom ("the embodiment of an artistic philosophy"[64]) on that truth-yielding mutual dependence of actor and character is represented by Stoker through a trope of languor. The terms in which Stoker evokes a shared and fertile moment are of a kind that literary convention has associated with environments ripe for bodily abandon, rather than for a meeting of *bons esprits* kinned by aesthetic values: "Irving and I were alone together one hot afternoon ... ."[65] Stoker's ensuing explication of the "Philosophy of his [Irving's] Art" is prefaced by remarks on how artistic genius is bound to deliver, live, a core of truth. In order to be duly relayed, such truth will require an understanding mind, able to host and nurture a manifestation of "intellectual or psychic fire" with all its "penetrative force," combined with proper discursive talents "to put into words and the words into some sort of ordered sequence" the artist's "manifested wisdom."[66] Indeed, it involves a rarity of skill, empathy, and good fortune that the author of the *Reminiscences* is pleased to acknowledge in himself and believes proven in the insights vicariously provided by his text. Further, this capacity asserts itself—largely in a tacit manner—as homologous to the great actor's ability to "understand the dramatist's intention" and "represent the abstract idea as a concrete reality."[67] In this light, the proposition with which Stoker opens a section on the "Essence" of "Character"—"We think in abstractions, but we live in concretions"[68]—is both generic, referring to the *humanum genus*, and specific, concerning the two individuals brought into an indissoluble bond by collaboration at the Lyceum and the account it obtains in the *Reminiscences*.

Stoker's sense of the enactment of "a concrete reality" on stage certainly encompassed the literalism of Irving's mimetic practice (already mentioned above). And this in fact provides another revealing link between a commitment to the world of facts and a belief that dramatic representation crucially depends on a psychologized and spiritualized understanding of character. Indeed, the same impulse that led Irving, in Stoker's account, to test every stage prop for "accuracy" justified an event-based approach to characterization. At an anecdotal level, this finds a memorable instance in a stunt that Stoker narrates. Irving wanted to provide dramatist Frank Marshall with direct, personal knowledge of an emotional state he was to represent in a play; and, for that to be possible, Irving suddenly recreated the sound of a window bursting to give the unwitting and nervous playwright a sense of what a sudden rebellious attack would feel like. Having seriously frightened Marshall, Irving then remarked: "You are in the rare position now [...] of the dramatist who can write of high emotion from experience. The audience are bound to recognise the sincerity of your work."[69]

This sense of the need for direct experience if drama is indeed to prove a source of truth, be it the experience of the playwright or of the actor–manager, or indeed of anyone involved in their collaborative artistic rapport, becomes an important basis for Stoker's self-vindication as more than Irving's trusted factotum. As Catherine Wynne notes in the "General Introduction" to her edition of Stoker's writings on drama,

> Neither actor, nor playwright (although he attempted to write some plays), but business manager, Stoker, though instrumental to the Lyceum's success in his public relations, management, financial and administrative roles, nonetheless occupied its cultural margins.[70]

That he could easily be perceived as a subaltern with motley powers is in fact made clear by Stoker himself in the *Reminiscences*. This is acknowledged with remarkable sincerity on a couple of occasions, possibly the most striking of which being when he cites the observation of an American journalist about, an individual who *called himself* Bram Stoker […] who seems to occupy some anomalous position between secretary and valet. Whose manifest duties are to see that there is mustard in the sandwiches and to take the dogs out for a run; and who unites in his own person every vulgarity of the English-speaking race.[71]

The candor of this inclusion in the *Reminiscences* is suggestive of great self-confidence: rhetorically, the author behaves with the self-assurance and nonchalance of someone who knows with great certainty that his readership will take such a description as ludicrous—how else? It could indeed be so if it were not for the significant amount of self-justification that the book also includes. In a passage from the *Reminiscences* that one may see as directly balanced against the above, since it explains to outsiders the nature of Stoker's job with Irving by resorting to a high-flown analogy, he describes himself as "Chancellor of the Exchequer to his Absolute Monarchy."[72] Elsewhere, the credentials that Stoker repeatedly invokes stake his claims with regard to drama and criticism: in his 1894 essay on "Dramatic Criticism" he reassures his readers that he "speak[s] with a considerable knowledge of dramatic criticism and dramatic critics in both England and America;"[73] and in yet another passage from the *Reminiscences* he cites, with barely concealed pride, Irving's praise of his talent within the scope of Irving's own art:

> I well remember at one of our meetings in 1876 when after dinner we had some "recitations," according to the custom of that time, Irving was very complimentary to my own work because I antici-pated words by expression, particularly by the movement of my eyes.[74]

Such evening "recitations" provide, in fact, the setting for the passage with which I will close my argument. In one of the earlier chapters of the *Remi-niscences*, Stoker recalls an episode that acquires an almost foundational value as regards his relationship to Irving, while also confirming the extent to which it rested on a dramatic and character-based understanding of human bonds. At the climax of an evening spent with a small group of friends, Irving was reciting a poem theatrically,[75] and he conveyed the ostensible truth of a character in a way that Stoker exalts and commemorates as above nature (indeed, extra-ordinary), as if detached from the world of fact and matter. The impact on Stoker of what for him was a unique, superlative experience proved an instance of *crisis*, also etymologically—a decisive turning point:

> Irving's genius floated in blazing triumph above the summit of art. There is something in the soul which lifts it above all that has its base in material things. If once only in a lifetime the soul of a man can take wings and sweep for an instant into mortal gaze, then that "once" for Irving was on that, to me, ever memorable night.
>
> As to its effect I had no adequate words. I can only say that after a few seconds of stony silence [...] I burst out into something like a violent fit of hysterics.[76]

This passage of the memoirs—as indeed happens with other candid revelations in the *Reminiscences*—prompts Stoker to proceed to a lengthy self-justification:

> Let me say, not in my own vindication, but to bring new tribute to Irving's splendid power, that I was no hysterical subject. I was no green youth; no weak individual, yielding to a superior emotional force. I was as men go a strong man—strong in many ways.[77]

Ostensibly, Stoker's ensuing self-description as an athletic, sturdy thirty-year-old is justified by the hagiographic exercise: it intimates that Irving was so exceptional that no one could but be transfigured by his power to reveal and exacerbate character. However (as has been noted), this oft-quoted incident is rich in implications that go far beyond the triviality of an autobiographical vignette.[78] Stoker's claim not to be offering "[his] own vindication" is clearly disingenuous, and this is not only because the episode chimes with other passages in which Stoker insists on his emotional and intellectual perceptiveness. What crucially undermines Stoker's self-justification at this point is that the relevance he accords to it involves a claim for a revelatory power which reflects not just on the actor but also on himself as a privileged spectator whose superior sensitivity qualifies him for a special partnership, acknowledged and granted by Irving himself:

> Irving seemed much moved by the occurrence.
>
> On piecing together the causes of his pleasure at finding an understanding friend, and his further pleasure in realising that that friend's capacity for receptive emotion was something akin in forcefulness to his power of creating it, I can now have some glimpse of his compelling motive when he went into his bedroom and after a couple of minutes brought me out his photograph with an inscription on it, the ink still wet:
>
> "My dear friend Stoker. God bless you! God bless you!! Henry Irving. Dublin, December 3, 1876."
>
> In those moments of our mutual emotion he too had found a friend and knew it. Soul had looked into soul! From that hour began a friendship as profound, as close, as lasting as can be between two men.[79]

The exercise, indeed, in self-vindication is also *critical* in the judicative sense. It amounts to a rite of passage in emotion and intellect, and it follows a discussion that Stoker recalls from an earlier moment in the same evening. That discussion had concerned Stoker's reviews of Irving's *Hamlet*, with regard to which he noted Irving's willingness "to argue to the last any point suggested *on equal terms*."[80] To this, Stoker adds a remark made by Edward Dowden, in private conversation with him, apropos "Irving's acting: 'After all, an actor's commentary is his acting!'—a remark of embodied wisdom."[81] Stoker thus emphatically endorses the argument for a co-extension of the actor's revelatory talent and the critic's hermeneutic powers. By citing a critical authority (Dowden) who advocates a homology between Irving's stage talents, construed as a form of interpretation, and the explication offered by a man of letters, Stoker implicitly positions himself as the scholarly partner who stands by Irving, the artist, to make up an ideal concomitance. Further, the sequence of events that he reports allows him to combine that co-extension of critical acumen and artistic excellence with the ensuing record of a signed mutuality by which the object of his admiration was also the subject of a (self-)inscription that confirmed the dedicatee. Additionally, the memorialist's self-fashioning is of one piece with the ability he claims to share with the object of his efforts, a mutual understanding and internalization of character that he emphatically defines as the very core of dramatic art; and this is an argument, again, for mirrored (or at least complementary) talents, against the rich background of late nineteenth-century drama theory and stage practice. Through these and other imbrications, Stoker makes his *Personal Reminiscences of Henry Irving* into an integrated exercise that combines biography, hagiography, and lengthy but intermittent criticism—and indeed becomes a verbal memorial for the two men.

CHAPTER THREE

The Impress of the Visual and Scenic Arts on the Fiction of Bram Stoker

Matthew Gibson

Stoker, as Acting Manager of the Lyceum Theatre, had a somewhat unique relationship with the visual arts and with the artists of his day. His correspondence shows a large number of dealings with contemporary painters, from the older Pre-Raphaelites to later, more Impressionist-style painters such as John Singer Sargent. He acted more or less as a fixer and arranger for portrait sittings of Sir Henry Irving himself (one of the most painted subjects of the late nineteenth century); as an agent, practically, for his friend John B. Yeats[1] (whose drawing of Sir Henry is included in *Personal Reminiscences of Henry Irving* (1906)); but, above all, worked with scene painters such as W. L. Telbin and Joseph Harker, while managing one of the most visually sumptuous theaters of its time.

Lisa Hopkins has looked at the extensive references to Shakespeare, in particular *Othello* and *Hamlet*, which shape *Dracula* and *The Jewel of Seven Stars*.[2] Catherine Wynne has recently explored the means by which techniques of the late nineteenth-century "Gothic stage" made an impress on Stoker's fiction, with Ellen Terry's portrayal of Ophelia apparently affecting the character Teuta in *The Lady of the Shroud* and Irving's production of *Macbeth* also affecting the portrayal of *Dracula* and the rest of Bram Stoker's fiction.[3] Stephanie Moss has even seen the influence of the famous stage trick "pepper's ghost" in Dracula's inability to see his own reflection.[4]

However, it is also perhaps necessary to observe how Stoker's visual language and portrayal of both characters and settings were affected by the actual scenic arts of the theater, and by the more general trends in painting, which changed effectively from the Turneresque to the luscious later Victorian Pre-Raphaelite style and, finally, towards the more elliptical classicism of Art Nouveau and Fin-de-Siècle by the time Irving had lost the management of the Lyceum. The following chapter will examine firstly what Stoker's early reviews for the *Dublin Evening Mail* reveal about his attitude to both the scenic arts and towards painting generally; how the use of color on the stage affected his use of color in fiction; how the different schools of art, from the Pre-Raphaelite to the more elliptical Art Nouveau, are present in the iconography of his creative work; and, finally, how Stoker presents the practices of scene-painting and art in his fiction.

The Impress of Scenic Arts, Costume, and Painting on the Style of Stoker's Fiction

Throughout his career as Irving's Acting Manager at the Lyceum we find Stoker dealing with artists in his correspondence, in particular in relation to commissions for portraits of Sir Henry Irving. A letter of September 23, 1879 from John Butler Yeats confirms that the painter and Dublin friend of Stoker was providing him with paintings with which hopefully to interest buyers, while there are even two undated letters in French from Bastien Lepage arranging for a sitting to paint Irving's portrait.[5] A much longer sequence of letters is penned by Edward Burne-Jones to Stoker, including one that sheds light on how interaction with the theater contributed to Burne-Jones's own art. On May 2, 1895, the painter writes a letter to Stoker asking:

> I should very much like to have a suit of armour like the one that is worn by Sir Lancelot or Sir Percival and I should be most grateful to you if you could tell me how I could procure it and what the cost would be—I hope this would not be giving you any trouble and perhaps you might depute someone to help me in this matter as I know you are so very full of work.[6]

This letter shows how props that were used in plays were of use to painters like Burne-Jones in creating his medievalist works, and that there was thus an obvious confluence between the stage arts and the fine arts in this period. Burne-Jones had, of course, already painted the backdrop against which these suits of armor had been ranging in the first production of J. Comyns Carr's *King Arthur* (1895),[7] indicating how the performance on stage may have contributed an important link in the visualization of his own vibrant paintings, but what is also to be noted is that the letter may lead us to infer the unreliability of Stoker's *Reminiscences*, since there Stoker recalls that Burne-Jones designed the suit of armor himself and that it was "most picturesque."[8] Nevertheless, since J. Comyns Carr was himself attempting to bring the mystique of the Pre-Raphaelite aesthetic to his play, it is hardly surprising that one of the later Pre-Raphaelites should have been asked to paint the backdrop; this in itself demonstrates the extent to which painting and theater were closely interlinked in this period and further underlines the observations of Ellen Terry and Sybil Rosenfeld that Irving's goal was more beauty than historical accuracy in his productions.[9]

Regardless of Lyceum practices, the role of the visual arts in informing theatrical production was one of which Stoker had been well aware since his youth. As early as his twenties, when he was writing reviews for the *Dublin Evening Mail*, we observe a tendency to understand the problems of color and space in the theater in a way based on the appreciation of painting as an art form. In these reviews we can see the establishment of patterns indicating Stoker's own important tastes in the visual appearance of theater that were later to make an impact on his fiction as well. In a review of a pantomime at the Gaiety, Stoker makes an important declaration of his understanding of how stage craft communicates with the audience:

> The most important part of dress is colour. There is a natural symbolism in colour so perfect as any of the artificial symbols of the old masters ... and this symbolism can be carried to great perfection in theatrical dress. A photograph uncoloured is the truest means of reproducing expression, since it is a mere combination of light and shade, and possesses no power of prejudicing the mind of the beholder, for either good or evil, by the colours affecting his sight, but on the stage everything must be coloured, and highly coloured too, or else it will be absolutely without expression, since mere natural colour is lost in the great blaze of light.[10]

This comment, which compares color in stage costume to the "artificial symbols" of the old masters in art, and which eschews the comparison with the monochrome photograph made from natural—and thus more "real"—light, indicates two important elements in Stoker's attitude to the stage, and to art itself. Firstly, it demonstrates that Stoker's understanding of the visual effects of stage drama is linked to and based on the effects intended and achieved by painters—hardly surprising, as most scene-painters were also picture-painters, and the photograph was still a relatively new medium. However, this was an aesthetic model that he understood also as extending to costume design and other visual effects on the stage. In another early review of *Pygmalion and Galatea*, Stoker records how Pygmalion's "appearance is heightened by the adoption of the style of hair and beard which most painters deem so perfect that they have almost unanimously agreed in representing it in their picture of our lord."[11] In another review, this time of Miss Bateman in *Leah*, he describes the force of her acting this part as follows: "[her] face at the conclusion of this scene might well serve a painter for the study of the head of a Fury."[12] The intimation is that she is utterly convincing and hence a potential life model; however, the reference also intimates the importance of comparison with portraiture when observing the stage.

Indeed, Stoker frequently uses artists' metaphors in his descriptions of the productions, as though successful drama is in fact a form of *tableau vivant*. In one review of *Richard III* at Theatre Royal he calls Barry Sullivan's "pourtrayal" of the protagonist a "masterpiece of dramatic painting."[13] The visual touch-base for creating stage and scene effects, and in particular the characters themselves, was thus still the painting or artist's drawing—the most common visual image of the time—and the realistic, naturalistic photograph as yet played no part in the visual vocabulary needed by directors and set designers for creating theatrical illusion.

Scene-painting itself was of course closely aligned to conventional painting, and with this some of the popular fashions that informed the wider art world. For example, many years later Stoker notes that W. L. Telbin "painted some scenes worthy of Turner" as backdrops for the classically themed play *The Cup*, but that he and the other artists did so on the advice of Alexander Murray, Assistant Keeper of the Greek section of the British Museum, who researched Etruscan designs for them.[14] Again, this is hardly surprising as W. L. Telbin himself, in a series of articles on scene-painting for *The Magazine of the Arts*, acknowledges the need for "archaeological" knowledge on the part of the scene-painter along with the "artistic and the mechanical."[15] The style of Turner's own sublime, classical compositions was surely Telbin's goal, and the popularity of this style was not least because of the mid-century rise in archaeology, and of Turner's own ability to integrate mythology and modern interest in the discovery of ancient buildings, which further served scene-painters as the models for the backdrops of plays. As Sybil Rosenfeld explains, this had been the case with the Princess's Theatre, managed by Charles Kean in the 1850s. Kean, himself a devotee of the new enthusiasm for archaeology, had asked Thomas Grieve to reproduce Turner's *The Golden Bough* as a backdrop for "A Midsummer Night's Dream."[16] Therefore, comparison and allusion to known styles and visual clichés from the works of the great masters, many of them reproduced in illustrated books and magazines of the time, were important means of making the audience connect with and understand the play in accordance with an existing visual vocabulary.

Secondly, in returning to the above-quoted extract from Stoker's review of the Pantomime, it can be noted that the relation between painting and the visual effects of the stage is used to illustrate the importance of immediate symbolic effect, rather than purely naturalistic value or psychological plausibility of that time. While the Old Masters—perhaps allegorists such as Titian—achieved their techniques though "artificial symbols," color has a "natural symbolism" for Stoker, even if the color on the stage must itself be artificial and "not mere natural colour." Stoker repeats this importance of bright color for immediate effect on the stage in a review of Collins's *The Woman in White*, dramatized for a Dublin performance, when he observes that:

> Great use has been made of chromatic effect, and the attention of the audience is skillfully and subtly directed to the required points by the use which is made of the symbolical power of colour. Lady Glyde's dazzling blue dress in the second scene of the third act forms an admirable contrast to her gasoline appearance in the next scene, where she enters as Anne Catherick; and Fosco's dress in the "plot" scene is emininently suggestive of his character.[17]

The salient features of this passage are that the "symbolical power of colour" is used to "direct" the audience "subtly," and that colored dress is particularly suggestive of character. Since Fosco is a confidence trickster and charlatan, one must assume that this use of symbol belies the intentions of the characters considered as psychologically plausible persons, since drawing attention to one's own villainy is not what such people in real life do. Thus for Stoker the visual techniques of the stage have to be symbolic rather than simply naturalist or realistic—as suggested by his rejection of the analogy of the photograph—and, owing to the primitive nature of lighting at the time, this had to be achieved through bright, unnatural hues, despite the fact that the way in which color creates symbol is also entirely "natural." Hence Stoker would seem to understand the use of dress and color as being to present, in allegorical or essential fashion, the basic characters of the protagonists in a way akin to Romanticism and more recently melodrama, as opposed to the more metonymic and psychologically plausible tendencies of naturalism, where the salient features of characters are presented as being an effect of their psychological make-up, rather than an unconscious delineation of their true nature.

Both these aspects of the visual practices on the stage—the visual comparison with painting as a reference tool and the importance of color symbolism for portraying character—have a marked impress, I would argue, on Stoker's fiction. To begin with the framing of image through reference to painting, Stoker frequently refers to paintings or the painter's art when trying to direct the reader's "concretization"—to use Iser's phrase—of a scene.[18] Describing the villainous Don Bernadino in *The Mystery of the Sea*, we are told:

> Don Bernardino, with his high aquiline nose and black eyes of eagle keenness, his proud bearing and the very swarthiness which told of Moorish descent, was, despite his modern clothes, just such a picture as Velasquez would have loved to paint, or as Fortuny might have made to live again. (*TMS* 205)

There are two extant paintings of Moorish subjects by Velasquez, the one being the early *Kitchen Maid with the Supper at Emmaus* (1617–18), the other being the more famous *Juan de Pareja* (1650), a Moorish

Figure 3.1 *Portrait of Juan de Pareja*, Diego Velazquez, 1650.

indentured servant with a genuinely aquiline nose, whose portrait is one of Velazquez's most iconographic images. The reference to Marià Fortuny (1838–1874), a Catalan painter of Orientalist scenes, many with a historical bent, cements the idea that Don Bernardino is really a character who more properly belongs to a former age. Since the major protagonists in *The Mystery of the Sea* are descended from combatants on either side of the failed Spanish invasion of England of 1588, the comparison with the subjects of both these painters helps to manifest the historical basis of the two main rivals: Marjory Anita Drake, an American heiress, and Don Bernardino, a modern Spaniard—both of whom are attempting to reclaim old Spanish gold off the coast of Aberdeen, originally claimed by their rival ancestors.

At the beginning of *The Gates of Life* (1908) (*The Man* in its earlier British manifestation of 1905), the narrator actually sets the scene by describing its suitability for being painted:

> The scene would have gladdened a painter's heart. An old church-yard. The church low and square-towered, with long mullioned windows, the yellow-gray stone roughened by the waste and stress of age and tender-hued with growth of lichens. Round it clustered many old tombstones tilted and slanted in all directions; amongst them a few stately monuments, rising patrician fashion. Behind the church a line of ancient yews so gnarled and twisted in their thick brown stems […]
>
> The churchyard was full of fine cedars. Here and there amongst the dotted tombs and headstones many beautiful blossoming trees rose from the long green grass starred with wildflowers. The laburnum glowed in the June afternoon sunlight like a glory of burnished gold. The lilac, the hawthorn and the clustering meadowsweet which fringed the edge of the lazy stream mingled their heavy sweetness in sleepy fragrance which intensified the hum of myriad insect life […] The yellow-grey crumbling walls were green in places with wrinkled harts-tongues dwarfed by the stricture of their roots, and were topped with sweet-williams and spreading house-leek and stone-crop and wild-flowers whose delicious penetrating sweetness made for the intoxicating, drowsy repose of perfect summer.
>
> But amid all that mass of glowing colour the two young figures seated on the grey old tomb stood out conspicuously. (*GoL* 5–6)

In making this description, Stoker is drawing upon the reader's acquaintance with existing well-known graveyard paintings of the Victorian era: a favorite scene of the period. One would be Charles Rossiter's *Children in a Church Yard*, in which a young girl is seated on a flat tomb talking

Figure 3.2 *Children in a Church Yard*, Charles Rossiter, c. 1860?

to a smaller, standing child, against a backdrop almost identical to the one described in the first paragraph of Stoker's novel, with its line of trees trailing behind a lichen-spotted, square-towered church of grey and yellow stone, and "blossoming trees" amongst the tombstones; or, indeed, it could recall Arthur Hughes's "Home from the Sea" of c. 1862, in which a young boy wearing a sailor's uniform is lying in grief in a churchyard on his front, hands clasped as if in prayer, while a young girl in black, seated beside him, watches on. Or, indeed, it would recall William Holman Hunt's "The Old Church, Ewell" of 1847, which displays the church of that village as the impressive backdrop to an older woman, presumably a governess, leading a young girl through the graveyard. All of these paintings present a scene of the moral and emotional education of the young, reminiscent of Wordsworth's poem "We are Seven" (or, indeed—in a more ironic sense—the first chapter of *Great Expectations*). To cap it all, Stephen (a fourteen-year-old girl) and Harold (a nineteen-year-old youth) are overhearing the argument of two "off-stage" village girls, who are arguing over whether it is better to be a God than an angel (*GoL* 5). Such a scene is ironic, as Stephen's masculine attire is, as David Glover notes, a "'foreglimpse' of the 'trouble' that follows,"[19] as Stephen shows a similar hubris to the two village girls by taking on masculine distinctions, and never listens to the sensible Harold.

However, if we look further at the portrayal of Stephen in the following passages we can discern other salient features that recall famous paintings, or painting motifs, of both the time and before. Stephen's costume is described in great detail in keeping with the traditions normally associated with portraits of English women in hunting attire, but with special attention to her "red-golden hair" (*GoL* 6). However, we later see a description that bears relation to familiar tropes in more recent paintings:

> Even in her fourteenth year Miss Stephen Norman was of striking beauty; beauty of a rarely composite character [...] The firm-set jaw, with chin broader and more square than is usual in a woman, and the wide fine forehead and aquiline nose marked the high descent from Saxon through Norman. The glorious mass of red hair, full, thick, massive, long and fine of the true flame colour, showed the blood of another ancient ancestor of Northern race, and suited well with the voluptuous curves of the full, crimson lips [...] The black eyes, deep blue-black, or rather purple-black, the raven eyebrows and eyelashes, and the fine curve of the nostrils spoke of the Eastern blood of the far-back wife of the Crusader. Already she was tall for her age, [...] Long-legged, long-necked, as straight as a lance from the crown of her head to the sole of her foot, with head poised on the proud neck like a lily on its stem. (*GoL* 6–7)

The passage ostensibly draws on her racial features, which can be found in the eugenic work of Beddoe, who attributed red hair to Norman—and thus to aristocratic—ancestry, and with this the qualities of being "crafty, capable, energetic, brave and industrious"[20] (although here we are told that this red hair is from "another ancient ancestor of the Northern race," possibly the Norse people from whom the Normans were descended). Curiously, her "aquiline" nose is here related to this Norman ancestry, and not to the "Moorish" or eastern side of her progenitors, as it certainly is in the description of Don Bernardino in the comparison with a Velazquez painting in *The Mystery of the Sea*, and it is instead the "purple black eyes" and "fine curve of the nostrils" which indicate this trait. However, despite the trace of eastern influence in her racial heritage, it is her shape, hair, and skin color that conform most to clichés of painting, since her mass of golden red hair, her pale face on a long neck, "like a lily on its stem," and "voluptuous curves of full crimson lips," draw upon the visual cliché of the Pre-Raphaelite woman. In Rossetti's paintings it is the redheaded heroine who has all these features and is also, like the Virgin Mary, associated with the pale lily of chastity, as present in his painting *The Blessed Damozel*. In describing these features the image and the association of the Pre-Raphaelite would have been an obvious image cliché for his audience for innocent sensuality, as was the woman with pale face, red lips, and dim red hair described in Yeats's poems in *The Wind among the Reeds*, published six years earlier than the original, British version of the novel.

However, another feature of the description here is the importance of color for portraying the innate characteristics of a character. Stephen's red hair relates her to Pre-Raphaelite innocence as does the paleness of her face, while her black eyes—a common feature in Stoker's heroines and anti-heroines—relate her to a certain ambivalent masculinity, which she shares with the equally Eastern Margaret Trelawney and with Mimi in *The Lair of the White Worm* (*LWW* 23). Her portrayal thus has a psychological complexity between classic femininity and the more masculine features of aggression and mastery, which later in the novel she eventually learns to subdue. Such complexity could never have been presented on the stage in the forms of characters like Count Fosco, but nevertheless color, as in the scenic arts and in costume design, is always Stoker's foremost method for suggesting character, in a way that not only draws from the traditions of religious allegory and stage melodrama but which is actually more akin to the use of color by Symbolist and Modernist writers such as Yeats, rather than the more Realist, nineteenth-century traditions of fiction. Color is used to suggest mood, character, and even spiritual state in Stoker's work, but in a way that is often quite complex and which draws from artificial, not natural, color schemes. Rather than suggesting character metonymi-cally, as in the more usual realist traditions of nineteenth-century fiction,

Figure 3.3 *The Blessed Damozel*, Dante Gabriel Rossetti, 1875–78.

color relates immediate, unconscious, and symbolic aspects of personality, as in the scheme of Joyce's *Dubliners*.

The use of artificial color to represent spiritual state is obvious in *The Mystery of the Sea* (1902), and Stoker's reading in Alchemical and Rosicrucian texts makes itself known with his description of Lauchlane Macleod, whom the hero Archie Hunter—cursed with second sight—soon realizes will die off the rocks on "Lammas-tide" (the first of August):

> He was a fine-looking fellow, well over six feet high, with a tangled mass of thick red-yellow hair and curly, bushy beard. He had lustrous, far-seeing golden-brown eyes, and curly, bushy beard, and massive, finely cut features. His pilot-cloth trousers spangled all over with silver herring scales, were tucked into great, bucket-boots. He wore a heavy blue jersey and a cap of weasel skin. I had been thinking of the decline of the herring from the action of the trawlers in certain waters, and fancied this would be a good opportunity to get a local opinion. Before long I strolled over and joined this son of the Vikings. (*TMS* 10–11)

Macleod shares some similarities with Stephen in having red-golden hair (in her case a result of Norman, in his case Viking ancestry), and such a feature also relates him to virtue. However, his "golden-brown eyes," "silver herring scales," and blue jacket speak of a different set of features. The narrator describes the man as one who is marked out for death and spiritual transmogrification by the sea on Lammas-tide, after which event Archie sees the ghost of Macleod in a grim procession, with now wholly "golden beard" and "golden eyes" (*TMS* 30; 35). Stoker would have known of the potential of the alchemical metals gold and silver for representing the union of respectively Spirit and Soul purified beyond the body. Such is the symbology of the work of John Dee, whose attempt to make "trans-muted gold" from the philosopher's stone Stoker describes later in *Famous Impostors*,[21] and whose use of color symbolism he surely knew from his works such as the *Monas Heiroglyphica*, which uses the "marriage of moon and sun" to represent soul and spirit unified[22] (he had also read all about the famous alchemist Cagliostro, whose Rosicrucian symbols he described in some detail).[23] The complexity present in Stephen's portrayal is absent here, as Stoker uses color to suggest the transmogrification of this fisherman who is sacrificed to the sea, rather than to indicate his personality, but the development of artificial color as a form of immediate symbolism for character and spiritual state is as evident here as it was in the productions at the Gaiety Theatre in Dublin in the 1870s.

Greater complexity can be discerned in the use of color for portraying Margaret Trelawney in *The Jewel of Seven Stars* (1903), again drawing from Stoker's readings in the occult and from his understanding of painting: although in a manner which also indicates a movement away from the taste for the Great Masters and Pre-Raphaelite art which informs other novels. While Roger Luckhurst, in his work *The Mummy's Curse*, understands the inspiration for this novel as issuing from contemporary archaeological finds in Egypt and especially the recent interest in Queen Hatshepsut,[24] and David Glover notes the importance of H. Rider Haggard's *She* for inspiring the tale,[25] Stoker had, we must remember, seen archaeological discovery portrayed in the theater as well, one early example being the Assyrian forms displayed in "Sardanapulus" on the Irish stage in the 1870s.[26] In *The Jewel of Seven Stars*, a Gothic tale based on Egyptology, and in particular a fascination with the Queen Hatshepsut, the heroine Margaret Trelawny—herself an incarnation of the Egyptian Queen "Tera"—is likewise described in terms which use color to portray character:

> Miss Trelawney was of fine figure; dark, straight-featured. She had marvelous eyes; great, wide-open, and as black and soft as velvet, with a mysterious depth. To look in them was like gazing at a black mirror such as Doctor Dee used in his wizard rites. I heard an old gentleman at the picnic, a great oriental traveller, describe her eyes "as looking at night at the great distant lamps of a mosque through the open door." The eyebrows were typical. Finely arched and rich in long curling hair, they seemed like the proper architectural environment of the deep splendid eyes. Her hair was black also, but was as fine as silk. Generally black hair is a type of animal strength and seems as if some strong expression of the forces of a strong nature; but in this case there could be no such thought. There were refinement and high breeding; and though there was no suggestion of weakness, any sense of power

there was, was rather spiritual than animal. The whole harmony of her being seemed complete. Carriage, figure, hair, eyes; the mobile, full mouth, whose scarlet lips and white teeth seemed to light up the lower part of the face—as the eyes did the upper; the wide sweep of the jaw from chin to ear; the long, fine fingers; the hand which seemed to move from the wrist as though it had a sentience of its own. All perfections went to make up a personality that dominated either by its grace, its sweetness, its beauty, or its charm. (*JSS* 28–29)

This passage deserves some delicate attention. To begin with it uses color symbolism, and in particular black. Like Stephen, Margaret has oriental black eyes—a recurring motif in Stoker's fiction—which he later uses in *The Man/The Gates of Life* (to suggest masculinity and transgressive power (*GoL* 7)). As in *The Mystery of the Sea*, however, color is used not necessarily naturally, but to suggest a moral and spiritual state whose roots are in occult, supernatural strength, as the color black here is related to the "black mirror" of John Dee, whose work Stoker would write on later in *Famous Impostors*.[27]

However, the comparison of Margaret's forms with the harmony of architecture points to the scenic arts, rather than the visual arts, as having the greatest effect on this passage. In a book whose first part is set in a replica of a museum space, Margaret herself is described very much as though she is a temple holding some greater spiritual secret. Her "finely arched eyebrows," much like architraves, are an "architectural environment" for the black eyes that, through their color, suggest the opaque spiritualism already referred to through the "black mirror" of Dee. However, the most important aspect of the description is that of "harmony" in this architectural beauty, as though the parts all cohere into a rhythm. The comparison of her with an architectural form of course calls to mind the Turneresque, archaeological backdrops painted by Telbin, Grieve, and others in the decades before, as though we are being invited to see a human being's face as architectural scenery. The further combination of architectural comparison and insistence on "harmony" in the form also draws obvious comparison with Hegel's discussion of the "symmetry" of religious architecture as part of the early Symbolic phase in art history, in which the subject sees the "sublime"—for Hegel a form of ideality related to religious spirituality—as something external to that which suggests it.[28] While for Hegel this "Symbolic" phase is inferior to the later "Classical" phase, in which the material is able to blend with the ideal seamlessly (in particular through sculpture, and often through the anthropomorphic portrayal of gods),[29] its representative forms were beginning to make a return in the artistic referentiality of Europeans through the ideas of Art Nouveau and the "Advanced Movement,"[30] which began to deny personification in art—not least through the scene design of Ellen Terry's son Edward Craig for the Purcell Operatic Society.

We have therefore seen the effects of the scenic and visual arts specifically on Stoker's fiction; how the comparison with well-known paintings on stage prompts the same comparisons in his work; how the use of artificial color on the stage for symbolic effect also impacts his own use of color in fiction; and how he incorporated the styles and motifs of various different painterly styles into his work.

One question which remains to be addressed, however, relates to the clues given to us by the novels and short stories in relation to Stoker's view of the profession of the painter and its role within his novels.

Scenic Artist and Painter in Stoker's Fiction

In his late collection of short stories, *Snowbound* (1908), we see direct reference to the art of the scene-painter in the collection's very last piece, "A Moon-Light Effect." After a series of short stories all told by different members of a travelling theater company stuck on a train in a snow drift, the scene-painter of the troupe, Turner Smith, recounts how he was involved in a "sting" performed by a bankrupt theater manager called "Old Schoolbred." Asked to do the scene-painting for Byron's *Manfred*, his canny solicitor makes him take a lease on the atelier in the theater rather than just simply work there (*SnB* 147). Things soon change, as his boss is offered the chance to tour his opera company in the Americas, but cannot do so as receivers are claiming all his property. Old Schoolbred decides to pay this off by planning a new play set in an artist's atelier, and asks the scene-painter to recreate the workshop he is leasing on the stage itself, and also to create a moon on the backflap behind a window, to assure the receivers that he is serious about paying them back by preparing the stage for a new drama. The receivers admire this scene, in particular the moon, over alcohol that sends them to sleep. When they are asleep Old School-bred manages to "sho[o]t the moon" (*SnB* 159) by doing a moonlight flit: having asked Smith to re-create the atelier—the only objects in the theater that cannot be claimed because of the artist's lease—Old Schoolbred quickly takes the rest of the company and its props out to hired steamers for their American tour. The moonlight effect itself appears to have been an elaborate visual joke and a reminder that all on the stage is unreal. This use of the moon to create a false sense of perspective issues from Stoker's own very keen understanding, registered on more than one occasion in *Reminiscences*, that perspective on the stage is all falsehood, one particular example being Irving playing the role of Napoleon in *Madame-Sans-Gêne*, using very tall actresses and large scenery to make the otherwise tall Irving appear like the diminutive Napoleon.[31]

One of the first texts Stoker published concerning the visual arts is his short story "Lies and Lilies" (1881), all about the little girl Claribel, who is told by her schoolmistress that to lie is a sin, and that those who lie will be left outside the gates of the eternal city when they die. Claribel is a good girl, but when finding a sum too hard she decides to trace a painted lily on a slate, aided by the distracting demon Skooro, and then lies about this to her teacher. At night she is shown in a dream the lilies of the celestial city by the Child Angel, who informs her she will now not see them, and, despite the attempt of Skooro to distract her, the remorse absolves her of the guilt, giving her a love of real lilies for the rest of her life.[32] Since the lie comes from Claribel copying a painted lily which accompanies her lying, we might wish to interpret this as the equation of painting with falsehood, a substitute for reality, at least as part of the engine through which the moral of the story is conveyed. While it is unlikely that Stoker entertained such a distrust of art, given the deep respect for painters and scene-painters he presents in *Reminiscences*, one of Stoker's later fictions does demonstrate an understanding of the pitfalls of the artist's mindset and the results of their education, as well as its potential advantages.

The only novel of Stoker's to make art and painting central as an activity and profession is *The Shoulder of Shasta* (1895), in which the novel's heroine, Essie Elstree, comes back to life in the mountains of California after an illness, accompanied by her mother and by her protectress, Miss Gimp. Chaperoned and aided by her first youthful romantic enthusiasm, the manly frontiersman Grizzly Dick—which character, as Carol A. Senf has noted, was modeled on the real-life Bill Cody[33]—she finds her senses awakened in exposure to both the picturesque and the sublime traditions of poetry and painting by contemplating the landscape of the mountains. In one long passage, Stoker shows not only a remarkable knowledge of the work of Wordsworth, Coleridge, and the "Lakers" but also an appreciation of the (pre-Hegelian) German aesthetic ideas of the sublime that underpin the later thought of Coleridge:

> Esse stood watching and watching, and drinking in consciously and unconsciously all the rare charm and inspiration of Nature, and a thousand things impressed themselves on her mind which she afterwards realized to the full, though at the moment they were but unconsidered items of a vast mutually-dependent whole. Like many another young girl of restless imagination, at once stimulated and cramped by imperfect health, she had dipped into eccentric forms of religious thought. Swedenborgianism had at one time seemed to her to have an instinctive lesson, which was conveyed in some more subtle form than is allowed of by words. Again, that form of thought, or rather of feeling, which has been known as of the "Lake School," had made an impression on her, and she had so far accepted Pantheism as a creed that she could not dissociate from the impressions of Nature the idea of universal sentience. (*SoS* 37)

This passage moves from Esse's aesthetic apprehension of landscape to explaining the two schools of thought that help govern her impressions: firstly, Swedenborgianism, with, presumably, its beliefs in correspondence between the material and the spiritual and that the three layered heavens in Swedenborg's work contain the metaphysical prototypes of the objects of nature and human life;[34] and, secondly, the Pantheism of the Lake school of Wordsworth and Coleridge, which Coleridge had initially understood through the Unitarian belief that matter is an effect of energy and part of a preordained "Great Design" in history,[35] and in his later view through the Schellingian belief that the finite soul or consciousness of a human being is able to connect through imagination with the infinite soul of God through interpreting the works of nature, which symbolize God's mind (an idea arguably represented in his view that a harmonious poem is a "*tertium aliquid*," resulting from the imagination connecting with a spiritual other).[36] Stoker's reference to Swedenborg may result from his own independent studies, given his acknowledged interest in occult ideas (not least, perhaps also, his reading of Le Fanu), and his reading of Wordsworth and Coleridge—whose *The Eolian Harp* he later quotes to illustrate Esse's own worship at "the shrine of nature" (*SoS* 38)—would have been an obvious part of his education. However, the earlier description of her apprehension of the landscape and description of the process does seem distinctly similar to Kant's description of the sublime, or mathematical sublime, as the inability of the imagination to harmonize the innate reason and the acquired, conceptual understanding as it attempts to comprehend the form it sees and judge it, since the idea of reason manifested in nature is beyond that present in man's own so there is no finality, but simply a feeling of awe.[37] So, unlike with the beautiful, the free play of the *Urteilkraft* or Imagination—which allows the imagination to present the ideas to the understanding in judgments of the beautiful and find formal satisfaction[38]—fails to approximate the experience and allow the form to pass into the understanding and find that sense of finality.[39] That Esse is capable of later recalling the "thousand impressions" of the "vast mutually-dependent whole" may be no more than Stoker's consideration of Wordsworth's concept of "emotion recollected in tranquility," in which a powerful experience is recalled but then tempered by the lack of immediacy and the new ability to center on the details which prompted the emotion with more leisure, such as in the poem "I Wandered Lonely as a Cloud" where the poet saw "Ten thousand" daffodils "at a glance," but later sees them "in vacant or in pensive mood" as they "flash upon the inward eye."[40] The sense of being unable to comprehend and harmonize all the impressions at a time, as well as the sense of "unity" in the impression, may point to a wider reading into the aesthetic of the sublime on Stoker's part than knowledge of Wordsworth and Coleridge may have provided him.

Whatever the case, Esse's aesthetic sense and supporting Pantheism does not encourage her to write poetry, but rather to draw and paint the scenes that inspire her. Her tastes would certainly appear, however, to be in keeping with the tradition of landscape painting that was contemporary with late eighteenth-century poetry: namely, the "picturesque." Indeed, this term is used almost constantly to describe Esse's first tentative love interest, Grizzly Dick, whose hunter's dress she finds fascinating, and who is described as "the most picturesque figure" she meets when arriving on Shasta (*SoS* 27). The term is then used to describe Esse's perspective when at night she sees "the red flare of burning pine," and we learn that "Esse felt like some barbaric empress, and could not take her mind off the picturesque and romantic aspect of the whole thing" (*SoS* 31). The reference to "some barbaric empress" in relation to the torches that the Indians have lit for her hints at the sense of power she feels both through the importance the event accords her but also at the empowerment the aesthetic observer acquires in seeing the "picturesque." It may even recall the famous story about another empress (whose country Stoker most definitely understood as "barbaric"), Tsarina Caterina the Great, who famously ordered a ship to be burned to allow the painter Jakob Philipp Hackert to paint his celebratory painting "The Destruction of the Turkish Fleet in the Bay of Chesme," an event which she also orchestrated and observed (the ship upon which Dracula returns to Transylvania is of course also called the "*Czarina Catherine*" (*D* 311)). In calling the scene "picturesque," Stoker is of course using a term chiefly defined by William Gilpin as "*some quality, of being illustrated by painting*," but also as a kind of middle phase between the harmony of beauty and the vast and more disordered feature of the sublime, since Gilpin also asserted that "*roughness* forms the most essential point of difference between the *beautiful* and the *picturesque*."[41]

As mentioned above, the term is mainly used in this novel in relation to Esse's perspective on Grizzly Dick. When looking at Dick's "strong face, jolly with masculine humour and exuberant vitality" (*SoS* 40), and then at the Indians' "saturnine faces," Esse "contrasted his picturesqueness, which was yet without offence to convention, with their unutterably fantastic, barbarous, childish, raggedness" (*SoS* 40). The picturesqueness would appear to be a form of controlled wildness, or roughness, as opposed to the too-great wildness of the Indians, which, perhaps owing to their proximity, fails to complement his own powerful appearance with any sublime experience. The term is used not long afterwards, when she describes the golden hair of Miss Gimp as a "picturesque tangle" (41), again an image that hints at a form of controlled wildness, in the unbinding of normally plaited hair. Later we are told that Esse is continually sketching, but has soon exhausted "all the picturesque possibilities of the plateau," and so she decides to move to a location "further than usual down the steep side of the mountain." It is there that, having set up her easel and canvas, she sees Grizzly Dick again:

> There was a fallen tree, which served for a seat, and here, having unstrapped and mounted her portable easel, she began to make her sketch. There was a drowsy hum about the place, for these were regions of honey bees, and in the delightful solitude her thoughts took their most pleasant way, their central point being none other than the picturesque figure of Grizzly Dick. (*SoS* 67)

Here, just before the fateful encounter with the bear that leaves Dick badly wounded, and which further cements their relationship, Dick is not only picturesque but has blended in with the "picturesque" landscape—a sure sign that, despite the seeming closeness between them, Dick will eventually become less an individual whom she understands and more part of a decorative experience that plays upon her memory once she has left the mountains and is in the social whirl of San Francisco.

Once there her aesthetic education on Shasta creates the peculiar effect of both nostalgia at all these scenes but also remorse for her abandonment of Dick. We see the signs of an over-emotionalism comparable to the overly impressionable imaginations of Ann Radcliffe's heroines:

> Since Dick was only a memory, he became one with that particular nimbus of softening effects which is apt to accompany and environ a memory which is pleasant one—that which is to a memory what a halo is to a pictorial saint, at once a distinguishing trait and an aid to fancy. (*SoS* 84)[42]

Able to relate this "picturesque" charm to her friends, their advice leads her to the catastrophic decision to allow her friend Peter Blyth to go and ask Dick to join them in San Francisco—which the latter eventually does after she has agreed to marry the artist Reginald Hampden.

It is perhaps in this way that Stoker demonstrates the pitfalls of the artist's temperament, particularly when applied to relations with other human beings. While Dick and Esse forged a union through helping each other's survival when attacked by the bears, her lasting impression of him is his aesthetic appearance in the wilderness. That his "picturesque" aspect is ultimately associated with his surroundings ensures that Esse adds charm to the impression through memory, which allows her, initially at least, to create an exaggerated sense of attachment to what is really an aesthetic experience rather than a more deep-rooted encounter with an individual, as through the "tricks" of memory, "[s]he construed in her own soul the indifference of their parting into a wrong for him" (*SoS* 85). While Stoker also links her vacillation and self-delusion to her feminine need to love, and "something in the feminine nature which seems to have a distinct need of expressing itself in some form of self-abnegation," it is the cultivation of her artistic sentiment while on Shasta and her attachment to the "picturesque" that are the major spurs to this process. Thus the aesthetic education of Esse helps lead her onto the path of a deluded sense of romance and then remorse, which quickly evaporates when she meets Reginald. As Andrew J. Garavel writes, "[a]s she is in a sense aestheticized by the painter, so in turn she makes the memory of her former love into a work of art … [a] safe and sentimental icon."[43]

If we see the pitfalls of the artistic temperament in the over-impressionable nature of Esse after long dedication to landscape painting, then Reginald Hampden presents a more positive aspect of the aesthetic education in relation to its effect on social habit. We are told of Reginald that:

> He was one of those who had not attached himself to any art school long enough to be cramped by its inevitable littleness. He had skipped lightly through the various schools of the world, learning and adapting all their methods to his own genius, and keeping his mind and imagination fresh by a perpetual study of Nature in all her moods. Partly by nature, and partly by merit of his varied training, he was of a most charming personality, with

gentler manners and keener refinement than might have been
expected from his strength and stature. (*SoS* 109)

Unlike Esse, who has embraced purely the Romantic trends in painting,
Reginald has moved through more than one school without being dominated by any of them, meaning effectively that he has learned to look at
nature from more than one point of view. However, what also differenti-
ates him from Esse is that he is perhaps more dispassionate, making a
"study of Nature in all her moods" (109). This effectively means that he
has no particular bias in his observations, and is thus more capable of
observing nature objectively, as it is by observing the varieties in nature,
and thus its plurality, that he is capable of stirring his aesthetic abilities
while avoiding the type of fixation on one type of aesthetic and mood
which so far condemns Esse to her morbid memory. While Esse is, as
Garavel has written, "portrayed as a Romantic,"[44] it is fair to say that
Reginald cannot be classified in any particular way, as an insistence on
observing nature objectively—that is, in terms of its own varied moods
rather than the artist's subjective impression—is a prerequisite for artistic
schools as different as those of Jacques David, the synthesizing classicism of
Ingres, and even the early Pre-Raphaelites.[45] Through his "varied training"
of exposing himself to nature's plurality he has also allowed himself to
develop "keener refinement" than might be expected, the narrator tells
us, from someone of his size and strength—and we later see this quality
in application.

What this "keener refinement" appears to be is his ability to judge
character and temperament in others when the situation demands it, and
in particular when assuaging Grizzly Dick and allowing him to keep face
once he has been humiliated through his very public rejection by Esse
at her engagement reception. Just as Dick threatens to attack everyone
as he realizes his humiliation, Reginald's aesthetic education solves the
situation:

In the midst of the silence Reginald Hampden stepped out, and
Esse felt glad, and a new sense of relief, as she noticed his calm
and gallant bearing. He moved towards Dick, and said with
courtly sweetness:

"I hope I may speak here, since it is my privilege to speak for
Miss Elstree! Look, sir! Look; the young lady! You are distressing
her! I know you to be a brave man, and, from all I have heard her
say to your honour, I am quite sure you would not willingly cause
her harm or humiliate her." (*SoS* 124)

Reginald's refinement and ability to judge "Nature in all her moods," in this
"potent, reckless, fatal force," includes his ability to judge the parallel sense
of gallantry within Dick indicated by the fury of his own crushed honor
and acute feeling of humiliation, allowing Reginald to calm the hunter.

Thus, while Stoker shows how scene-painting in the theater is apt
for creating "trickery" and "trompe l'oeil," his portrayal of the artist's
temperament and education appears to favor classical objectivity over
the picturesque of the late eighteenth century and later, self-indulgent
Romantic period. While the artist can be self-indulgent and prone to
objectifying people as part of an aesthetic experience, as Esse does, leading
her paradoxically to confuse the aesthetic with the ethical, the empirical
artist who studies nature without prejudice can also develop refined
psychological insight, as does Reginald Hampden.

Conclusion

The major impress of the visual and scenic arts on Stoker's fiction, among
the many other influences which inform his work, would appear to be the
use of painting as a comparative form to allow his readers to concretize
the appearance of characters; the use of artificial color to suggest character
and spiritual state, as on the stage; and the adoption of stylistic movements and ideas ranging across the Turneresque, the Pre-Raphaelite,
and the post-Hegelian forms of Fin-de-Siècle art as inspirations for his
portrayal of scene and character. While he understands the role of the
scene-painter specifically as being to create false perspective, his novel *The
Shoulder of Shasta* displays a very fine knowledge of Romanticism and
the picturesque, and also acts as a form of analysis of different styles and
predispositions in the artist's temperament to assess the possible pitfalls
and advantages of being an artist.

Science, Technology, and Ideas

CHAPTER FOUR

"Sure we are all friends here!"

Bram Stoker's Ideal of Friendship
and Community in the Context of
Nineteenth-century Bio-social Thought

Sabine Lenore Müller

"Never in any other man have I seen such a capacity for devotion to a friend," Hall Caine writes about Bram Stoker in his obituary in 1912.[1] Stoker's friends and correspondents, as well as his biographers, agree that he was a sincerely devoted and appreciative friend, Dacre Stoker, in *The Forgotten Writings of Bram Stoker*, noting that "Bram was clearly a man who valued and was valued by his circle of friends." Ellen Terry, Henry Irving, and Hall Caine were among his closest friends, to whom he dedicated effusive notes of appreciation and appraisal.[2] When reading Stoker's novels, especially those from the 1890s—*The Snake's Pass* (1890), *The Shoulder of Shasta* (1895) and *Dracula* (1897)—friendship, loyalty, even sacrifice for the sake of a community of friends appear as unshakeable ideals and the only antidote to social injustice and an omniscient, threatening form of bio-power. Stoker's novels unfold their narratives in the wider context of Victorian theories on population growth and social development, in which questions about "how we live and how we might live, became questions that were believed to have biological answers."[3] The theories of Charles Darwin and Robert Malthus, and a host of scholars and critics in their wake, were the foundation of a climate in which biological, sociological, and political questions were discussed in close connection. Hence, it is not surprising that throughout Stoker's prose and fiction this nexus is apparent. But what is surprising is that Stoker, perhaps inspired by the outspoken socialism of his friend the Manx-man Thomas Henry Hall Caine, himself expressed views critical of Darwinian principles of natural selection and also opposed the fatal bio-politics resulting from combining economic laissez-faire with Malthusian population theories. This paper will explore Stoker's social ideals and his vision of friendship in the frame of nineteenth-century bio-sociological and bio-political thought and—owing a great debt to Piers J. Hale's *Political Descent: Malthus, Mutualism, and the Politics of Evolution in Victorian England* (2014)—will draw special attention to the numerous resonances between views expressed in Stoker's texts and those developed by Victorian socialist critics of Malthus, Darwin, and their followers.

It seems that Bram Stoker not only outlined ideals of friendship in his fiction but also adhered to them in life. Yet, William Hughes warns us not to accept this mythicized image of Stoker—"'faithful Bram'" and his big heart, gentle nature, and bottomless loyalty in the midst of devoted and deserving, selfless friends—without noticing the deliberate ways in which his image was created.[4] This paper will explore some of the ways in which Stoker and his notion of friendship and community were constructed and reconstructed by himself and his contemporaries in a wider force field of bio-sociological debates concerning whether altruism or self-interest were the true determinants of individual and societal evolution, and which, in turn, would be the most advantageous form of social governance. In the Darwinian frame, as Hale notes:

> It seemed reasonable to doubt that a compassionate regard for others could possibly result from a process that appeared only to reward self-interest. In a struggle for life in which even the smallest advantage could make the difference between life and death, surely, on the average, the selfish would prevail and the selfless would be driven to extinction—this much seemed evident for the way in which Darwin had applied Malthus.[5]

Yet, ever since the publication of *The Origin of Species* (1859) this view had been and still continues to be fiercely debated because of its direct implications for understanding human behavior. Richard Dawkins, in *The Selfish Gene*, popularized and radicalized the view that altruism is nothing but a "rare case of natural selection getting it wrong," and is proposed only by "men who have allowed themselves to be persuaded by what they want to be true rather than to accept the cold hard truth of scientific fact."[6] Meanwhile, at the other end of the spectrum, Matt Ridley, in his *The Origins of Virtue* (1996), bases his argument on evolutionary biology reaching back to the beginnings of the discipline, exploring the evolutionary origins of the "surprisingly social nature of the human animal."[7] This argument and schism reaches back to the nineteenth century and beyond. The idea that nature is an "arena of pitiless struggle between self-interested creatures,"[8] propagated by the followers of Darwin—first and foremost "Darwin's bulldog" Thomas Henry Huxley—reaches back "through Malthus, Hobbes, Macchiavelli and St. Augustine to the Sophist philosophers of Greece, who viewed human nature as essentially selfish and individualistic unless tamed by culture."[9] On the other hand, the notion that virtue, altruism, and cooperation are, likewise, innate and naturally evolved was passionately defended in the nineteenth century by thinkers such as the Russian exiled anarchist Peter Kropotkin, this tradition going back via Godwin, Rousseau, and Pelagius to Plato.[10] Piers J. Hale offers a valuable synthesis and historically contextualizing reading of the two "distinct and mutually hostile traditions."[11] This debate, as Hale shows, evolved around the ideas of the political economist Thomas Robert Malthus and the significance of his 1798 *Essay on the Principle of Population*. Malthus had argued that "because population increased exponentially [...] while resources could at best increase in only a linear, or "arithmetic," ratio, then scarcity, starvation, and struggle would always be a part and parcel of the human condition."[12] This was an attitude which, adopted into theories of governance and economy, led to catastrophic neglect and mass mortality in the wake of the Irish famine. Darwin, intrigued by Malthus's thought, as were many of his contemporaries, considers his own *Origin of Species* "the doctrine of Malthus applied to the whole animal and vegetable kingdoms."[13] Much historical and cultural studies research has been dedicated to exploring the impact of Malthus and Darwin on nineteenth-century discourse and politics. This dominant focus also has its impact on Stoker studies, with various scholars having pointed out Darwinian repercussions in *Dracula* and beyond.[14] Yet, here as well we can observe a noticeable gap in that, as Hale observes, so far there are only a few studies on the "anti-Malthusian radical-cum-socialist tradition" and its impact on nineteenth-century thought, literature, and politics.[15] The tradition of philosophical radicalism, "steeped in Lamarckian ideas," fuelled a "socialist revival" in the decade and a half from the mid-1880s to the end of the century, as Hale observes, and as a result a plethora of socialist organizations were established that also "turned to evolutionary ideas in order to press their agendas."[16]

Bram Stoker never directly confessed any socialist leanings yet, like his closest friend, Hall Caine, who had a "rooted belief in socialism," he developed visions of human co-existence in his novels.[17] William Morris's brand of socialism had influenced the development of Caine's own political ideas, which manifested as a form of idealist Christian socialism in his novels.[18] Without a doubt, the lively debates surrounding evolutionary biology, ethics, and sociality have to be seen as the fertile climate in which Stoker's own novels of the 1890s, especially *Dracula*, *The Shoulder of Shasta* and *The Snake's Pass*, unfold their narratives. Visions of community, friendship, and altruistic behavior in these novels take shape in the direct vicinity of predatory threats, individualism, and the "Darwinian nightmare" of the vampire. The vision of friendship and community, which he outlined in his prose writings and correspondences, is relevant to the question of Stoker's position in the Victorian debate surrounding sociality, ethics, and bio-politics. His views on Ireland, his own native country, whose fate had in his own living memory been so adversely affected by the political manifestations of Malthusianism, will also be explored in the following analysis.

Fashioning and Self-fashioning of Friendship: Irish Stoker in Victorian London

Stoker's own presence in his 1906 memoir, *Personal Reminiscences of Henry Irving*, as Hughes points out, includes a somewhat telling admission: "In the doing of my work, I am painfully conscious that I have obtruded my own personality, but I trust that for this I may be forgiven, since it is only by this means that I can convey at all the ideas which I wish to impress."[19] It is not only ideas but *ideals* that motivate Stoker's self-fashioning as well as his depiction of social harmony in *Reminiscences*. His correspondents, first and foremost Manx author Hall Caine, co-create this image of a mutually supportive sphere of intimate male friends. If Caine says of Stoker that he expressed "the strongest love that man may feel for man,"[20] Stoker does Irving the same favor, calling their relationship "as profound, as close, as lasting as can be between two men."[21] Friendship is essential for Stoker, who, as the manager of Irving's Lyceum Theatre, finds himself among the *Who's Who* of the Victorian world, which he took an "obsessive delight" in listing in *Reminiscences*. As Hughes delineates, he conversed with political celebrities implicated in Irish, British, and Imperial politics, including Gladstone, Disraeli, Justin McCarthy, Lord Randolph Churchill, Asquith, and Balfour. The list of guests over the years is diverse and included many of the physicians, explorers, scientists, novelists, painters, zoologists, and religious thinkers of the day. Certainly, Stoker was in an "ideal position from which to observe the current preoccupations of late nineteenth-century English society [...] as gender politics, religious controversy, the ethics of fiction and the integrity of national identity" were all on the menu.[22] Paul Murray reminds us that the relationship between Stoker and Irving had "undergone a sea change at the very start, from close friendship to that of a subordinate to a superior."[23] Stoker, however, seemed to bear no resentment toward Irving, and in general seems to have taken no offense even when insulted.[24] Yet, the myth of a tense Jekyll and Hyde-like rift between a public real-life Stoker and an angry, repressed, private Stoker who siphoned his demons into Gothic fiction has manifested in a broad scope of Freudian readings of repressed sexuality in Stoker's works. It is, in a nascent form, already present in Hall Caine's obituary in *The Telegraph*, which claimed that Bram was a man of the theater only for his "great love for its leader"—Irving—and that:

> his true self was something quite unlike the personality which was seen in that environment. Those who knew him there only hardly knew him at all. Some hint of this world would occasionally reveal itself among the scarcely favourable conditions of a public dinner, when as speaker (always capable of the racy

humour which is considered necessary to that rather artificial atmosphere), he would strike, in that soft roll of his Irish tongue, a note of deep and almost startling emotion that would obliterate the facile witticisms of more important persons.[25]

"Genuine" Stoker, here, is shattering the clamor of societal wit with the resounding deep notes of his emotional nature and his Irish tongue. Yet, Caine is anxious to add that Stoker nevertheless possessed those credentials—that is, the "racy humour"—that was a prerequisite to thriving in such an "artificial atmosphere." Caine's Stoker displays a kind of Irishness which his contemporaries were happy to accommodate and admire: the gentle giant with a big heart who sacrifices himself for his master Irving, not out of some unwholesome idolization but out of "the strongest love that man may feel for man."[26] Despite Caine's and later biographers' reservations, the myth of perfect harmony between Irving and Stoker is somewhat perennial. British actor Michael Kilgarriff, in a piece published on The Irving Society's website entitled "Henry Irving & Bram Stoker: A Working Relationship," insists that "[t]heir comradeship was without friction or rancour [...]. True, theirs was not an equal partnership for HI was unquestionably the Guv'nor, but together they made a matchless team."[27] This image of Stoker as a peaceful, successful, and subservient Irishman was and is politically useful, as it manifests the myth of a happy Union with Ireland in which one party was to be unquestionably superior while the other was to be a good sport and overlook the regrets of its servile condition for the sake of the strength that comes from the unity of a "matchless team." In the face of violence springing up in the aftermath of the abortive Fenian uprising in 1867 and the specter of Home Rule looming, it was more important than ever that Victorian society had reason to believe in a healthy "working relationship" to which acts of violence were not indicative of mass dissent but rather to be considered random and unjustifiable exceptions.[28] Successful Irish "Micks on the Make" such as Stoker, smoothly integrating into London society, perpetuated the myth that there was equal opportunity for all within the Empire, as R. F. Foster perhaps somewhat dubiously puts it: "[c]onquering, then as now, can be a two-way process,"[29] with Stoker the epitome of an Irish good sport, even in the face of abuse.

However, there is much to suggest that Stoker himself had a deep-seated belief in social harmony and in keeping peace and friendship even in the face of tension and grievances. This is clearly expressed in his stance on Ireland. On November 13, 1872 Stoker gave a speech for the Trinity Historical Society in the university's dining hall to fellow students and the public. Entitled "The Necessity for Political Honesty," the speech was very well received and to some extent represents the "opinions, beliefs and incisive vision of Bram Stoker as a young man."[30] In his speech Stoker showed an acute awareness of external threats (United Germany and France, the Slavonic nations, "Russia with her millions" challenging British colonial rule in India, America being on the way to testing the "merits and de-merits of ideal democracy").[31] He was also not blind to the discontents that enveloped Ireland and the union: "The strife of arbour and capital" and "the hollowness and artificialness of society within and its wastefulness and extravagance without" continues, while "actual want stares many of our people in the face," education is unevenly accessible, and, finally, "[s]tatesmen [try] to subordinate every circumstance to their own scheme," forming an impenetrable "maze of political combinations."[32] In the midst of degeneration and corruption, however, Stoker observes that "the Celtic race is waking up from its long lethargy." He attributes an "energy that is unparalleled," an intellect "which only requires to be directed by experience to make itself felt and an instinct for right and wrong almost poetical in its intensity:" it is "these powers" that will make the Irish the "leavening race" to shape the future US, where Stoker proclaimed the change to be already in progress. This self-ascertained, high-spirited, passionate Irishry, full of courage and devotion that "the suffering of centuries" could not break, and which "in the midst of all her sorrow" proved its valor in "every great battle in Europe," however, was in dire need of being educated (by cultural torch-bearers like himself), and in order to realize its ambitious calling and for a "new order" to take hold in Ireland "the old animosities have to be forgotten and the dead past left to rest in peace—there have been wrongs, but they have been atoned for—there have been errors, but they have been corrected—there have been insults, but they are wiped away."[33]

Stoker's idealistic vision of reconciliation would not become manifest as the grievances were too deep and the efforts at reconciliation too shallow. Stoker goes on to make an argument here for the Irish being "noble" as an "advancing race"[34] against the overwhelming presence of a Victorian discourse based on Darwinian–Malthusian thought, which cast Ireland as racially inferior. L. Perry Curtis's study *Apes and Angels: The Irishman in Victorian Caricature* (1971) investigates this overwhelming presence of "simian" and other stereotypes in Victorian cartoons and shows clearly to what extent grossly simplified and popularized Darwinian thought had fueled racist politics. Further supported by Malthusian population theories that saw "famine as the last, most dreadful" and yet inevitable "resource of nature,"[35] the Irish famine was viewed by many Victorians as a positive check on population growth. Yet, Stoker, as an Irishman, would not adopt such a murderous stance. In his *Reminiscences* he reflects on the oratory of John Bright, a radical reformer who proposed "almost universal" suffrage for Ireland.[36] Stoker recounts being swept away "heart and brain and memory and hope" by Bright's powerful words, "moving all who remembered how in the Famine time America took the guns from her battleships to load them fuller with grain for the starving Irish peasants."[37] Stoker, here, celebrates this act of humanitarian aid, which contradicted the logics of struggle and self-interest. The sense of reconciliatory virtue, which he advocates in his Trinity speech, must be understood as an appeal to forsake the state of nature and its logics and means of aggression and retaliation. In his novels, too, Stoker creates fictional encounters between civilization and the state of nature.

The Shoulder of Shasta

As Carol A. Senf points out, in *The Shoulder of Shasta* (1895) Stoker addresses a host of cultural and social concerns, such as the changing roles of women and the relationship between the United States as a major emerging political power and England.[38] Beyond these, the novel also reflects on inter-cultural encounters, relations between native Americans and settlers, questions of wilderness and civilization, and, finally, questions concerning conflict resolution and forgiveness.

In this romance, the "primitive" "frontiersman bearing the memorable if unfortunate name of Grizzly Dick," wearing a "point-for-point description of Cody's costume," encounters Esse, a city girl with refined Romantic attitudes inspired by the Lake Poets and Swedenborgian mysticism.[39] The name "Grizzly Dick" encapsulates the fundamental question the novel raises about humanity in its relation to wilderness and Otherness (that is, is this a man who is determined by his proximity to bears or is this an imbruted, uncanny, *grizzly* man?). In his descriptions of Grizzly Dick and the conditions of life on the frontier, the Shoulder of mount Shasta, Stoker outlines a "state of nature" similar to the one Huxley had described in "The Struggle for Existence in Human Society," where men "preyed upon things weaker or less cunning than themselves," and were not "to be praised or blamed on moral grounds."[40]

We first encounter Grizzly Dick in his own habitat, the great outdoors, his "complete absence of fear, and even of misgiving" characterizing him as "the King of Beasts in his own sphere" (*SoS* 28). The uncertainty is playfully thematized by Esse, who, after having her fingers nearly crushed by his healthy handshake, asks "'By the way, are you Mr Grizzly Dick or Mr Dick Grizzly? If that is your friendly shake, I must look out for a real grizzly when I want a mild one,'" prompting Dick to laugh so wholesomely that henceforward there cannot be any doubt about the soundness of his heart and "all his other vital organs" (*SoS* 29). Esse, on the other hand, is severely anaemic and arrives at Shasta on doctor's orders to be reinvigorated by the healthy and pure mountain air and water. She hails from "that great country" in which, as Stoker had insisted in his Trinity speech "the native Anglo-Saxon race is dwindling and can never be restored to equal vigour," and which he suggested as a "fertile venturing ground for the vigorous spirit of the Irish."[41]

Yet this story does not feature anything readily recognizable as an Irish invigoration, but what appears rather as an English reaffirmation of supremacy, when "manly Englishman Hampden" rises to the task of plucking a quasi-Arthurian gauntlet from the floor, proving his "right to lead,"[42] claiming Esse for his bride, and returning her to civilization. This reading misses a vital point, however: namely the elaborate and noteworthy peace agreement which allows Grizzly Dick, who had nearly committed murder prompted by a misunderstanding, to be considered a valuable member of a peaceful community. On one level, the story can be read as celebrating deference in the face of societal conventions and the superiority of the "muscular" Englishman, who is "invariably the most complete of gentlemen."[43] Yet, there are a few unusual aspects to the detailed and almost contractual achievement of peace and *friendship* at the end of the story that deserve some further attention.

To everyone's embarrassment, Grizzly Dick appears at Esse and Reginald's engagement party outrageously clothed and groomed, intending to propose marriage to Esse. "[C]hained to the social stake," she does not find it within herself to go over and talk to Grizzly Dick or send her mother to "take care of Dick and find out his purpose," and in turn Reginald too is "chained to the stake by the exceptional circumstances of his social duty" (SoS 118). Afraid of the danger Grizzly Dick poses to society and to herself, however, she later sets out to look for him. Convinced by one of Esse's insincere acquaintances that he should propose marriage to Esse publically and on the spot, Grizzly approaches Esse, suffers rejection and ridicule by the "smart set," and puts a knife to Peter Blyth's throat, whom he perceives to have been causing the deception. Like Stoker, Grizzly Dick is unable to mask his accent and his emotions, but unlike his creator he does not possess the wit or "racy humour" to survive the vicissitudes of polite society, nor can he sublimate his anger.

As a result of provocation he sinks into a "blood-madness" and becomes "more dangerous than any wild animal," but Reginald manages to relax the situation and assures Grizzly Dick that he is welcome to stay and join the party, never mind he just tried to murder one of the guests (SoS 123). What sounds like a polite or anxious dishonesty might be Reginald revealing his heart-felt opinion:

> "No, no, Mr Grizzly Dick, you must not go! *There is no one who can come into my house that I could be more glad to see.* You must stay and show us all that you forgive us that we have amongst us made you, for a time, uncomfortable" [...] "Never mind, Dick" said Reginald heartily; "we are all friends of yours here! If there are any who are not so, then they are no friend of our hostess or of me either, and I'll stand back to back, if you'll let me, when we slice up the last of them!" (SoS 127; my emphasis)

The English gentleman does not flinch in the face of Grizzly Dick's readiness to enact violence in the midst of society but, what is more, he promises to drop his civil compliance and launch a relentless back-to-back attack against anyone who disagrees with the terms of this newly established union. In *The Shoulder of Shasta* the English gentleman and his society are symbolically reunited with their dark double, the primitive and potentially violent frontiersman, in an agreement of mutual aid. In this, as in many other examples, Stoker sides with the anti-Malthusian side of Victorian evolutionary debates. One of its most influential proponents, the geologist and anarchist Peter Kropotkin, succinctly formulates a reading of Darwin's evolutionary biology and consequently of sociology Stoker would have subscribed to: "'Don't compete!—competition is always injurious to the species, and you have plenty of resources to avoid it!'"[44]

Dracula

The exegetic tradition of the "Imperial Gothic" is certain that Stoker was a staunch defender of the British empire and, seeing its slow erosion, expressed fears of infection, infiltration, penetration, or corruption by some evil outside *Other*. As "a conquerer and invader,"[45] Dracula is seen as representing Turkish, Balkan, Russian, German, Anglo-Irish and Irish, Catholic, Muslim, and Jewish identities, yet, strangely enough, others have found in Dracula elements that identify him with the British empire, Christian missioning, and capitalist and aristocratic expansion of power.[46] Jeanne Dubino, providing instances for each reading, thus convincingly argues that Dracula "becomes a figure for whatever critical constructions we want to project onto him," an instance of "Othering" "transforming fragments of Otherness into one Body."[47] Characterized by the "anxiety of reverse colonization," the vampire is enduringly read by critics as "a metaphor for the upheaval that threatens all imperial projects."[48] Yet, when looking at the coincidence of opposites that characterizes Stoker's *Dracula*, a very different situation than this type of binary threat in fact presents itself: one in which any fear of invasion is futile because the monstrous "Other" already occupies the very center of the "Self" to be invaded.

Perhaps this is one of the conclusions we can draw from the fact that *Dracula* (1897) is able to accommodate so many even contradictory allegorical readings with ease.[49] It is a Victorian *Leviathan* whose commentary on "sovereign power and bare life"—to borrow Giorgio Agamben's title phrase[50]—is more encompassing than has so far been assumed. Dracula contains a speculation on the mystic union of man and beast, which Stoker certainly had the opportunity to reflect on during his times as manager of the Lyceum.

In *Reminiscences* we can variously witness Stoker associating the baring of canine teeth with a "militant instinct" in notables of the Victorian empire, such as laureate Alfred Lord Tennyson and colonial explorer Sir Richard Burton. Stoker tells us how at one of the Lyceum dinner parties Burton recounts an undercover journey to Mecca where, dressed as an Arab, instead of risking discovery, he kills a boy. This prompted many guests at the dinner party to get up and leave. When Stoker asks him about the incident, Burton replies that it had "never troubled" him much because in the desert in the East "it is a small thing to kill a man," yet "as he spoke he lifted his upper lip and his canine tooth showed its full length like the gleam of a dagger."[51] In instances like these, upon seeing the saber-tooth of the British empire bared, it becomes hard to sustain the view that it was merely an anxiety of reverse colonization that motivated *Dracula*, out of a feeling of colonial guilt and an anticipation of retaliation or a fear of "the ease with which civilization can revert to barbarism or savagery."[52]

Certainly, such encounters as these convinced Stoker that savagery and barbarism were not the dark "Other" but inhabited the gilded throne of the collective "Self" of British feudal imperialism from the beginning and in principle. Dracula, comprised of various predatory aspects of animality combined with self-interest and a ruthless will to multiply, can be seen as a direct representation of that threatening specter of the "eternal competition of man against man and of nation against nation" which must "grow continually worse"—the Darwinian–Malthusian and, in its pessimistic interpretation, Huxleyian understanding of evolutionary biology. Dracula, then, poses what had to Huxley become "'the true riddle of the Sphinx,'" in the face of which "'every nation which does not solve it will sooner or later be devoured by the monster itself has generated.'"[53]

In the face of the revelation of evil holding dominion and occupancy of the center of self, the prime concern would certainly have been about how to *remove it from its current position*. And that, in fact, is the exact dilemma of *Dracula*—one of non-immunity. Evil is not just the looming outside threat, but it has already seen, arrived, and conquered *from within*: "Your girls that you all love are mine already" (*D* 285). The Count "'know[s] and speak[s] English thoroughly'" (*D* 22), and, having the assets and the legal entitlement to buy a house in Piccadilly or anywhere else, he owns it already; actually buying it is a trivial afterthought. The threat lies not in whatever national identity we can decipher in Dracula's body but the intent and pattern of action that characterize the predatory principle and may, like a virus, take over any nation, polity, or community.

The Carpathian Count is as much happenstance to this principle as is Lucy Westenra. After take-over is complete, the vampiric corporate identity enacts itself in an ever homogeneous, ever self-repeating and self-proliferating embodiment of violent self-interest.[54] The "undead supremacy" is characterized by its relentless and uncontrollable will to live: Dracula and his minions cannot choose to cease to consume and exist. The Crew of Light, in turn, is characterized by the renunciation of that will. Mina requests her friends to assist her free will and kill her, in case of evil taking over: "'Because if I find in myself—and I shall watch keenly for it—a sign of harm to any that I love, I shall die!'" (*D* 287). Being reminded that her death would help, not harm, Dracula, she embraces life but only in renunciation, as she agrees to stay alive not for herself but for the greater common goal and the will of God to be done.

One might wonder why Stoker, in his manuscripts, in his correspondences, and in his fiction, shows so little rejection or resentment whenever he recounts or narrates encounters with "beast-man-ship," such as the bared canines of Burton. Perhaps it is that he saw a counter-productive moment in showing hatred as a response to a principle that relishes and provokes it. As he stated in his Trinity speech, if Ireland ever was to be great it had to forgive transgressions, past or present: "if we are ever to be noble we must begin by generosity."[55] Stoker did not envision revaluing good and evil but overcoming a set of divisions that would otherwise limit understanding and be harmful to communal peace. Stoker perhaps saw what Kropotkin saw—that in Darwinian England this was already the common belief: "The theory which maintains that men can, and must, seek their own happiness in a disregard for other people's wants is now triumphant all round—in law, in science, in religion ... and to doubt of its efficacy is to be a dangerous Utopian."[56] If Dracula embodied the violent "natural state of man," which had such continuous, prior residence within "Self," the solution for the Crew of Light lies in embracing the diametrically opposed principle, namely that of altruism, and striving for counter-infection: the Eucharist manifesting the presence of Christ's self-sacrifice is extended into Dracula's abodes. Christ's atoms, his endlessly dissembled body, a sacrificial gift to whatsoever or whomsoever it touches, will vanquish Dracula by *saving* him: to touch this principle, to be connected to that counter-circuit of forgiveness, ends the self-cloning circuit of Dracula's anxious egomania.

The Crew of Light in the course of the story overcomes its rejection and revulsion in the presence of Dracula's impurity developing a sense of faith that they will not be usurped by it. They establish among them-self a *reserveless unity*, established through blood transfusions, circulation of letters, news media, information—yet, overcoming Dracula means keeping him connected to their circle: Mina actively maintains both her telepathic connection with their opponent and a sense of hope even after having drunk his blood.

If the opponent is able to access a smooth circuity of media, insti-tutions, chains of command, and states of being, then those who try to defeat him must also aspire to form some kind of communal circulation. In one noteworthy episode in *Dracula's Guest*, namely chapter three, "The Dream in the Dead House," which, as Elizabeth Miller shows, was origi-nally intended to be included in *Dracula*, we see the smooth circuity of the military, of wolves and aristocracy.[57] Dracula obviously embodies the kind of privilege that allows him to utilize the structures and organs of the system he finds himself part of. He can command the military by power of his fortune and his ancient name. He uses the latest technologies, yet he can also mesmerize and paralyze minds and has enough of a pact with animality that wolves do his bidding. When the narrator, Harker, finds out that he was saved on the orders of the Count, he begins to experience severe vertigo at something "so weird and impossible to imagine" and falls into mental paralysis: "I was certainly under some mysterious form of protection. From a distant country had come a message that took me out of the dangers of the snow-sleep and the jaws of the wolf" (*D* 352–62, at 362). The paralyzing realization here is that he is subject to a power that is ready to kill and from which there is no ulterior salvation. He lives because evil itself has decided to make a "guest" of him, an exception.

Dracula orders the military to search for Harker and keep him safe *from himself*, as long as this serves his purposes.

Giorgio Agamben considers the basic injunction that forms the premise of the modern sovereign state: "human life is included in the juridical order [ordinamento] solely in the form of its exclusion (that is, of its capacity to be killed)," a notion that for Agamben becomes an access point to understanding sovereignty in general.[58] Sovereignty assumes the form of bio-power, in Agamben's view, by making decisions about life and the body—that is, retaining within itself the prerogative to decide at any given instance what kind of life it agrees to hold sacred and what kind of life it is ready to outlaw and kill. Agamben takes as a starting point of his own elaboration Foucault's observation that it was possible to bring about bestiality within civilization through the sophistication of political measures and judicial clauses, at the same time protecting the "sacred" life of one group of citizens while removing all legal protection from another. Sovereignty, one must add, creates myths of "limited resources" and "immediate threats" to bolster the sense of an urgent need to protect its arbitrarily erected demarcation lines. The collective acceptance of such demarcation lines makes it possible for one group of citizens of the same polity to thrive, be sheltered and well nourished while another group perishes from the "dangers of the snow-sleep" of eviction and the "jaws of the wolf" of starvation. Mystified by the machinations of power, one might mistakenly consider one's own safety an indicator of its goodness, yet even a minimal amount of human compassion would urge one to wonder—for what reason or purpose was I spared? This, I would argue, is exactly the question that makes "Dracula's guest" dizzy.

In turn, to defeat Dracula the Crew of Light needs to let go of its desire to attain immunity or safety from Dracula. They create a circulation among themselves without clinging to notions of purity and they have to profane the sacred in a radical submission to pragmatism: sharing blood, violating the dead and their tombs, kneading crumbled-up Eucharist wafers into an effective mortar. The measures of the Crew would have made not just nineteenth-century Catholics but also Protestants very uncomfortable. Stoker, obviously, believed that an evil as multiform and contradictory as Dracula could be slain only by a *community* ready to understand and accept that they are not immune to that evil yet that they can triumph in self-sacrifice and in surrendering whatever they hold sacred to their common cause and to each other.

The Snake's Pass

This is a stance also predominant in *The Snake's Pass* (1890). In this novel, again, it is a community of friends that overcomes their opponent by means of creating circulation, both between themselves and symbolically by re-establishing the free flow of a watercourse after greed and ignorance had blocked it. The novel displays a robust social and economic idealism in sketching the unlikely romance and marriage between Arthur Severn, a wealthy Englishman who inherited land and title from a deceased relative, and Nora Joyce, a poor Irish peasant girl. Arthur Severn is not so much coming to rule and take possession as to be moved and changed by Ireland and the fate of the people he encounters. Upon arrival he is entering into an awakening: "I felt as though I looked for the first time with open eyes on the beauty and reality of the world" (*SP* 11). The protagonist describes himself as having been made to feel an "'outsider'" by his own family (*SP* 12). His aristocratic father, who had married a woman from the lower classes, found himself cut off from his family, and after both parents died at sea an aunt had provided for the "rudiments of an education" that were supposed to prepare Arthur for the life of a country gentleman (*SP* 12). On his aunt's death Severn finds himself the heir to all her possessions, entitled to "take a place among the magnates of the country" (*SP* 13). He embarks upon a tour of Europe and, after meeting new friends, who invite him to their place in County Clare, he decides to improve his "knowledge of Irish affairs by making a detour through some of the counties in the west" (*SP* 13). He finds himself profoundly fascinated and changed by the experience.

Stoker chooses a vantage point and entrance into the novel of virtual innocence and ignorance of any grim realities in Ireland.[59] Arthur Severn encounters Ireland with a sense of curiosity and humility, and a desire to be of use to the people he encounters. Thus his story becomes the transformative "fool's journey" of classical fairy tales, in which the protagonist, who appears to be too simple to enact the "ways of the world," assists in lifting a curse from the land by following his pure and noble disposition, thus gaining sovereignty over the land and usually the hand of the princess in marriage. This, in essence, is Arthur Severn's story, which Stoker quite consciously frames as a fairy tale of Victorian social wish-fulfilment: "'Arthur, you are the Fairy Prince!'" Norah Joyce enthuses towards the end of the novel, when she learns that her future husband bought the entire neighborhood: "'There is nothing that I can wish for that you have not done—even my dresses are ready by your sweet thoughtfulness'" (SP 208).

At the outset of the novel Arthur Severn, after escaping a severe thunderstorm, joins the local community gathered in Widdy Kelligan's shibín (an illegal inn). He asks to buy the evening's drinks for the entire house (SP 17) and joins a dinner reminiscent of early Christian gatherings in its austere simplicity:

> The herrings were cut in pieces, and a piece given to each.—
> The dinner was served. There were no plates, no knives, forks
> or spoons—no ceremony—no precedence—nor was there any
> heartburning, jealousy or greed. A happier meal I never took a
> part in—nor did I ever enjoy food more. Such as it was it was
> perfect. (SP 16–17)

He then eagerly listens to folklore and legend associated with the nearby mountain and pass. The first speaker retells an ancient tale of the king of snakes leaving Ireland. Angered by St. Patrick, the snake disappears only after burying his crown in a nearby hill and forcing the water of a lake into the surrounding land, eventually turning it into the shifting bog that presently makes the area unsafe.

With the image of a crowned snake, not unlike the Egyptian Uraeus, Stoker creates another symbol for sovereign power: "I'm the whole govermint here, and I put a nexeat on meself not to lave widout me own permission" (SP 21–22). The snake has power over the hill and when the general conversation later turns to the "gombeen man," a widely recognized token of legal mismanagement and parasitism,[60] this figure is in turn considered a personification of the principal of governance represented by the snake. As Arthur Severn is initiated into the basics of rural life in Ireland he learns about the local gombeen man "Black Murdock," and about the belief of the locals that he cannot leave the area despite his great wealth because "the Hill houlds him" (*SP* 27). He and his neighbor Phellim Joyce, a poor farmer, both own land on the hill. Joyce's is the better land, of which Murdock is jealous, believing treasure to be buried there. On this dramatic night, Severn and the reader witness a confrontation between Murdock and Joyce, learning that by means of a deceitful contract the former had gained the right to arrange an exchange of property.

There are only two institutions that Stoker depicts as standing in the way of Murdock's power. One is the village priest, who proclaims a prophecy over Murdock: "You have used your powers without mercy; you have made the law an engine of oppression. Mark me! It was said of old that what measure men meted should be meted out to them again" (*SP* 37). The other institution capable of confronting the evil of the gombeen man is the local community: "Tell us, Phelim, *sure we're all friends here!* how Black Murdock got ye in his clutches? Sure any wan of us would get you out of thim if he could" (*SP* 38, my emphasis). Yet, certainly none of his poor contemporaries are in any position to intervene when Joyce is forced to leave his property.

Arthur Severn, however, through the course of the novel is characterized as the kind of good-hearted, wealthy Englishman that was needed to set things right in Ireland. He falls in love with Norah Joyce, Phelim's daughter, and proposes to marry her, agreeing to pay for her schooling. He buys first their old property and eventually the entire hill with a prospect of joint future prosperity not just for him: "'With a quarry on the spot, we can not only build cheap and reclaim our own bog, but we can supply five hundred square miles of country with the rudiments of prosperity'" (*SP* 203). This lofty vision expresses the social idealism of William Morris and in turn Hall Caine, but it also embodies the central promise of the Home Rule movement, namely that of a greater and more widely spread economic prosperity. Justin McCarthy—friend to both Gladstone and Stoker, fellow emigrant who became chairman of the Irish Parliamentary Party in 1890 and who campaigned widely in England, impressing his views certainly also on Bram Stoker—told the House of Commons in 1886: "Our capital under a Home Rule government would be induced to flow, for we should have industry and trade. We would bring all the resources of the country into play," and that a Home Rule parliament would not be a "parliament of politicians, but one of ernest, energetic, practical men, anxious to restore the prosperity of their country."[61] Englishman Severn thus becomes the exact opposite of an absentee landlord. When he finally comes into ownership of the hill his friend Dick exclaims: "'The Mountain holds—and it holds tight.' [...] It is yours now, every acre of it and, if I don't mistake, you are going to make it in time —and not a long time either—into the fairest bower to which the best fellow ever brought the fairest lady!" (SP 204) Indeed, Norah's innate nobility and thus suitability and her wish to become "worthy" of her husband's station are emphasized repeatedly, as is Severn's idealization of work: "'When a man has once tasted the pleasure of real work, especially work that taxes the mind and the imagination, the world seems only a poor place without it'" (SP 54).

The Snake's Pass presents its reader with the same "sentimental version of Christian socialism" that characterizes the works of Hall Caine.[62] Evidently, the close friendship between Bram Stoker and Hall Caine was a major inspiration for the novel and biographical facts of Hall Caine's life were even adopted into the novel's narrative parameters. For a brief period of time in the late 1870s Caine became an environmental activist, joining the Thirlmere Defence Association along with Ruskin, unsuccessfully opposing the damming of the lake which runs from Grasmere to Keswick in order to create hydro-electric power.[63] Caine's efforts are symbolically turned into the success that The Snake's Pass celebrates, as evidenced in the free flow of water, which establishes the protagonists' victory at the end of the novel.

Some of the facts surrounding Hall Caine's marriage likewise found their way into Stoker's novel and provided the detail necessary to give substance to his social idealist vision. In 1882, whilst renting rooms at the Clements Inn, Caine and Robertson had their dinners sent over from a local coffee shop, delivered by two teenage girls who worked there. The girls soon took to waiting while they finished their meals and then joined in whatever entertainment was going on. One night, however, their fathers appeared, pressuring Caine and Robertson to marry them in order to avoid scandal, even though "nothing but a bit of flirting had taken place," and the fathers merely saw a chance of getting the girls "off their hands."[64] Caine was pressured into accepting responsibility for the future of then 13-year-old Mary Chandler, whom he settled in Sevenoaks, arranging for her to have an education, "to make her a fit wife for a rising intellectual and author."[65] This idea of marriage forged across class and economic boundaries becomes central to several of Caine's novels, especially *The Deemster* and *The Master of Man*. Kate Cregeen in *The Deemster* (1887) teaches herself French to become a good wife to her husband and Bessie Collister in *The Master of Man* (1921) burns a candle every night as she works to improve her grammar and spelling so as to become a suitable wife to her future husband. Stoker, likewise, has Norah Joyce spend two years in France working arduously to improve herself in preparation for marriage across class divides. In an essay devoted to his friend, titled "The Ethics of Hall Caine," first published in the August 1909 issue of *The Homiletic Review*, Bram Stoker admires mostly in Hall Caine's romances that they are "productive of good" and that they are "morally and often spiritually didactic," conveying in modern terms "great lessons of the Master, on which all worthy teaching must be based."[66] He mentions Caine's social engagement in so-called "rescue work," which is reflected in his novel *The Christian* (1897)—in Stoker's eyes "a sermon put in the attractive form of narrative."[67] Stoker emphasizes Caine's "tenderness for the poor and the oppressed," and insists that Caine "persistently preaches on some principle of righteousness."[68]

In this essay Stoker also quotes at length from Caine's *The White Prophet* (1909), showing appreciation for Caine's ability to expose "ethical defects"—that is, in Western Christianity. Stoker quotes at length the protagonist of Caine's novel, a Mahdi called Ishmael Ameer, who finds that Western Christianity is "little better than an organized hypocrisy, a lust of empire in nations and a greed of gold in men," and warns that "such sordid and squalid materialism is swallowing up religion, morality and truth."[69] It seems that some of the political outlook, at least in its basic tenets, was shared by Stoker. He saw embodied in Hall Caine a "sense of duty" solidly realized in his life and literature; "A gift implies a duty; a duty implies self-sacrifice, if only in the shape of labour." Stoker observes in Caine the dual ideal of Christian Socialism that underlies many of his novels, especially *The Snake's Pass*.[70] It is in the light of this notion of unceasing labor pitted against the hypocrisy of the wealthy and society's "sordid materialism" that his own labor and that of his friends made a greater sense.[71]

In many of Bram Stoker's novels, including *The Snake's Pass*, characters have reason for envy or jealousy yet, after some internal struggle, manage to return to a higher vision of friendship and community. Arthur Severn's childhood friend Dick Sutherland, for example, like his author, had turned from "a slight, pale boy" into a "burly, hale, stalwart man, with keen eyes and a flowing brown beard" (*SP* 52). Owing to the typically triangulated visions of romance that characterize both Caine's and Stoker's novels, in *The Snake's Pass* Dick has to learn the hard way that Arthur is engaged to the girl he loves. Yet, realizing that Arthur did not know that he was courting his best friend's love interest and had even intended to give him a piece of land that would enable him to marry her, Dick eventually is able to let go of his anger, forgive his friend, and praise the virtue of friendship:

> Thank God for loyal and royal manhood! Thank God for the heart of a friend that can suffer and remain true! And thanks, above all, that the lessons of tolerance and forgiveness, taught of old by the Son of God, are now and then remembered by the sons of men. (*SP* 136)

These lessons of forgiveness are repeated by the community at the death of Bat Moynahan and Murtagh Murdock as the novel comes to a close and reaches a threefold satisfaction: the lost crown of the pre-Christian snake king is found in a cavern, justifying the community's belief in its indigenous myth. The fabled gold of the fugitive soldiers is found and donated for the sake of developing rural Ireland, confirming Protestant McGlown's insistence on the accuracy of this legend. Finally, as the greedy gombeen man Murdock is killed by the shifting bog the village priest considers the will of God to have restored justice and reminds Joyce of the value of being patient, as god can save by the very measures by which he seems to punish (*SoS* 244).

In Stoker's symbolic Ireland there is enough space for a happy co-existence of all of the above. Under the wise and benign stewardship of its new owner, Englishman Arthur Severn, the hill continues to "hold them all." Stoker had many opportunities to discuss Irish matters with Gladstone, who regularly attended Lyceum opening nights and "was especially interested in a case of oppression by a gombeen man over a loan secured on some land," thus giving him the initial idea for "The Gombeen Man" which was published in the London magazine *The People* in 1890 and became a

chapter in *The Snake's Pass*.[72] Gladstone, who received a personal copy of
the story, was deeply impressed. Richard English remarks that "this latter
tale would indeed have echoed—and surely reinforced—some of Gladstone's conceptions of Ireland."[73] Gladstone's views certainly encouraged
Stoker's pragmatic Christian idealism in *The Snake's Pass*, and his avowed
"commitment to the politics of Christian conscience and responsibility"
and "pragmatic approach toward historically-minded, gradual change" are
certainly echoed here.[74] For him, who, unlike Arthur Severn, could not solve
the multiple crises afflicting Ireland at the time, the novel certainly provided
some distracting comfort. In constantly insisting that the Irish characters
depicted, though being poor, have good characters and thus deserve to be
exempted from cruelty and injustice ("'Oh! and he's the fine lad, God bless
him! An' the good lad too!'"), the novel pleads with an implied readership
in favor of recognizing the depicted subjects as worthy of redemption from
their abject circumstances (*SP* 38). Arthur Severn, the practical, selfless,
wealthy Englishman, who educates his local Irish bride and in persona
ends all present woes, remained a wishful fiction. Yet, he was created to
further the cause of Home Rule. As Sara J. Butler points out, evolutionary
biologists towards the end of the century also began to indirectly benefit
that cause by proliferating the view that "the Britons were a mixed race,"
perhaps due to a "steady decline in optimism over the Empire's future,"
and certainly the momentum of the Home Rule movement "made it more
attractive to view Britain as one unit."[75] Thomas Huxley, a strong propo-
nent of Darwinian ideas in 1870, argued for a unified genetic background
of Britonic and Celtic peoples on the British Isles in an article published by
the *Anthropological Review*, yet his views were met with considerable resis-
tance from Victorian readers, which indicates the "strength of anti-Irish
feelings" at the time.[76] Stoker, however, directly conforms with Huxley's
view in *The Snake's Pass*, that in Ireland as well as in Cornwall was to be
found "Iberian blood … although all traces of the language may have been
obliterated."[77] Huxley's view of a shared genetic heritage directly supported
Unionist ambitions in a political discourse that had throughout the second
half of the century become increasingly reliant upon evolutionary biology,
and Stoker's image of Norah Joyce as a personified Hibernia attempted to
create an idealized vision of a noble Irish peasantry: "How lovely she was!
I had heard that along the west coast of Ireland there are traces of Spanish

blood and Spanish beauty" (SP 75). Norah's beauty is presented as yet more perfect because it was "tempered with northern calm," adorned with perfect features and proportions, and Stoker measures out the perfection of her face with an almost mathematical precision, employing the widespread Victorian belief, according to Lavater's physiognomical theory, that a beautiful appearance was precisely indicative of a beautiful soul.

Arthur Severn was invented to rescue the Irish peasantry symbolically from the evil of the gombeen man and the yoke of poverty, yet, the bright hero, using a racial slur, indicates that no matter how far apart in social status Irish peasants and English gentlemen were in Victorian society, they could always find common ground in having a good shared laugh at the expense of people considered inferior and hence fair game to such ridicule. After Severn emphasizes that he had fallen in love with a "dark" woman he uses a slur to clarify that it is her hair not her skin that is dark. The Irishman, who ignorantly confesses that he has "niver seen a faymale naygur meself, but I suppose there's such things," is amused and the two men share a hearty laugh, illustrating the good relationship between them (SP 101). This casual callousness, indicative of the toxicity that characterized Victorian racial discourses, is all the more surprising to see considering that Stoker had such deep admiration for Lincoln, not least for having ended slavery. He admires Lincoln first and foremost as a "man of principles:"

> There was a distinct guiding purpose in his life from which his every action sprang. Every height which he won, every power which he achieved, every honour accorded to him was in distinct logical and dramatic sequence with his own efforts to an noble end.[78]

Stoker, the social idealist, certainly saw himself and his friends in pursuit of equally lofty goals and, as we have seen, consistently pursued ideals of friendship and communal harmony in his fiction. Yet, in instances such as this it is clear that such visions in Victorian times were neither global nor inclusive of all humanity, but on occasion collapsed back into the bog or quagmire of racial hierarchy that the bio-sociological thought inspired by Darwin and Malthus had fostered.

CHAPTER FIVE

Communication Technologies in Bram Stoker's *Dracula*: Utopian or Dystopian?

Anne DeLong

Introduction

Bram Stoker's 1897 novel *Dracula* opens itself to two distinct interpretive readings: one utopian, in which a fellowship known as the Crew of Light vanquishes the forces of evil; and one dystopian, in which heroes are fumbling and faulty and evil is never fully purged or vanquished, but rather disseminated into the vampiric dust motes that are the reader's last glimpse of Dracula. These two interpretations are fully linked to—in fact, depend upon—the reader's utopian or dystopian reading of technology, specifically communication technologies. *Dracula* is a text that examines and employs the most cutting-edge writing technologies of its day, from shorthand and phonographs to telegrams and typewriters. While a utopian reading celebrates the triumph of these technologies over the vampire, dystopian readings critique these very technologies as inherently vampiric.

It is easy to imagine an original utopian reception of Stoker's novel by a Victorian audience that is traditionally assumed to have unilaterally embraced the promises of the new steam era and its attendant scientific marvels, a culture that presumably delighted in the use of such technology to forestall the return of an age-old repressive foreign feudal lord. But Stoker's novel also appears at a historical moment on the verge of an emerging modernist wave of dystopian fiction, including Jules Verne's 1879 *The Begum's Fortune* and H. G. Wells's 1898 *War of the Worlds*. In many ways it ushers in an era dominated by a humanistic fear of tyranny. In its portrayal of the vampire as an Eastern threat to Western liberty, *Dracula* anticipates twentieth-century dystopian fiction. More particularly, Stoker's depiction of communication technologies inspires readings of the text itself as dangerous, even deadly.

In *Dystopian Fiction East and West: Universe of Terror and Trial*, Erika Gottlieb observes that "fear of the emergence of a totalitarian regime is the major component of the dystopian impulse."[1] As an Eastern European feudal lord who aims to infect and dominate Western culture, Count Dracula bears some affinities with the threat of fascism that Gottlieb identifies as dystopic. For Gottlieb, utopian fiction is characterized by faith in the values of justice, democracy, and enlightenment. While most contemporary reviewers of *Dracula* accept the triumph of the modern Crew of Light over the ancient vampire, several more recent critics have examined textual nuances that suggest otherwise. Furthermore, even some of the Victorian responses to the novel express a dystopian fear that the taint of *Dracula* may infect its most vulnerable readers.

Recent critical work on utopian and dystopian responses to twenty-first-century communication technology suggests that the utopian viewpoint sees these innovations as potentially humanizing and democratizing. In a study entitled "On Utopias and Dystopias: Toward an Understanding of the Discourse Surrounding the Internet," Dana R. Fisher writes "Perhaps the most salient aspect of the utopian position is the implied notion that there are technological solutions to social problems [...]. These problems are often described in terms of technology's effects on communitarian and populist forms of democratic participation." Conversely, the dystopian view of technology emphasizes the dehumanizing aspects of communication technologies: "The dystopian argument claims that democracy crumbles as the social fabric of society becomes fragmented and people become more isolated from one another."[2] While the networking aspect of the medium has a democratizing potential, the dystopian view fears the possibility that the medium might affect negatively the nature of the communication itself. Similarly, cutting-edge Victorian communication technologies in *Dracula*, including shorthand, voice recordings, newspaper clippings, telegrams, and manifold typewriting, serve to create intimate and immediate bonds among the novel's protagonists. But these same technologies also mimic and duplicate the dehumanizing aspects of the mass cultural reproduction of texts. For utopians, technology defeats the vampire. For dystopians, technology *is* the vampire.

Writing as Technology:
When the Medium Becomes the Message

In his 1992 essay "The Judgment of Thamus," Neil Postman argues for a moderate reception of technological advances that is neither uncritically celebratory nor unreasonably condemnatory. Postman recounts a tale from Plato's *Phaedrus* in which the Egyptian king Thamus argues with the god Theuth over the introduction of a new technology: writing. While technophile Theuth touts the wonders of writing as an improvement to memory and wisdom, from the technophobic perspective of the king this new technique of recording information will have detrimental effects because it will become a crutch to aid memory and a substitute for actual wisdom.[3]

The notion of writing as a technology informs utopian and dystopian readings of *Dracula* in several important ways. First, it prompts an exploration of the utopian benefits of writing as therapeutic. Secondly, this conception enables an examination of various justifications for writing as both textual plot devices and tools for the development of characters' motivations. Finally, viewing writing itself as a technology forces an engagement with the dystopian implications of the difficulty in rendering the spoken word as written text.

Stoker's *Dracula* is noteworthy for its own metatextual awareness of itself as a text. Not only is the novel a compilation of various types of writing, it is composed of writings that communicate their own purposes, audiences, and rationales. Beginning with Jonathan Harker's journal, which comprises the novel's first four chapters, these texts are littered with authorial interjections that comment on their existence and *raisons d'être* as texts. Even before he arrives at Dracula's castle and its "strange night-existence [begins to] tell [...] on" him (*D* 27), Jonathan habitually and repeatedly writes himself to sleep (*D* 37, 50). Dr. Seward also remarks upon the soporific powers of journaling: "This diary has quieted me, and I feel I shall get some sleep tonight" (D 98). Ironically, like writing, Dracula also has a tranquilizing effect. When Lucy expresses her aversion to sleep, Seward is oblivious to its dystopian possibilities: "Afraid to go to sleep! Why so? It is the boon we all crave for" (D 118). Lucy's cryptic reply inverts the utopian notion of sleep as healing: "Ah, not if you were like me—if sleep was to you a presage of horror!" (D 118).

As Lucy vacillates between sleeping and waking, her attachment to Dracula waxes and wanes. Slumber intensifies the vampiric bond, and it is sleeping Lucy who attempts to destroy the writing of waking Lucy. While cognizant, Lucy writes a memo detailing the experience of her mother's death, which contains important clues for the vampire hunters, and she secretes it in her bosom. But "[w]hilst still asleep she took the paper from her breast and tore it in two" (D 143). Vampire Lucy views writing as the enemy, a dangerous threat that must be destroyed.

Several of the characters employ the technology of writing as a means to make sense of strange events by recording them. As Harker speculates in his journal, "[t]here was a certain method in the Count's inquiries, so I shall try to put them down in sequence; the knowledge may somehow or some time be useful to me" (D 31). The Captain of the *Demeter*, author of the ship's log that is excerpted in the *Dailygraph* cutting, subtitles his account "*things so strange happening that I shall keep accurate note henceforth till we land*" (D 79). Lucy writes to duplicate Mina's journalistic ambitions: "I must imitate Mina, and keep writing things down" (D 103). Seward also justifies his diary-keeping for its informational value: "Jonathan Harker has asked me to note this, as he says he is hardly equal to the task, and he wants an exact record kept" (D 305). Later he expresses a utopian fondness for his lost technology: "How I miss my phonograph! To write diary with a pen is irksome to me; but Van Helsing says I must" (D 311). Mina also extols the virtues of technologically enabled writing: "I feel so grateful to the man who invented the 'Traveller's' typewriter, and to Mr. Morris for getting this one for me. I should have felt quite astray doing the work if I had to write with a pen ..." (D 325).

Harker frequently comments on the therapeutic properties of writing as a means to preserve his sanity. Like Hamlet, whom he misquotes, Harker records his need to write to stave off madness:

> Up to now I never quite knew what Shakespeare meant when he made Hamlet say:—"My tablets! quick, my tablets! / 'Tis meet that I put it down, etc.," for now, feeling as though my own brain were unhinged or as if the shock had come which must end in its undoing, I turn to my diary for repose. (*D* 37)

Much later, Harker returns to diary-keeping to process the trauma of having witnessed his wife's vampirization: "As I must do something or go mad, I write this diary" (*D* 268).

From a utopian perspective, these written texts assert themselves to be both necessary and useful in the pursuit of justice. But from a dystopian perspective, the written word may be unreliable as a representation of reality. Harker's failure to correctly interpret the note written by working man Joseph Smollett illustrates class divisions in terms of literacy. Smollett's note, written on "a dirty scrap of paper [...] with a carpenter's pencil in a sprawling hand," reads: "Sam Bloxam, Korkrans, 4, Poters Cort, Bartel Street, Walworth. Arsk for the depite" (*D* 244). "Misled" by "phonetic spelling," Harker has some difficulty in locating this person, arriving eventually at Potter's Court, where Bloxam identifies himself as the "depity," or deputy (*D* 244). This misreading of the directed envelope demonstrates the inability of written language to convey truth. Dystopian readings interpret this communication breakdown as indicative of vast class divisions within England that are more unbridgeable than those between cultures. As the Norton Critical Edition editors note, "the British characters have more difficulty communicating with each other than with the Romanian vampire."[4]

Not for Public Consumption: Shorthand as Coded Language

In compiling their meticulous record of the vampire's comings and goings, Stoker's heroes avail themselves of the tools of modernity to conquer the monster of antiquity. The first communication technology mentioned in Stoker's text is shorthand. This technique, developed by Isaac Pitman in 1837, consists of a phonetic notation which records spoken language. The Preface to Pitman's *Shorthand Instructor* explains that with the adoption of the systematized methods of abbreviation developed in the briefest or Reporting style of writing Phonography, this method of shorthand can be written with the speed of the most rapid distinct articulation, while it may be read with the certainty and ease of ordinary longhand writing.[5]

Hence, it was extremely useful for taking dictation in office environments before the widespread emergence of voice recording devices, as the term "writing Phonography" suggests. Pitman's Preface also notes that this system may be employed "as a vehicle for private communications or for use in various ways in business or professional life."

Mina and Jonathan Harker employ shorthand for both professional and personal interactions. Mina links the practice to both her wifely duties and her own professional ambitions:

I want to keep up with Jonathan's studies, and I have been prac-tising shorthand very assiduously. When we are married I shall be able to be useful to Jonathan, and if I can stenograph well enough I can take down what he wants to say in this way and write it out for him on the typewriter, at which also I am prac-tising very hard. He and I sometimes write letters in shorthand, and he is keeping a stenographic journal of his travels abroad. (D 53)

She also outlines her plan to keep her own shorthand diary as an "exer-cise-book" in which she will mimic "lady journalists:" "interviewing and writing descriptions and trying to remember conversations:" techniques she will employ throughout the text (D 53).

Apart from its Utilitarian domestic and professional functions, Mina also considers writing in shorthand to be therapeutic, perhaps because of the privacy it seems to afford. As she muses in her own journal, "I am anxious, and it soothes me to express myself here; it is like whispering to one's self and listening at the same time. And there is something about the shorthand symbols that makes it different from writing" (D 69). Harker's journal, the novel's first four chapters, is initially intended as a private communication between lovers. Mina's sealing of her husband's diary of events at Castle Dracula without reading it becomes part of their marriage vows, "an outward and visible sign" of mutual trust (*D* 100).

Conversely, shorthand sets up an adversarial relationship between the young solicitor Jonathan Harker and the elderly Count Dracula. As Jennifer Wicke remarks, "[s]tenography is a fortuitous code for Jonathan, since Dracula, who seems to know everything else, does not take shorthand."[6] Harker is secure in the knowledge that he can write to his fiancée Mina "in shorthand, which would puzzle the Count, if he did see it" (*D* 33). Upon discovering the coded letter to Mina, Dracula is not only puzzled but also enraged, calling it "'a vile thing, an outrage upon friendship and hospitality,'" before consigning it to the flames (*D* 42). Later in the novel Mina cannot "resist the temptation of mystifying [the much older Van Helsing] a bit," by handing him the shorthand diary to decipher (*D* 170). For the utopian reader, new technology empowers a younger generation against an older, less informed one.

The fate of coded language in *Dracula*, however, suggests that the privacy it seems to afford is an illusion. Concerned for her husband's sanity and wellbeing, Mina eventually feels compelled to break her vow, unsealing her husband's journal and not only reading it but also translating and transcribing it by typewriter. She justifies these actions in her own journal by explaining, "[t]hen we shall be ready for other eyes if required" (*D* 167). Mina's decision to transcribe the record of Jonathan's trauma is a reminder that written communication, however intimate, always risks exposure. From a dystopian perspective, communication technologies contain the potential to make the personal public.

Dystopian readings of *Dracula* also explore the intersections among the novel's communication technologies and the vampirism they seek to foil. In an article called, simply but tellingly, "Textula," Robert Ready draws an analogy between Harker's shorthand journal and Dracula's coffin: "The box is where Dracula keeps the Un-dead version of himself undetected just as Harker's journal is where he keeps a version of himself undecoded. Hence, the Un-dead hosts the un-read and vice versa."[7] Ready's comparison suggests that the writing and the vampire both mirror one another and hide from one another in an uneasy truce.

In a more contextually informed argument, Jennifer Wicke's dystopian reading considers that shorthand's "feminization of the clerical work force [and] standardization of mass business writing" represent a type of mass cultural vampirism, one that replicates workers and the information that they process endlessly and uniformly.[8] Pamela Thurschwell analyzes the complex set of identities that get mapped onto the figure of the secretary. On the one hand, the female clerical worker brings a comforting domestic presence into the workplace that is humanizing from a utopian perspective: "[t]he angel in the house becomes the angel in the office." On the other hand, the technological functions that the secretary performs make her one with the machine: "the word typewriter originally meant both the machine itself and the person who worked it."[9] The dystopian discourse surrounding clerical workers becomes that of the automaton: robotic, dehumanized, even vampirized.

Phonography and Voice Recognition: When the Confessional Invades the Professional

Another cutting-edge Victorian communication technique in *Dracula* is Dr. Seward's phonograph, an early voice-recording device that enables him to keep an audio diary. Mina's excited reaction to his new technology ("'Why, this beats even shorthand!'" (195)) hearkens back to Pitman's notion of shorthand as "writing Phonography." As Jill Galvan notes,

> Edison and other designers mainly saw [the phonograph] as an alternative to the stenographer's shorthand—a Victorian synonym for which, *phonography*, sums up its historical link to the phonograph's method of inscribing sound (in the case of shorthand, the human voice).[10]

Edison actually imagined a wide variety of applications for this new technology. Like most inventors, Edison was optimistic about the possible uses of his innovation. Among the many kinds of communication he envisioned this instrument enhancing were business practices such as letter-writing and record-keeping of a more personal nature, including family records and dying people's last words.[11] But Edison also ended his endorsement with a veiled caution:

The phonograph, in one sense, knows more than we do ourselves. For it will retain perfect mechanical memory of many things which we may forget, even though we have said them. It will become an important factor in education; and it will teach us to be careful what we say—for it imparts to us the gift of hearing ourselves as others hear us—exerting thus a decidedly moral influence by making men brief, businesslike and straightforward, cultivating improved manners, and uniting distant friends and associates by direct vocal communication.[12]

The inventor's caveat thus anticipates some of the ongoing challenges that plague our contemporary milieu of digital communications; namely, privacy and permanency.

Seward keeps his log or journal as a professional record of his cases, including descriptions of his visits with his patients and his speculations on the causes and treatments of their disorders. Occasionally, however, the doctor's personal emotions invade this professional record, as when he speaks of the dearly departed Lucy, for whom he still carries a torch. Mina's offer to transcribe Seward's recordings is initially presented as a technological innovation, a means by which Seward can locate and access specific sections of his journal with more ease than the phonographic medium provides. But this professional transaction also has a personal and intimate consequence, as Mina's description of the phonograph attests:

"That is a wonderful machine, but it is cruelly true. It told me, in its very tones, the anguish of your heart. It was like a soul crying out to almighty God. No one must hear them spoken ever again! See, I have tried to be useful. I have copied out the words on my typewriter, and none other need now hear your heart beat, as I did." (D 197)

This interchange creates an emotional bond between these two relative strangers, one that solidifies around their mutual love for Lucy and grief at her untimely demise. Utopian readings of *Dracula* celebrate the exchange of writing in various forms for its ability to fuse alliances and emotional connections among the band of heroes. But technologically enhanced audio communication is also fraught with potential pitfalls.

Dystopian readings of Victorian voice technology emphasize its dehumanizing effects. In "The Victorian Aura of the Recorded Voice," John M. Picker notes that "[e]ndless repetition of a disembodied voice had the potential to distort even the most benign speech into a monotonous rant that sounded diabolical, perhaps even terrifying."[13] Wicke argues that "Seward's diary constitutes the immaterialization of a voice, a technologized zone of the novel, […] speech already colonized, or vampirized, by mass mediation."[14] According to this dystopian reading, the voice-recording technology vampirizes the authentic voice by duplicating the simulacrum of a voice. In other words, virtual reality is vampiric in that it is both a parasite and a corrupting influence on reality.

As Thurschwell argues in her analysis of *Dracula*, "both telegraphy and phonographs threaten to invade and discover the secrets of the insides of minds in the novel, just as vampires threaten to suck dry the insides of bodies."[15] Like the vampirized body, "the mind is open to invasion, and bodily intimacy becomes impossible to extricate from 'tele'intimacy: the all knowing intimacy created by a machine like the telephone, the distant but penetrating access to another."[16] Both vampirism and recorded-voice technology therefore threaten the boundaries of selfhood, rendering both bodies and minds penetrable, their contents exposed and colonized by invading forces.

Tabloid Journalism:
Sensationalizing the News

Another type of communication technology present in Bram Stoker's novel *Dracula* appears in the form of newspaper "cuttings" or clippings. A sense of immediacy, or synchronous pacing, is enhanced by the insertion of these pieces. The newspaper articles that Mina collates with the other written accounts provide narrative coherence and fill in the gaps in the vampires' activities, including Dracula's arrival in Whitby, his visit to the London zoo, and Lucy's nocturnal ramblings as the "Bloofer Lady." While these insertions arm the heroes with knowledge of their enemy, they also provide examples of the potentially dehumanizing effects of sensationalism.

Emerging during an era that saw the proliferation of periodicals, *Dracula* mimics both the urgency and aggrandizement of yellow journalism. News in Britain had been sensationalized since at least the mid-eighteenth century. The popularity of the Newgate Calendar, a sordid collection of crime dramas focused upon the inhabitants of Newgate Prison, attests to the public appetite for scandal. Salacious stories of the type that characterize today's tabloids proliferated throughout the nineteenth century. In addition to newspapers, cheaply available Penny Dreadfuls fictionalized true crime stories. While more fully developed as literary narratives than their contemporary counterparts, newspaper articles like the ones found in *Dracula* illustrate the power of both the written word and the technology that disseminates it to construct reality.

The account of Dracula's arrival on British shores is related in two Whitby newspaper articles detailing the wreck of a mysterious unmanned ship complete with an embedded captain's log that is a literal message in a bottle. Written for an audience comprised mostly of vacationers at a seaside town, these articles present newsworthy items at a surprisingly leisurely pace. The first cutting from the *Dailygraph*, dated August 8, begins with a detailed account of "[o]ne of the greatest and suddenest storms on record" (*D* 72). The description of the storm is developed at length and includes the sort of literary references that one would not expect to find in a news story. The *Dailygraph* correspondent quotes Samuel Taylor Coleridge's poem *The Rime of the Ancient Mariner* ("As idle as a painted ship upon a painted ocean" (*D* 74)) to describe a becalmed Russian schooner. While the story seems to be about the storm, the real news, of course, is this ship's dramatic arrival on Whitby shores with a corpse "lashed to the helm" (*D* 75). This revelation is delayed for dramatic effect—a technique that journalists call "burying the lead."

Despite the leisurely development of the first article, the real-time pacing of these events is enhanced by the status update of the second piece, dated the next day. This follow-up contains more specific detail about the vessel, as well as a warning to the public about "the fierce brute" (*D* 78) of a dog who disembarked from it. Most interestingly, the second clipping includes a translation of the ship's captain's log. This journalistic account embeds a second narrative that corroborates and enhances the first, particularly for the band of vampire hunters, specifically Mina, who eventually not only collates but also correctly interprets all of these materials. Journalistic technology thus aids the heroes in their quest.

Another journalistic technique, the interview, comprises most of the second cutting that Mina includes in the record. "The Escaped Wolf: Perilous Adventure of Our Interviewer: Interview with the Keeper of the Zoological Gardens," from the *Pall Mall Gazette* of September 18, aims to tell a sensational tale in order to amuse its London readers. Since the escaped wolf returns before the piece concludes, the sense of urgency of a public warning can here be sacrificed for the sake of a good story.

The interview with zookeeper Thomas Bilder takes the form of a "slice of life" vignette, a conversation with an eccentric character in his own natural habitat, his home. The journalist attempts to faithfully render Bilder's speech by transcribing his dialect phonetically. He also allows Bilder's sly and somewhat off-color humor to emerge, as it becomes clear that the keeper is much more interested in the wolf's safety than the public's. Bilder's attempts at humor communicate one of the novel's most disturbingly dehumanizing elements: the callous disregard for the well-being of infants and children.[17] As he speculates on the damage the wolf might do, Bilder casually surmises: "If he can't get food he's bound to look for it, and mayhap he may chance to light on a butcher's shop in time. If he doesn't, and some nursemaid goes a-walkin' orf with a soldier, leavin' of the hinfant in the perambulator—well then I shouldn't be surprised if the census is one babby the less. That's all" (*D* 131). Although this account helps Mina and the others to synchronize the wandering wolf's nocturnal ramblings with Dracula's activities, the filtering of this story through macabre humor creates a distancing effect from the possible horrific consequences of the actions of both predators, the wolf and the vampire.

Perhaps the most sensational of these journalistic insertions is *The Westminster Gazette's* tabloidization of Lucy as the "Bloofer Lady," who is apparently feeding on the neighborhood children. Comparing this "Hampstead Mystery" to salacious headlines such as "'The Kensington Horror,' 'The Stabbing Woman,' or 'The Woman in Black,'" this piece establishes Lucy's plight as another chapter in a long list of scandals (*D* 165). That the children refer to this predator as the "bloofer lady," a childish pronunciation of "beautiful lady," attests to her allure. The tone of this article is particularly disturbing. Although it ends with a serious warning to parents to safeguard their youngsters, the piece also delights in both the titillating aspect of this mysterious figure and the children's attempts to imitate her:

> the favourite game of the little ones at present is luring each other away by wiles. A correspondent writes us that to see some of the tiny tots pretending to be the "bloofer lady" is supremely funny. Some of our caricaturists might, he says, take a lesson in the irony of grotesque by comparing the reality and the picture. It is only in accordance with general principles of human nature that the "bloofer lady" should be the popular rôle at these *al Fresco* performances. Our correspondent naïvely says that even Ellen Terry could not be so winningly attractive as some of these grubby-faced little children pretend—and even imagine themselves—to be. (*D* 165–66)

The reference to Lyceum Theatre actress Terry contributes to the sexualization of these children, a precociousness that is simultaneously admired and mocked. From a utopian perspective, the proliferation of vampiric behavior by these children constitutes a horrific foreshadowing, another clue to the looming threat of Dracula's proliferation. But in dystopian terms the article's humorously inappropriate tone performs the same dehumanizing functions as today's tabloids: sexualizing and shaming victims and distancing readers from horror through humor.

While more extensively and more novelistically developed than today's journalistic accounts, these cuttings nevertheless provide a sense of the novel unfolding in real time. This sense of urgency pits the pace of modern life against the timelessness of the vampire. And, in practical terms, as Leah Richards points out, "if the information is provided quickly enough, the audience can respond while the news is still relevant."[18] For Stoker's characters, this entails reading between the lines of these newspaper accounts and having enough foresight to include them in the record. Tracking Dracula's movements through technologically enhanced communications becomes an essential part of the quest to destroy him.

But the communications themselves ironically comment upon the ways in which writing technologies can distort reality.

Speedy Delivery:
The Telegram, Instant Gratification, and Technology Failures

In an era of rapid technological advancements in communication the telegram is another of the contemporary tools used to battle the ancient vampire. The delivery of the telegram must have seemed nearly instantaneous to contemporary Victorian readers of the novel. Indeed, at one point in the novel, Mina sends a message that actually beats Dracula to their mutual destination. During the time that Van Helsing and company are infiltrating Dracula's Piccadilly property, Mina figures out that Dracula is on his way there also and sends the following telegram: "Look out for D. He has just now, 12.45, come from Carfax hurriedly and hastened towards the south. He seems to be going the round and may want to see you: Mina" (*D* 282). Luckily for the slayers, this communication beats the vampire, and they are thus prepared for his arrival. Earlier, during Lucy's decline, a series of three telegrams from Seward in London to Van Helsing in Amsterdam, printed in succession, also communicate a sense of rapid pacing, especially because the last one reads: "Terrible change for the worse. Come at once; do not lose an hour" (*D* 111). Van Helsing's timely receipt of this message avails Lucy of additional time but ultimately fails to save her.

Dependence upon technology becomes particularly problematic when the technology fails. The telegram sent by Van Helsing from Antwerp to Seward at Carfax, urging him to spend the night at Lucy's, is "delivered late by twenty-two hours," a technological failure that results in Lucy's mother's death (*D* 133). And, near the novel's end, the telegram from London to Varna stating that the *Czarina Catherine* has entered Galatz arrives too late for Dracula's pursuers to reroute their course. Jill Galvan neatly sums up the dystopian implications of these "tech fails," acknowledging that utopian interpretations fail to account for the novel's subtler nuances:

These shortcomings reinforce the superiority of the Count's communication methods and, at the same time, indicate the inadequacies of some of the most spectacular achievements of late Victorian civilization. Inasmuch as the group's media practices, hypnotic as well as technological, condition the way they access, record, and process reality, the way they shape it into something called knowledge, their media failures symbolize and, more covertly, partially effect the failures of their systems of knowledge—their science—to apprehend and comprehend the actual. That is, though it may be tempting to view *Dracula* as a narrative of the triumph of positive knowledge, in which the forces of modernity synthesize information to squeeze out of existence the mystery Dracula represents, the triumph is illusory at best.[19]

These delayed messages highlight the precarious nature of relying on the technological transmission of written communication.

Manifold Typing and Mass Market Publishing: The Proliferation of the Vampire

Utopian readings of *Dracula* value communication technologies for their ability to foster intimacy and immediacy. Sharing of information through cutting-edge technologies serves both to bond Stoker's characters and to enable them to outpace Dracula. The resulting sense of intimacy and immediacy extends to the reader, who is pulled into the circle of slayers by becoming privy to their private documents in a timely fashion. Mina employs a cutting-edge writing technology known as manifold, an early version of carbon paper, to produce three simultaneous versions of her typewritten account, thus increasing the pace at which the stories can be disseminated and shared. For Wicke, however, the manifold function is "positively vampiric" in its ability to replicate itself, and thus manifests cultural anxieties about "mechanical reproduction."[20] This use of technology to proliferate the vampire's story suggests a proliferation of the vampire himself, disseminated endlessly into the many readers who devour the legend and perpetuate Dracula's immortality.

Glimpses of dystopian interpretations of the text as vampiric may be seen even among Victorian reviews of *Dracula*. The reviewer for the *Belfast*

News-Letter thinks the book's cover should include an announcement in red letters "warning off all nervous individuals."[21] *The Bookman* reviewer cautioned, "Keep 'Dracula' out of the way of nervous children."[22] Most explicitly, the *Pall Mall Gazette* review begins with the following warning:

> Mr. Bram Stoker should have labeled his book 'For Strong Men Only,' or words to that effect. Left lying carelessly around, it might get into the hands of your maiden aunt who believes devoutly in the man under the bed, or of the new parlourmaid with unsuspected hysterical tendencies. 'Dracula' to such would be manslaughter.[23]

While *Dracula*'s potential fatal effects are seemingly offered in jest, these reviews suggest that the book itself was perceived as dangerous in its believed ability to infect and unsettle susceptible minds.

Roughly two-thirds into the novel there is a critical point at which the principal characters meet and exchange their written stories, which literally comprise the novel up to that point. Mina's decision to unseal Harker's shorthand journal and add it to the mix provides the characters with the first four chapters of the novel, creating a real-time pacing effect between characters and readers. As Mina relates: "I told them, as well as I could, that I had read all the papers and diaries, and that my husband and I, having typewritten them, had just finished putting them in order. I gave them each a copy to read in the library. [...] —it does make a pretty good pile—" (D 213). The exchange of this "pretty good pile" of writing, effectively the first two hundred pages of Stoker's novel, means that the characters are all caught up not only with one another but also with the reader, who thus takes part in both the intimacy and immediacy of the experience.

Utopian readings emphasize the novel's exchange of information as a bonding between the characters, one that serves to cement not only their relationships but also their common purpose. As Leah Richards argues:

> Within the context of the novel, it is not sufficient that the material be collected by firsthand observers and written down; it needs to be shared. To know everything about Dracula is to know how

to destroy him. It is information, gathered and arranged into a collaborative and comprehensive account, that enables the group to defeat Dracula.[24]

Ultimately, it is the process of collating and transcribing these materials that enables Mina to make the discovery of Dracula's escape route. Information sharing for a common collective purpose is in keeping with the utopian reading of technology as democratizing. Still, it is problematic from a utopian, democratizing point of view that only a privileged few can decode the original documents. As Richards notes, "in the case of *Dracula*, reproduction puts private documents in the hands of an expert, Van Helsing, who knows how to use the information in the originals but would not have been able to decode most of it." Thus even the utopian reading is fraught with "anxieties about [...] the technological spread of information, none of which is authentic when it reaches its audience."[25]

The final product which Mina collates is a multimedia presentation rendered as text. The audible components, Seward's wax cylinders, along with all the other original documentation, have been destroyed, consigned to the flames by a Dracula desperate to preserve the mystery that protects him. As Van Helsing notes, "in this enlightened age, when men believe not even what they see, the doubting of wise men would be his greatest strength" (*D* 298). Dracula's destruction of the original record reveals another way in which the novel anticipates dystopian fiction. As Gottlieb notes, "probably one of the most typical 'messages' of dystopian fiction is that access to the records of the past is vital to the mental health of any society."[26] Seward relates Arthur's tale of Dracula's vandalism:

> "He had been there, and though it could only have been for a few seconds, he made rare hay of the place. All the manuscript had been burned, and the blue flames were flickering amongst the white ashes; the cylinders of your phonograph too were thrown on the fire, and the wax had helped the flames." Here I interrupted. "Thank God there is the other copy in the safe!" (*D* 265)

Thus the vampire is foiled again by technology, this time by Mina's manifold typewriting. According to Christine Ferguson's utopian interpretation, "[l]anguage proves too mobile a force to be absorbed by the vampire."[27] The other copy in the safe, although a simulacrum of the original, becomes not only the novel itself and the bedrock of their hopes for defeating Dracula but also insurance against legal prosecution. As Harker, the lawyer, notes, "perhaps some day this very script may be evidence to come between some of us and a rope" (D 311). But, at the end of the novel, Harker admits to the lack of authenticity of their written record:

> in all the mass of material of which the record is composed, there is hardly one authentic document! nothing but a mass of type-writing, except the later note-books of Mina and Seward and myself, and Van Helsing's memorandum. We could hardly ask anyone, even did we wish to, to accept these as proofs of so wild a story. (D 351)

While the utopian reading accepts the authenticity of the typewritten mass—that is, the novel—the dystopian reading questions not only the authority of the text but also its conclusion.

To accept that technology defeats the vampire is to accept Dracula's demise, which Stoker renders ambiguously. Dracula's "final dissolution," in which his body "crumble[s] into its native dust," somewhat resembles his initial entrance into Lucy's chamber, in which "a whole myriad of little specks seemed to come blowing in through the broken window, [...] wheeling and circling round like the pillar of dust that travellers describe when there is a simoom [i.e. hot wind] in the desert" (D 345, 134–35). Thus, this dissolution could be read as a vanishing or shapeshifting, rather than an annihilation. Additionally, Stoker excised a paragraph detailing the implosion of Castle Dracula, which many critics read as a denial of the finality of Dracula's ultimate defeat.[28] The utopian interpretation reads this textual ending as complete, closed, and final, while the dystopian interpretation probes the textual gaps and holes left open by these ambiguities.

Utopian interpretations view communication technologies in Dracula not only as effective and efficient in neutralizing the threat of the foreign invader but also as humanizing in their ability to enable intimate and immediate connections among the novel's characters. Dystopian readings, on the other hand, probe the questions left open by the novel's ambiguous close. Was Harker bitten? Does Mina fully recover? If their son embodies the soul of Quincey because he was born on his death day, does he also embody the soul of Dracula (provided the vampire also died on that day, which remains another open question)? Such interpretations examine the hypocrisy and fallibility of the heroes, the lack of a definitive demise for the Count, and the possibility of the proliferation of vampiric contagion through the surviving characters. In questioning not only the defeat of the vampire but also the efficacy of the technology that brings him down, dystopian readings acknowledge the triumph of the vampire as both predator and proliferator of texts.

CHAPTER SIX

Tracking the Unruly Cadaver
Dracula and Victorian Coroners' Reports

Rebecca E. May

Introduction

Coroners have worked to assess sudden or mysterious deaths and to ensure that justice is served since about the eleventh century. In the late Victorian period coroners still serve this purpose. They are ubiquitous in late Victorian lived experience and, though much has been said about the dead, the law, medicine, and professions in *Dracula*, scholars have yet to connect coroners as demystifiers of the strange dead to Stoker's novel. Given Stoker's connection to both the law and medicine, this is a rich area for exploration. But if the coroner *has* been around for so long, and if his duties are generally speaking the same whether we study him in 1500 in England or in 1800 in America, in what ways can we locate what is uniquely late Victorian about him, and how can that be connected to the ways in which Stoker built a late Victorian worldview into his novel? The answer demands that we discuss, via coroners' case files, Victorian professional expertise, forms of documentation and technology, and public health institutions, including how those elements of the period combine to make inquests an advanced and complicated bureaucratized procedure rather than a participatory feature of community life. Above all, the advanced codification of the police state, the law, medical expertise, and the state management of vital records make the process of certification at once essential to record-keeping and ever more complicated to manage.

Dracula in fact walks us through *many* tensions locatable in the coroner's case files: struggles to document authority, to discipline the disordered cadaver, to collate narrative, to fill up space with information, and to hold modern medical and judicial systems up as the apotheosis of demystification and truth-making. As a text obsessed with collation, transcription, and cutting-edge forms of documentation—all of which fail to impart any sense of comforting certainty or to control the social and promiscuous corpse—*Dracula* is the coroner's best Fin-de-Siècle literary analogue.

Broadly speaking, literature does not neglect the coroner's profession; although a coroner is not central to Stoker's novel, the Crew of Light knows enough to avoid an inquest into Lucy's, Renfield's, and Mrs. Westenra's deaths.[1] Coroners pop up often enough in mid and late nineteenth-century literary texts as a kind of social given, background function, or plot mechanism. Works by George Eliot, James Fenimore Cooper, Arthur Conan Doyle, and Charles Dickens mention coroners doing their duties or even defending their jobs, as in *Middlemarch*, but rarely do these coroners have names or much character development. I want to account for this absent-presence or, to put it another way, the accepted yet marginalized presence of the coroner, who does inquests, who is there as a local social formation, but who is not looked at too closely because, in the Victorian period, the coroner's authority was questionable, especially because of territorial jockeying between the medical and legal fields and an ongoing anxiety about the necessity of striking a balance between the public's right to participate in inquests and the more efficient private management that closed medical certification of deaths could provide.[2] While most coroners in the United Kingdom in the nineteenth century were legal experts, an increasing assertion that the position should be predominantly medical, prompted by diagnostic improvements and a belief that only a medical professional could appropriately assess the need for an inquest, caused a great deal of debate. This same debate raged in America. In some areas of the United States state and local governments voted to abolish the position of coroner in favor of medical examiners. There was no standard approach to the issue in the United Kingdom, United States, or Canada because most official documents simply asserted that "[a]ny fit person may hold [the position of coroner] who is not at the time an alderman or a councilor.

By custom it has gradually come to be limited to barristers, solicitors, and members of the medical profession."[3] Thus, the coroner's position already points us to one uniquely late Victorian issue: that expertise and professional codification and fracturing, medical technology, the clinical gaze, public health movements, and national records of vital statistics complicate who the coroner is and what kind of knowledge he must produce and how. Frederick W. Lowndes goes on to assert that

> considering the nature of the coroner's duties, this meeting of the Liverpool Medical Institution is of the opinion that they can be more efficiently performed by a medical man, who has thoroughly acquainted himself with the legal bearings of medical questions than by any gentleman who has not had the advantage of a medical training.[4]

Professional forms collide with methods of knowledge-making and the certification of certainty in particularly potent, late Victorian ways. What should be most predominant in a death investigation: medical ways of knowing or legal–judicial ways? Which is the most complicated or liable to error? Is the certification of cause of death most important?

John B. Carey's 1891 novel *The Oddities of Short-hand, or, the coroner and his friends* is populated by a cache of unnamed professionals (the Lawyer, the Engineer, the Stenographer, the Real Estate Man). The central thrust of the text is to call into question the veracity of documentation technologies such as shorthand and to show how often professionals can make destructive mistakes, even when they are bolstered by modern technological advancements. Carey counters conservative representations of the police state professional, who perceives accurately enough to take disparate forms of evidence and integrate them into a seamless narrative of resplendent, uncovered truth. In the Coroner's narrative, the Coroner misnumbers his deputy's shorthand transcription of a wounded man's last words. The story shows that, read one way, the notes indicate the man identified his attacker, but when the pages are turned another way they indicate that the man could not identify his attacker. This mistake's consequences obviously hamper the pursuit of truth and justice, and it is all because the coroner does not have a careful or foolproof filing system.

Carey's characterization of his unnamed coroner is the most detailed and significant I have found in Victorian fiction, not only because it showcases the failure of accurate and reliable protocol but also because it depicts the coroner as both educated and defiled:

> The Coroner was an Irishman, educated, witty, polished, and inclined to be cynical. His horror of what he called "rum" and the rum traffic was only equaled by his intense affection for the weed. He had been thrice elected coroner, and his professional duties brought him in close proximity to the lower strata of society, in "the slums and alleys of a great sinful city."
>
> The pictures he drew of gaunt poverty, willful murder, unexplained suicide, the ghastly morgue, the police court and the hospital, were startling, vivid and gruesome.[5]

Carey's coroner's Irishness here seems to imply that he is ethnically fit to work "in close proximity to the lower strata of society," but that he is also "educated, witty, polished." He is horrified by alcohol consumption, perhaps because many coroners' reports catalogue whether or not the deceased was "intemperate," but he is not uptight enough to abjure tobacco. Most importantly, he is "a conscious possessor of a mine of narratives from his own personal experience that was seemingly inexhaustible."[6] He can tell engaging, hair-raising stories of abject behaviors and the workings of mysterious places inaccessible to the public: the morgue, the hospital, the police court.

Carey's Coroner is precisely the kind of character I am interested in using to understand Stoker's novel because his professionalism is his identity, as is the case with Van Helsing, Harker, and Seward, and because he exemplifies the Victorian professional's work to confront death and violence through documentation with the belief that medicine and the law can discipline social ills, even as documentation is shown to be faulty. Like Van Helsing, and even Mina, he is a collector of exclusive narratives. He is a compiler, translator, and interpreter of corpses. He takes disparate fragments of information and forms them into verdicts; his files take shape like the Crew of Light's dossier on the vampire. In many ways the public sees the coroner as someone who touches "undesirables," yet, because of his work, the masses can consume lurid details in the popular press.[7] His files are the archive I examine in this essay, alone at first, and then with *Dracula* to show how their form is so much like the papers Stoker asks us to imagine in our hands as we read the novel: stacks of tiny papers tacked together, heartbreaking and violent narratives of death and truncated accounts with a dispassionate telos.

Contents of Coroners' Case Files

Coroners' case files are indexes of micro and macro forms, not the least of which is a record of things that could suddenly kill late Victorians, including trains, mills and mines, rivers, poisons such as carbolic acid, suicide, gangrene, consumption, heart failure, falls, exposure, heat stroke, apoplexy, explosions, fire, sudden infant death, and so on. Coroners also index constructions of narrative, body-as-text, truth, and authority. Their records can impart warm feelings of community as neighbors provide statements, tell stories of someone's final moments, or identify bodies, but they can elicit skeptical responses as suspicious-sounding testimonies result in verdicts of accidental or natural death. Coroners infiltrate intimate domestic structures, visiting homes broken by violence or addiction; they come in the aftermath of medical distress, and they respond in moments of terrible accident and social crisis. Their case files document intimacy, vulnerability, tragedy, and suffering, but their form and style work as a palliative agent via the process of certifying cause of death and determining responsibility. In many ways, his function as a social balm relies heavily on the psychosocial power of closure even though his work is never complete.

For this project I reviewed archived files of the Allegheny County Coroner at the University of Pittsburgh Archives Services Center from about 1885 to 1905.[8] I studied what kinds of paper, certificate, form, report, and statement are in the files to determine how file contents changed during the period, thus indicating changes in protocol, technology, statutes, regulations, institutional expectations, and larger public health structures. The closer the files get to 1900 the more standardized and formalized the documentation process becomes, indicated by blank form documents for the coroner or physician to complete. Such standard forms lend the files an increasing sense of dispassionate and mechanized protocol and forge a strong connection between protocol, closure, state-mandated record keeping, and social satisfaction. It ostensibly simplifies the job, as well, and reduces the risk of error.

The files look like this: papers tacked together (see Figure 6.1). Through the 1880s and into the 1890s the coroner's notes are pencil on lined or unlined paper.[9] These notes include witness statements, jury verdicts, and correspondence from attending physicians. One file might include three small sheets of paper with close-crammed writing on both sides. There are typewritten documents only if the deceased is a prison inmate, occasional telegraphs, receipts indicating family members receiving the personal effects found on a cadaver, and, only once, laboratory toxicology reports, in fragments from March 26, 1887. What is fascinating about these early reports is how ephemeral the technology of documentation seems in relation to the social need for an official determination and the state's demands for certification. It appears that the coroner's authority does not at all rest in these files. He only matters, it seems, in determining whether or not a jury should be called and then shuttling them together to pronounce cause of death, which, once heard, cements closure or opens up a case for criminal prosecution, not handled by the coroner. The forms of documentation collide in interesting ways with the (re)formation of the profession in, especially, the late Victorian period.

In many ways, the coroner is a mediator amongst competing social formations: medical–legal, family–community, state–local, home–hospital, dead–living, bureaucratic documentation–public press. Moreover, any single coroner jostles against other coroners because each locale constructs the profession slightly differently, even, as I have indicated above, at the level of documentation. While basic duties are consistent across states and counties, and indeed nations, protocol and educational background vary, even well past the Victorian period, yet the same kinds of variation and continuity can be found in documents on both sides of the Atlantic. For example, while Massachusetts votes in 1877 to abolish the elected coroner in favor of an appointed medical examiner, it is only in 2005 that the coroner as elected position is abolished in Allegheny County, Pittsburgh, Pennsylvania and replaced with the position of medical examiner appointed by the mayor. Thus, while all counties have someone who fulfills the duties of a

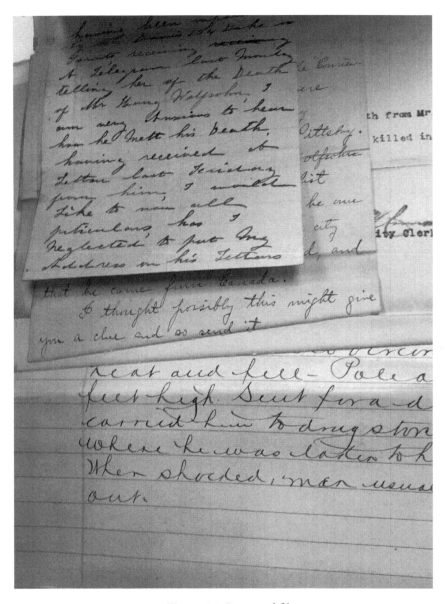

Figure 6.1 Coroners' files.

coroner, not all coroners operate in the same ways, have access to the same facilities, are liable to the same laws and statutes, or have medical or legal degrees.

The case files in many ways occlude the coroner's daily activities and interpersonal skills, but it appears that information traveled efficiently and that coroners were able to close out cases quickly. The time between a death and a verdict was as little as one or two days and, indeed, delay was a punishable offense on the coroner's part. It is also clear that people felt either comfortable enough or compelled enough to speak with him. Elizabeth T. Hurren also notes that the everyday duties of coroners are difficult to trace, but she uses the notebooks of Edward Law Hussey, Coroner for the City of Oxford from 1877 to 1894 to overview his career from doctor to the poor, to surgeon, and finally to coroner.[10] His notes uncover his commitment to exploring especially cases of infanticide, his empathy for the poor, and his very difficult relationship with the staff of the Radcliffe Infirmary, where he had resigned a position as House Surgeon under contentious circumstances, which often made it difficult for him to complete his work as coroner because his old colleagues often did not report deaths to him. She notes that he had to gain the trust especially of the poor, who treated him with distaste and suspicion:

> It was moreover a fact of his working life that the truth was often told to Hussey quietly. In effect this meant that he was powerless to act without official proof. Problems of concealment and cultures of secrecy were common, which explains why those coroners that lacked social contacts were so confounded by silence.[11]

It is not difficult to see how these cultures of secrecy especially surrounded infanticide, abortion, and domestic violence. However, Hurren finds that Hussey possessed a great deal of interpersonal empathy and tact and filled the position well. He successfully campaigned for the city to build a mortuary to house the dead, rather than relying on public houses or graveyard sheds. Ian Burney further contextualizes the coroner's professional and interpersonal skills in the context of the medical–legal debates. While total transparency between the coroner and the public was, he repeatedly emphasizes, an important part of the participatory nature of the inquest jury, physicians drawing up death certificates faced pressure to conceal controversial deaths or ones that might damage a family's reputation, especially in cases involving syphilis or alcohol abuse.[12]

Coroners toed a tough line between the intimate interpersonal circumstances of a person finding a corpse, a community's need to have narrative completion, and the dispassionate bureaucratic mechanisms that administer social balm to the chaos of sudden death by determining cause and seeking to hold responsible suspect parties. Coroners no doubt assuaged a powerful social anxiety. However, they aroused anxieties too, because they are indicative of social illnesses such as disaster, abuse, "mental derangement," disease, and, frequently, industrial accidents, as seen in this Jury verdict pronouncement of March 3, 1887 (see Figure 6.2):

> To the Coroner
> We your jury in the case of Jacob Konuaska (?), age 15 years, came to his death at the Homeopathic Hospital on Monday, 3/2 about 8:40 am, 2nd Ave Pgh from the effects of having his leg crushed between 21st and 22nd St South Side on the track of the Pgh McK & Y (or T) RR on a moving freight train driven by __ and GE. Engine #3 and not having received the proper medical attention at the time. The jury also censures Dr. SF Scott for his inhumane treatment of the case and exhonerates [sic] the RR Co. from any responsibility.[13]

While the content of this verdict is formal and standardized, it is an example of a closure-providing document lacking a valence of official authority—or undervaluing the importance of the coroner's verdict document as a record of public value—as it is pencil on notepaper, not even given its own dedicated page. The quite ephemeral nature of these files acts as a poignant reminder of the vulnerable cadaver, isolated and in need of assistance in being classified and cared for as well as dispassionately assessed and moved through institutional structures. In this case, a 15-year-old boy fatally injured by a train was not given proper medical treatment, but the file does not indicate how. At times the coroner, here Heber McDowell, crams more onto a page than seems reasonable, making study nearly impossible. This may indicate that the files were for

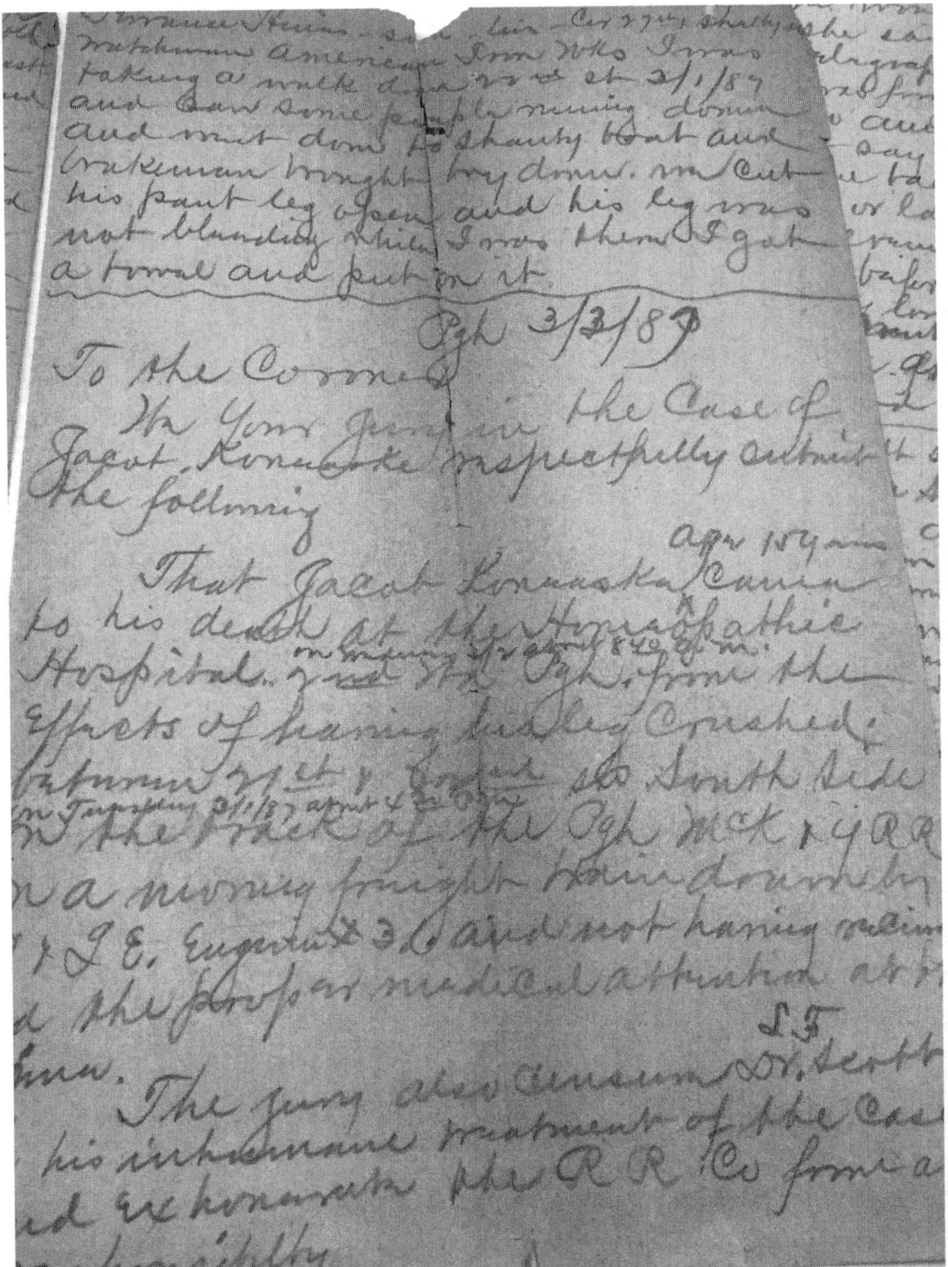

Figure 6.2 Jury verdict pronouncement.

the coroner's personal reference. Abbreviations, lack of punctuation, and incorrect spelling add to the personal feel. Despite this, narratives of social accountability and community intimacy emerge, as in this witness report of April 9, 1890 on the bodies of Robert and June Beattie, wherein David Phillips comments that a footbridge over a creek is dangerous and has caused the death of two children.

> David Phillips sworn.
> I heard that some children were in the run which was very high I saw a little girl float past me. But could not catch her. Wm. Mountain [?] and others were looking after the children in the run we found both of the children dead in the run about one half mile from the footlog I knew them to be the twin children of George Beattie I don't consider the footlog across Lobbs Run a Safe crossing for children as the railing had been broken off I believe it was put there by the Township.[14]

David Phillips clearly knew the twin children who drowned. Witness statements like this depict communities of people who know their neighbors and their neighbors' children. They come in the early morning when a mother awakens to find her infant dead; they call the doctor when a visiting friend has chest pains; they overhear arguments and violence; they know who is drunk and how often. The form of these documents cements the illusion of seamless forthcoming narrative, since McDowell's questions are not recorded. Witness testimonies do not record the coroners' questions until the twentieth century, though in an 1881 *Handbook for Coroners* a standard list of questions is recommended, taken from the British system:

> When did the death happen, when was the body found, was the deceased male or female? An infant, lunatic, or pauper, what is thought to have been the cause of death, is the body in a fresh or decomposed state, if it be supposed poison was the cause of death, what was the poison, if any medical practitioner was in attendance before death, what was his name, if the death was sudden was there any previous illness and for what length of time?[15]

While some of these questions could be answered by witnesses, others clearly demand a degree of medical expertise. Coroners did not perform postmortem examinations or autopsies, though they could call on physicians or surgeons to do so, and a medically educated coroner could save the community money by avoiding unnecessary postmortem examinations. If a patient died in hospital, physicians there could perform an autopsy if the coroner requested. Postmortem reports frequently took the form of letters, although in some counties forms were provided for completion, especially in cases when accountable institutions were involved, such as prisons, mines or mills, and railroads. The reports typically describe the body and any external marks of injury and then record the condition of relevant organs or internal markers of injury. The letter rounds out with the physician's pronouncement of cause of death.

Inquest requests for hospital deaths and railroad deaths made to the coroner are forms that, like pamphlets, are folded in thirds and printed on both sides (see Figure 6.3). Figure 6.3 shows a request from Allegheny General Hospital from 1897 for the death of one Addison W. Hunter, whose death was declared accidental. Hospital staff filled out this form requesting that the coroner McDowell perform an inquest. The deceased's name, residence, age, admission date, nativity, how arrived to hospital and from where, marital status, and occupation are listed. Below this the deceased's reason for admission is noted: "Shock due to crush of both legs and left arm." The attending physician notes how the injuries were received and what treatment was given. "Accidental while working on the P&W R.R. Run over by P&W locomotive at Wildwood 5.40 a.m. June 22nd 1897. // No operation." Date and time of death is recorded: "Tuesday, June 22nd 1897 at 9.40."[16] Remarks could be made below that might include whether the patient was conscious and what they said or what other treatments were given; sometimes postmortem notes are made here in cases of poisoning. In my survey of these forms, physicians rarely remark in this area. The physician signs the form. Notes at the bottom instruct the physician what to include on each of lines A–F. Other developments late in the period of study include a file form from the Coroner's Office to record the features of an unidentified or unidentifiable body, including the clothing and belongings found. Frequently, when someone died at home in the presence of a physician, the physician would write their own narrative of the event and

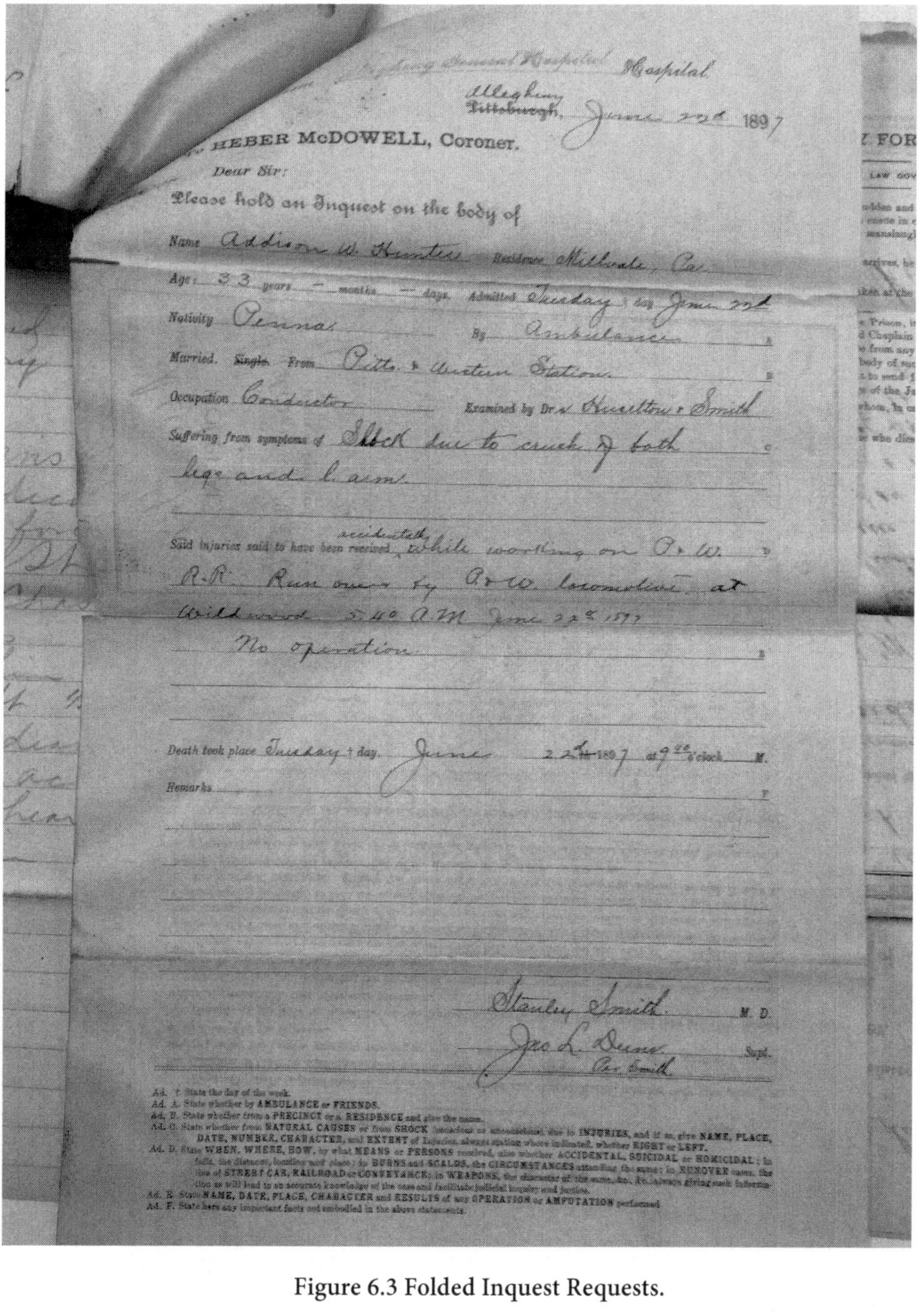

Hospital
Allegheny
~~Pittsburgh~~, June 22nd 1897

HEBER McDOWELL, Coroner.

Dear Sir:

Please hold an Inquest on the body of

Name Addison W. Hunter Residence Millvale, Pa.

Age: 33 years — months — days. Admitted Tuesday † day June 22nd

Nativity Penna. By Ambulance A

Married. ~~Single~~ From Pitts. & Western Station. B

Occupation Conductor Examined by Drs. Hazelton & Smith

Suffering from symptoms of Shock due to crush of both legs and l. arm C

Said injuries said to have been received accidentally while working on P. & W. R.R. Run over by P. & W. locomotive at Wildwood 5.40 A.M. June 22nd 1897 D

No operation E

Death took place Tuesday † day. June 22nd 1897 at 9.20 o'clock M.

Remarks F

Stanley Smith M.D.

Jno. L. Dunn Supt.
Per Smith

Ad. † State the day of the week.
Ad. A. State whether by AMBULANCE or FRIENDS.
Ad. B. State whether from a PRECINCT or a RESIDENCE and give the name.
Ad. C. State whether from NATURAL CAUSES or from SHOCK (accidental or self-inflicted) due to INJURIES, and if so, give NAME, PLACE, DATE, NUMBER, CHARACTER, and EXTENT of Injuries, always stating where indicated, whether RIGHT or LEFT.
Ad. D. State WHEN, WHERE, HOW, by what MEANS or PERSONS received, also whether ACCIDENTAL, SUICIDAL or HOMICIDAL; in falls, the distance, location and place; in BURNS and SCALDS, the CIRCUMSTANCES attending the same; in RUNOVER cases, the line of STREET CAR, RAILROAD or CONVEYANCE; in WEAPONS, the character of the same, &c. &c. always giving such information as will lead to an accurate knowledge of the case and facilitate judicial inquiry and justice.
Ad. E. State NAME, DATE, PLACE, CHARACTER and RESULTS of any OPERATION or AMPUTATION performed.
Ad. F. State here any important facts not embodied in the above statements.

Figure 6.3 Folded Inquest Requests.

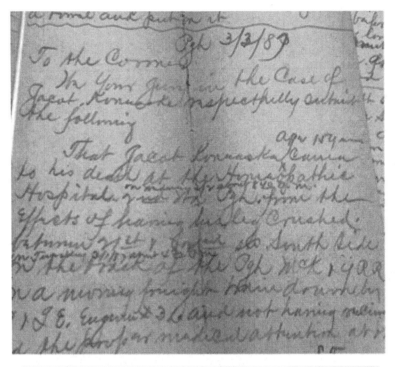

Figure 6.4 Jury verdicts, 1887 and 1905.

submit it to the coroner for filing. Here, a physician, in a letter from 1900, describes being called to the home of a man with chest pain:

> He said I have taken some whiskey and would soon be better."
> [*sic*] He was pale and pulseless with the surface cold and clammy.
> I at once appreciated the extreme danger and had him lie down
> on a lounge in an adjoining room. My wife and I walked on
> either side to be of any assistance that might be necessary. For
> a moment his pulse became quite perceptible but at once began
> to [indecipherable] and suddenly ceased to beat altogether, and
> no heart sounds could be heard. The time from the onset of the
> pain until he was dead, did not exceed eight or ten minutes. It was
> unquestionably a case of angina pectoria.[17]

The physician's unmistakable authority prevents the coroner from needing to take any further action, although, as stated above, Ian Burney notes that cases such as this could be complicated by pressure from the family for the physician to save embarrassment.

The year 1900 marks a significant year in the archive I studied: all files begin to follow a standard protocol consisting of: 1. a completed press report; 2. a proof of identity document; 3. a letter from the deceased's attending physician or an MD who has examined the body; and 4. a jury verdict form. Two documents from 1903 show changes in standardization based on larger institutional developments: a morgue view, as the county received a new morgue in 1903, and a physician's certificate of death in the wake of increased investments in public health indicating the use of proper diagnostic terms "to secure the greatest practicable uniformity." Physicians are instructed to avoid hybrid or indefinite terms such as "heart clot" and to indicate if intemperance facilitated death.

The Victorian Coroner and Institutional Structures

While the coroner collaborates, collates, and builds narratives, his reports show both a codification and an absence of (or a struggle towards) form in institutionalized forensic medicine, contradictions evidencing tensions amongst professional spheres and public health needs. The reports point to a social impulse to impose order onto the chaos of corpses found in suspicious circumstances and to build narrative out of testimony and postmortem evidence. However, they also indicate the fleeting nature of the coroner's authority and certification: early in the 1880s, the notes do not reflect a standard or organized protocol, while by the close of the century standardized forms simplify and even mask the nuances of his labor. The files do show a way of ordering death and managing concurrent social anxieties over narrative ambiguity, and the inquest does transform the social trauma of the mysterious corpse into a formed statement of certainty. Some of the tension can be explained by further examining some of the arguments about the coroner's expertise.

Late Victorian professionalization demands singular expertise. Victorian institutions, especially medical ones, become so complex, mediated by technologies and specializations, that it is argued that the coroner is simply unnecessary and outdated because no man can straddle the legal and the medical. John Lee in 1881 underscores how medical specialization can fracture an inquest's certainty:

The skillful diagnostician and therapeutist not unfrequently looks down upon the occasionally rough handiwork of his fellow-craftsman, the surgeon; the anatomist is frequently tempted to smile at the labors of the toxicologist, who perhaps, cares little for any other division of his profession; while the physiologist may have a poor opinion of the experimenter in therapeutics. The opthamologist is very liable to refer to all the symptoms of a disease which he may meet with some eye trouble while the gyneacologist blames the uterus; and so on ad infinitum. So that when an expert is to be called, it should be borne in mind that the science of medicine has grown so vast and been divided and subdivided into so many branches of special study, that its complete mastery is almost an impossibility.[18]

While increased specialization improves medical knowledge and treatments, these disparate ways of seeing can negatively affect the coroner's ability to mediate proclamations of certainty. As diagnostic technologies progress, as awareness of diseases and addictions proliferate, the answers available to the coroner proliferate as well, creating more potential for error and inaccurate claims; protocol seems to be a stopgap in the face of this.

The assumed authority of medical viewing, however, is emphasized in arguing that the coroner must have medical certification and that his legal/judicial duties should be dispensed with. In 1891 Dr. Henry O. Marcy argues in "The Coroner System in the US" that

> the coroner, no matter how skilled in any branch of special training could, under the law, scarcely be expected to discharge his duties in a satisfactory manner [because] the same person was expected to be competent as a medical expert, to serve as an administrator of the law, as a judge to hear evidence, to decide upon its admissibility, [and to] bring also a witness in the case.[19]

Marcy argues for reform in the entire system, to replace coroners with medical examiners, "able and discreet men, learned in the science of medicine," who would take into custody any body "supposed to have come to their death by violence" and in the presence of two witnesses perform an autopsy "and then and there carefully reduce[s] or cause[s] to be reduced to writing every fact and circumstance tending to show the condition of the body, and the cause and manner of death, together with the names and addresses of said witnesses, which record he shall subscribe."[20]

It was further argued that medical experience was necessary for the coroner because he should be exclusively tasked with transporting and examining the cadaver and screening the public from that indecency. The empaneled jury in many cases viewed the corpse at the hospital, morgue, pub, or undertaker, but the public was not permitted to do so. Ian Burney points out that, in the early twentieth century, a reform movement was undertaken in England to remove corpse viewing from the jury inquest on the grounds that it was a public health hazard and also emotionally damaging to juries; Burney also shows, however, that the corpse gave authority to the inquest:

> The "decorporealized" inquest in this way pointed unambiguously in the direction of an expert-based, efficiency-oriented

system of death management. But even as plans for restructuring the relationship between the lay public and the dead body were developed, it was clear that the elaboration of a quiet place for scientific contemplation opened up a new and rich field of anxieties. If the view of the body could be banished as a shared evidentiary fount, at other levels the inquest required a present body ... the project of decorporealization intended to produce a disciplined, scientifically purified inquest, might ironically result in a loss of the very dominion of medical expertise over the body that reformers were seeking to cement.[21]

Burney's argument is that this indicates the increasing control the medical community had over the dead in England, making the inquest more scientific and less public. The medical witness should intervene for the juror so as not to expose them to the corpse. Arguments made against the decorporealization of the inquest asserted that making it a purely "paper inquiry" takes away the realness.[22] Here it is obvious that paper mediation threatens to undermine certainty and authority, and that the coroner must be a medical professional trained to screen the public from the cadaver's disruptive presence. It is this very criticism over the flimsiness of the purely paper inquest that leads us into *Dracula*.

Stoker's Novel and the Failures
of Victorian Inquest Documentation

Stoker's novel *is* a failed inquest, and it enacts both the features and failures of Victorian inquest documentation, first in that the novel features institutional structures central to inquests, such as hospitals and morgues, and second in that the Crew of Light and their methods are repeatedly shown faulty when they avoid real inquests and when they undertake the more "decorporealized" inquest of researching Dracula's traits and movements. The novel and the coroners' case files stage the professional management of narratives of the mysterious dead, and *Dracula*, like inquest documents, fails to generate any substantial sense of certainty. The Crew of Light's trust in and adoration of the modern, found in their multiple professions, partial perspectives, and recording technologies that seem to bring order and illumination to their text, collapses when in the end all that survives is a "mass of typewriting" (D 351) and a record of questionable behaviors that undercut their authority, expertise, and reliability.[23] As we read *Dracula* Stoker invites us to imagine an ever-shifting form in our hands, calling into question how any paper form can be considered fixed or certain. At times we imagine that we hold Jonathan's shorthand journal, Lucy's letters to Mina, or articles that Mina has clipped from the newspaper, including the zookeeper's report of Berserker's return from his wild night with the vampire (much like a coroner's witness report). However, by the end, the whole stack has transmuted into a "mass of typewriting," which we wonder if we have held all along. In short, form itself is a juggle in *Dracula*: the novel's bid for verisimilitude and authority rests on immediate documentation, but we are finally asked to believe that the "mass of typewriting" should be just as acceptable, despite the fact that Dracula tossed manuscript and cylinders into the fireplace on the same night he desecrated Mina. The simultaneity of these events foreshadows the impurity of both things that will haunt the end of the novel: Mina's impurity as a mother who has fed from the vampire and the narratives that have been so mediated and remediated by the ill-equipped Crew of Light that it is difficult to believe in the purity of their final form. Moreover, we are ultimately asked to believe that the reduction of Dracula's body to dust on a wild road in the Carpathians means that the grotesquely boundary-crossing cadaver has been authoritatively disciplined for good.

At first it seems that the novel desperately wants to be believed, since it opens with the claim that "there is throughout no statement of past things wherein memory may err, for all the records chosen are exactly contemporary, given from the standpoints and within the range of knowledge of those who made them" (D 4). Here records are chosen and included for accuracy and immediacy to validate collaboration—there is a bid for reader investment. However, by the end of the text Harker and Van Helsing release themselves from the pressures of believability and accountability. Jonathan states, "We could hardly ask anyone, even did we wish to, to accept these as proofs of so wild a story," and, shortly after, Van Helsing claims, "'We want no proofs; we ask none to believe us!'" (D 351) Thus, while we begin with an almost judicial assertion of in-the-moment record-keeping—just as shown on certification of evidence statements in the case files—readers end with the assertion that the story is difficult to accept but none of the players care. In the same way, coroners' files undermine senses of larger social accountability and accuracy because we see papers crammed with nearly illegible and quickly edited text or sparsely completed forms. The Crew of Light, and the coroner, though intervening with unruly cadavers in the name of maintaining social order and protecting communal health, finally generate insular textual forms targeted to those who made them. It is not difficult to feel like an outsider at the end of the novel when Harker reports that they

> made a journey to Transylvania, and went over the old ground which was, and is, to us so full of vivid and terrible memories. It was almost impossible to believe that the things which we had seen with our own eyes and heard with our own ears were living truths. Every trace of all that had been was blotted out. (*D* 351)

Harker's choice of the word "blotted," with its implications of erased text, mimics the ways that a coroner's case file imperfectly stands in for the body. We are asked to accept the document that has replaced experience. Indeed, document blots out experience.

Inquests are discussed three times in Stoker's novel: after Dracula's ship docks at Whitby, after Mrs. Westenra dies, and after the Crew of Light finds Renfield fatally injured in his cell. The first establishes England's functioning system, while the others show how the Crew of Light perceive the coroner as a threat to their mission. An inquest is undertaken on the body of the corpse found lashed to the wheel of the *Demeter*—"The dead steersman [is] reverently... placed in the mortuary to await inquest"—and later "the paper found in the bottle, [is] produced at the inquest" (*D* 77, 78). The journalist presents these details in Whitby's *Dailygraph*, showing the functioning system and the press's digestion and mass dissemination of the inquest process: short and sweet, respectful of the corpse, and full of the juicy details of the *Demeter*'s log. However, this inquest results in an open verdict, a failure of closure, which early on indicates that events surrounding the vampire pinpoint places where certification collapses. The second and third references speak to the Crew of Light's efforts to *skirt* legal systems or to, like the coroner, be both of the professions and outside of them, as they work to avoid inquests into Mrs. Westenra's and Renfield's deaths, which would be disastrous to their obsession with privacy and their exceptionalism. Seward tells Van Helsing, "If we do not act properly and wisely, there may be an inquest … . I am in hopes that we need have no inquest … . Let us fill up the certificate at once, and I shall take it myself to the registrar and go on to the undertaker" (*D* 140). Even more brazen is Harker's report that, after Renfield's death, "Dr. Seward said to us, when we were alone … the question of an inquest had to be considered, and it would never do to put forward the truth" (*D* 269). He and Van Helsing exploit their medical credentials to deflect prying outsiders and maintain control by making and registering falsified death certificates.

Death certificates and press reports are present in the case files—the press reports are frequent through the 1890s, though the death certificates not until into the twentieth century, indicating the coroner's later collaboration with the Bureau of Health. Further documentation technologies and information networks found in both textual bodies include telegrams—indicating the importance of quick inquiry across space, especially to identify cadavers—and postmortem reports. These documents emphasize efficiency and collaboration—shown in Stoker's novel, of course, when the Crew of Light's disparate documents are shown to be dependent on each other. Physical spaces of the Victorian inquest found in the novel emphasize the interactions between medicine and the law, cordoning off the abject cadaver, and spaces of professional intervention, including the morgue where the seaman's body is taken, Seward's asylum, where the Crew of Light eventually sets up their War Room, and the hospital, where children attacked by the vampirized Lucy risk the Crew of Light's bid to stay out of the public eye. Thus, *Dracula* works to avoid the inquest and protect the ethically suspect behaviors of the Crew of Light even as it enacts the inquest's features—the attending physician's testimony, telegraphs, postmortems, Van Helsing's inquest-like questioning and testing of Seward, the typewriter, and so on.

The magnitude of late Victorian professional codification and the coroner's fractured profession are further evident in Stoker's novel as the many professions and perspectives that must collaborate to pull together narrative details and formulate as complete a picture of the vampire as possible. Much of chapter 18 involves Van Helsing sharing information about Dracula that he has culled from other sources, and, while he does provide substantial information, including that "The Draculas were … a great and noble race, though now and again were scions who were held by their coevals to have had dealings with the Evil One," the dossier on the vampire is partial and incomplete because the vampire does not provide his own narrative. Everything is filtered through the Crew of Light and texts written by those like them, such as Van Helsing's "friend Arminius, of Buda-Pesth University" (*D* 224). We never learn, for example, the story of Dracula's three vampire women. The Crew of Light builds narrative around the vampire: evidence is gathered and interpreted in his context much in the same way as the corpse is mediated by medical and legal structures and the popular press. At the same time, Van Helsing best represents the multiple professions of the coroner as resulting in a fractured perspective rather than a unifying vision. Over and over he undermines success—in not telling Mrs. Westenra about the importance of garlic he facilitates her death and Lucy's; by not being able to read Mina's shorthand journal his connection to the law is questioned; by planning to remove Lucy's head and heart and then dialing back on it … . One wonders how much he is really improvising, or how much he is unconsciously sabotaging their efforts to prolong the thrill of his power and involvement. His stilted English, even his name as an anagram for English, undermines the text's presentation of his authority, alluding to the broken and overtaxed man beneath who cannot work effectively. His incoherence and lack of authority, his authoritative posturing—these things all show the failure of modern professionalization to bring a whole and certain closure.[24]

Many have noted the unsatisfactory or ambiguous nature of Dracula's death and the Crew of Light's triumph—Carol Senf shows that by the end of the novel the Crew of Light has openly confessed to more violent and depraved behaviors than can be connected to the vampire, and Stephen Arata and Nicholas Daly both note that Mina's son has five figurative fathers, as if he is the product of all of their efforts.[25] The Crew of Light's modern impotence, then, and Dracula's fluid exchange with Mina reinforce the presence of the mysterious cadaver who has not disappeared but who inhabits the bodies of the protagonists. Inconclusive, ambiguous, uncertain: the novel ends as a failed inquest. It's not that the novel is not structured; there are efforts made, but there is enough uncertainty to undermine the narrative. What *has* happened? Who has committed acts of violence against whom? How can responsibility be assigned, especially in Lucy's death? Moreover, it is never clear what Van Helsing means when he tells Seward about the crucifix over Lucy's dead lips: "You need not trouble about the knives; we shall not do it ... it is too late—or too early" (*D* 155). When he dispatches the three vampire women he says, "it was butcher work ... I tremble and tremble even yet," as if when it is his turn to do the killing he is unprepared and overwhelmed (*D* 344). Even the killing of Dracula lacks any ritualization. Was Dracula dispatched according to proper protocol, or did the look of triumph in his eyes indicate simply that turning to dust is something he has done again and again, just like the vampire women, who Jonathan describes as appearing in "the tiniest grains of dust?" (*D* 44). There is no totalizing professional view because too many things remain inconclusive and too many variables exist for one man to be master of them all. Van Helsing must wield the surgeon's black bag, the priest's communion wafer, the forged death certificates, and the money for bribes.

Arguments into the early twentieth century both in favor of and against the decorporealized inquest are predicted by the novel's form, as the Crew of Light struggles with the vampire's very real effects even as his body is incorporeal and they find themselves awash in papers as they try to get a grip on a body that constantly shifts and flees. Dracula's body crosses borders, it affects characters, and its actions have consequences in the material world, but how substantial their claims are is questionable. Arguments for decorporealizing the inquest underscored the necessity to screen the public (and even, recall, the jury) from the infectious and upsetting presence of the cadaver, which should only be handled by medical professionals. However, it was also argued that an inquest without a body and jury members witnessing it was not really an inquest. The inquest's validity and officiality, then, in part rests on witnessing the corpse. The Crew of Light's desperation to wage their warfare in private follows this structure: do the work, interpret the vampire, pass judgment, control and eliminate its threat, and let the narrative stand in for the body. This is why they avoid inquests and why they must intervene as soon as The Bloofer Lady makes headlines. Thus, the pure "paper inquiry" of both the novel and the decorporealized inquest takes away the realness. Paper mediation, whether handwritten notes or a "mass of typewriting," threatens certainty and authority, undercutting the triumph and closure of the novel and the inquest.

The narrative thrust to both textual bodies is an organized effort to track and pin down the unruly cadaver-on-the-loose threatening to transform the social order, to impart chaos and illness. Although the coroner tracks and pins down the unruly cadaver in his documents, the case files ultimately represent a wasted effort and give the lie to documentation's ability to fix something. Even though the Crew of Light may track Dracula as he flees home, locates him by merging their documents and others' documents, and pins him down with their great knives, the look of triumph in Dracula's eyes before he crumbles to dust indicates that their efforts are wasted. Dust is not certainty or stability. Dust is the corpse's equivalent of the mass of typewriting. It is not the body, and it still threatens to disperse and disrupt. Thus, their triumph rings false and the inquest fails.

The two jury verdicts in Figure 6.4, from 1887 and 1905, give off very different valences of authority and even permanence: a verdict squeezed onto the bottom of a sheet of notepaper in McDowell's scrawl juxtaposed against the readymade form, typewritten, less a record of the coroner's individualism and more a representation of objective systems of meaning-making. This movement in the coroner's protocol, in addition to being uneven across states, shows the constant pressure coroners faced to update and remake what constitutes certification.

Conclusion: Forms and Fragments

Form [...] is conceptual and abstract, generalizing and transhistorical. But it is neither apolitical nor ahistorical. It does not fix or reduce every pattern to the same. Nor is it confined to the literary text, to the canon, or to the aesthetic. It does involve a kind of close reading, a careful attention to the ways that historical texts, bodies, and institutions are organized—what shapes they take, what models they follow and rework. But it is all about the social: it involves reading particular, historically specific collisions among generalizing political, cultural, and social forms.[26]

I have turned to Caroline Levine's words on strategic formalism as a way to connect the coroner's ambiguous neither-here-nor-there profession to other social formations and to account for the specific ways the cadaver is transformed into closure. There is obviously a process of "imposing order, of shaping and structuring experience" that is socially necessary, imperfectly satisfactory, and perpetually in flux.[27] I would like to end by commenting on the many forms of codification and disintegration—forms and fragments—happening in coroners' files and their late Victorian context.

I have already asserted that coroners work to impose a reassuring order by explaining sudden deaths, but this is constant, never-ceasing work, and their files are full of ellipses and blanks, incomplete lines, and dubious-sounding narratives. In the files the fragility and potential falsity of certification/certainty/closure is clear. The form of the body is fragmented into the pages, into the disparate reports, under the autopsy knife. The coroner hangs suspended to negotiate between the cadaver, the public, and the network of institutions invoked: departments of public health, state assemblies, prisons, hospitals, asylums, mills and railroads, distributors of alcohol, providers of abortions, domestic family economies, the language used by physicians to diagnose cause of death, morgues. The coroner fills out forms, and he forms empaneled juries who reach verdicts. He is not a detective, and he does not seem particularly gifted when we read his files. He is a conduit through which stories and evidence flow and a pronouncement comes out. The coroner is a site for the jostling of various forms of expertise. Oftentimes, especially by medical professionals, coroners are not trusted to be authoritative. They are seen as average men who use the position as a stepping-stone to politics, which is why we see the late Victorian push for state-controlled self-containment mapped out by Ian Burney. Further undermining accuracy and closure are errors in spelling, indecipherable text, added or edited text, and a lack of punctuation. Form's endless flexibility can be found in the recording of witness statements pieced together to give the fullest descriptive and narrative context; it is recording technologies such as pencil or ink, typewriter or stenograph; form is in the word "sworn" written after every witness name as a talisman against the uncertainty of identity, so prevalent in the cadaver; it is the phrase "injuries received" communicated by the physician who parses discrete biomarkers into a wholeness of cause-of-death. Form is found in the changes in protocol towards 1900, meaning standardization is an attempt at formation, which demonstrates a valuing of unity. Fragmentation can be found across the files and efforts at formation, too.

Fragmentation happens in order to make forms. The early reports are fragmented and in fragments. Witnesses bring fragmented subjectivities to the narrative. Forms come in fragments, too, as many are not completed. Injuries received and recorded come in fragments: crushed, drowned, shot, stabbed, fallen, heart disease, apoplexy, explosions, heat exhaustion. Fragments are the bits and pieces of stories and must be collated, pushed onto the same paper or into material proximity with each other.

Finally, on the largest scale, the late Victorian environment (in this case study) of Pittsburgh is formed and constructed in reading the files. We mentally construct working in the heat of the mills or the darkness of mines, falling asleep next to a boiler and being overcome, bathing in the river and drowning, toddlers starting house fires by knocking over lamps, people of all ages trying to cross the tracks or street and being crushed. Hot summers, dangerous storms, neighbors and streets, doctors running to homes, children being given harmful medicine, domestic violence or child abuse veiled. And these are all fragments that construct Pittsburgh's sensory imaginary. I am left with the ephemeral nature of the documents. Fragment is the verdict heard by the judge and coroner, noted, and then left to dissipate. Fragment is how unnecessary the papers are now, and yet how archivists feel protective over them. Fragment is their falling to pieces.

Most importantly, the coroner is a site whereupon medical and legal advancements overlap and rub against each other. Institutions think of themselves as always making progress and offering improvements to citizens, and the coroner is caught up in the pressures to automate via protocol or to sit squarely in the medical and not the legal. He must certainly at times face political or institutional pressures to hide forms of violence, whether in the home or in the prison. As a social ordering force, the coroner's work controls and manages social responses to curiosity or to panic because sudden deaths both fracture and unify local community structures. People panic or call for change or want to know what could have been done differently. He cannot be impervious to error, though changes in protocol work to reduce his chances of making serious mistakes.

Politics and Society

CHAPTER SEVEN

Bram Stoker, Geopolitics, and War

Jimmie E. Cain

O n February 3, 1892, Rudyard Kipling and his new bride Caroline Balestier boarded a train in London for Liverpool to begin a honeymoon excursion to the United States. Gathered on the platform to see them off were such literary notables as Henry James, who had given the bride away, Edmund Gosse, the publisher William Heinemann, and Bram Stoker. Although none of Stoker's biographers record his attendance at the train station that day, at least two Kipling biographers do.[1] Despite their failure to mention such a close relationship between Stoker and Kipling, Stoker's biographers have provided ample evidence that Stoker and Kipling could well have met and interacted since at least 1889. In that year, Stoker introduced his friend Hall Caine to Wolcott Balestier, Kipling's future brother-in-law and the London representative of a New York publishing house seeking to set up a new publishing firm with William Heinemann. In 1891, this imprint, The English Library, opened with the publication of Kipling's *The Light that Failed*.[2] Two years later, Stoker himself would appear in print alongside Kipling in *Pall Mall Magazine*.[3] Through the Pre-Raphaelite painter Edward Burne-Jones, Stoker might likewise have encountered Kipling, Burne-Jones' nephew. Edward was among the many celebrities of the day who frequented the Lyceum and shared meals with Henry Irving and Stoker in the Beefsteak Room. In 1888 Edward's son Phillip, whom Ellen Terry described as "one of the Lyceum's greatest admirers,"[4] helped design sets for productions of *King*

Arthur and *Coriolanus* at the Lyceum. In the same year in which *Dracula* was published, 1897, Phillip exhibited a painting titled *The Vampire*; to commemorate the occasion, Kipling, Phillip's cousin, published the text "The Vampire."[5]

Although the extent of their personal and professional connections are, admittedly, somewhat nebulous, Stoker and Kipling did share one abiding passion that would have drawn them to each other: a pronounced enthusiasm for the British empire and a keen awareness of the geopolitical threats to British hegemony. The child of English missionaries in India and a one-time student at the United Services College at Westward Ho!, a boarding school in Devon "intended to attract the sons of naval and military officers who could not afford the fees of the great public schools,"[6] Kipling early on manifested a precocious understanding of the perils facing the interests of the empire. For instance, in 1882, at age sixteen, Kipling engaged the headmaster of Westward Ho! in a debate over the proposition "the advance of the Russians in central Asia is hostile to British power," a topic suggested by Kipling himself.[7] As a mature writer, Kipling would further enunciate his animosity and distrust toward Russia in works such as *Kim*, a novel which gave "universal currency"[8] to the expression "The Great Game," the proxy war waged between Britain and Russia in Afghanistan during the nineteenth century.

Ten years prior to Kipling's debate Stoker himself issued an alarm against the Russian menace. As auditor of the College Historical Society at Trinity College, Dublin, Stoker opened the 1872–73 session of the Society on November 13, 1872 with a speech titled "The Necessity for Political Honesty." In his address, Stoker warns that European rivals would seek to contend with Britain on the world stage, noting that a "United Germany marches on us on the one hand, and Republican France on the other." Yet, of more concern, "The Slavonic nations awake from their long lethargy, and Russia with her millions threatens the future peace of Europe, and stretches already a greedy arm towards British India."[9] Undoubtedly, as his address proves, Stoker was cognizant of and animated by world events, especially as they affected Britain and her empire. Stephen Arata even goes so far as to argue that a "concern with questions of empire and colonization can be found in nearly all of Stoker's fiction" and that Stoker was intimately aware of the dangers of what Arata terms "reverse colonization."[10] Patrick

Brantlinger further contends that Stoker and Kipling were both practitioners of "imperial Gothic" literature, a genre which "expresses anxieties about the ease with which civilization can revert to barbarism or savagery and thus about the weakening of Britain's imperial hegemony."[11] An examination of Stoker's life reveals just how geopolitics and the military struggles that often eventuate from them helped to render him susceptible to this worldview. Moreover, a close reading of his novels *Dracula*, *The Lady of the Shroud*, and *The Mystery of the Sea* will demonstrate how the potential rivals to Britain highlighted in his Trinity address, especially Germany, Russia, and the Slavic peoples of the Balkans, gave him the plots, settings, and characters populating his imperial Gothic works.

Almost from birth, Stoker lived immersed in a world of gothic fantasies and accounts of martial exploits. According to Barbara Belford, during his childhood Stoker's "happiest times" were the evenings when his mother regaled him with "myths of Ireland" and "his father embellished the military exploits of ancestors."[12] An adolescent Stoker listened as his maternal grandfather, Thomas Thornley, spun "tales of his service as a subaltern in the Peninsular War, including the claim that he had marched all night *asleep*." Likewise, from his mother Charlotte Stoker further learned of the martial exploits of his great-uncles George and Manus Blake.[13] Harry Ludlam describes an adult Stoker enthralled by the "tales of army service in the Crimea and India" recounted by his future father-in-law, Lieutenant Colonel James Balcombe,[14] whose daughter Florence bore the first name of Florence Nightingale, the "Lady with the Lamp" of Crimean War fame or, perhaps, the town of Floriana on the island of Malta, where Col. Balcombe had served shortly after the war.[15]

His career as manager of Henry Irving's Lyceum Theatre would once again expose Stoker to accounts of geopolitical and military exploits from a host of politicians, revolutionaries, and writers who would help to mold further his outlook on the empire and the threats thereto. In the course of many gatherings in the Beefsteak Room at the Lyceum, Stoker conversed with, among others, Alfred Lord Tennyson, the author of such stirring patriotic poems as "The Charge of the Light Brigade," and William Ewart Gladstone, the chancellor of the exchequer in the Aberdeen administration, which had launched Britain's entry into the Crimean War.[16] They regaled Stoker with discussions of the war's causes, aims, and ends, and tales of the bravery of British arms. Moreover, they would have given Stoker a nuanced understanding of the military and governmental blunders that were a hallmark of the conflict and the extent of Russian savagery and ineptitude on the battlefield, as well as an inkling of the exotic Euro-Asiatic locales in which the war was waged. In an episode that may well have given Stoker the inspiration for Dr. Seward in *Dracula* and reinforced his impressions of the Crimean War, Stoker had occasion to hear Tennyson reading "The Charge of the Heavy Brigade at Balaclava" on a recorded cylinder in preparation for the staging of Tennyson's *Beckett* at the Lyceum.[17] The impact of the recorded recitation moved Stoker to observe that

> The poem of Scarlett's charge is one of special excellence for both phonographic recital and as an illustration of Tennyson's remarkable sense of time. One seems to hear the rhythmic thunder of the horses' hoofs as they ride to the attack. The virile voice of the reader conveys in added volume the desperate valour of the charge.[18]

Stoker would once again come face to face with the very real threat posed by Russia through his younger brother George, a physician. George had served with Turkish forces during the 1877–78 Russo-Turkish War. Upon his return to England, George lived with Bram, Florence, and their new-born son, Noel, in London. While thus lodged, George recorded his experiences "as a surgeon in the Turkish service," where he had "been Chief of Ambulance of the Red Crescent,"[19] in a memoir entitled *With the Unspeakables; or Two Years' Campaigning in European and Asiatic Turkey*, written with Bram's editorial assistance. Belford posits that this book "provided background for *Dracula*'s opening chapters, which so admirably evoke the geography, customs, and ethnic complexities of Transylvania;"[20] George's memoir provided Bram with much more than background material, however. *With the Unspeakables* clearly stoked Bram's and the British public's fears of Russia, fears which John Howes Gleason[21] traces as far back as the eighteenth century.

Twelve years after the publication of *With the Unspeakables*, Stoker made the acquaintance of "Arminius Vambery, Professor at the University of Buda-Pesth," who dined with Stoker in the Beefsteak Room on April 30,

1890. A "linguist" with command of "over twenty" languages,[22] Vambery had established himself as a prominent Russophobe by the time he met Stoker. Stoker illustrates Vambery's celebrity and unremitting indictment of nefarious Russian intentions when he recounts in *Personal Reminiscences of Henry Irving* a second meeting with the professor:

> We saw him again two years later, when he was being given a Degree at the Tercentenary of Dublin University. On the day on which the delegates from the various Universities of the world spoke, he shone out as a star. He soared above all the speakers, making one of the finest speeches I have ever heard. Be sure that he spoke loudly against Russian aggression—a subject to which he had largely devoted himself.[23]

Vambery's impression on Stoker was so profound that he would later make an appearance in *Dracula* and, shortly after hearing Vambery's speech, Stoker would once again befriend someone raising the alarm against Russia.

After a performance of *Faust* at the Lyceum on July 8, 1892, Stoker joined with the actors Sarah Bernhardt and Ellen Terry, a couple from Boston, and one Sergius Stepniak, a Russian émigré and revolutionary, for a late meal in the Beefsteak Room. Stoker notes of Stepniak that he "sat next to him at supper and we had a great deal of conversation together, chiefly about the state of affairs in Russia generally and the Revolutionary party in especial."[24] He had heard Stepniak speak previously in Hyde Park in May of that year before a crowd of many thousands. During their conversation over supper, Stepniak expounded on the fate of fellow revolutionaries who had been imprisoned in Siberia. Stoker summarizes his remarks thusly:

> Men of learning and culture, mostly University professors, men of blameless life and takers of no active part in revolution or conspiracy—simply theorists of freedom, patriots at heart—sent away to the terrible muddy shores of the Arctic sea, ill housed, ill fed, over worked—where life was one long, sordid, degrading struggle for bare life in that inhospitable region.

Palpably "interested and moved" by Stepniak's story, Stoker eagerly implored him for more information about the plight of Russian revolutionaries, eventually reading all of Stepniak's books and issues of *Free Russia*, a radical newspaper edited by Stepniak.[25]

Aside from these personal relations fomenting anti-Russian sentiment, Stoker lived most of his life in a social and cultural environment replete with warnings of impending Russian incursions upon Britain's imperial dominions and her allies, especially the popular reaction to Russia in the run-up to and during the course of the Crimean War of 1854–56. Two particularly relevant cartoons appeared in *Punch* just as the war was about to commence. The first, "CONSULTATION ABOUT THE STATE OF TURKEY," is an allegorical depiction of the major players in the war—Britain, France, Russia, and Turkey. Turkey, which Czar Nicholas had described as "the sick man of Europe," lies prostrate on a sick bed attended by John Bull and his French counterpart, depicted here as physicians attending the patient. Unbeknownst to them, emerging from a cloud hovering above Turkey is a human skeleton adorned with the czar's crown and scepter and what appear to be bat wings, an unmistakable parody of the Romanov's dynastic symbol, the two-headed eagle, and, in all probability, an image meant to conjure up the association of bats with nocturnal predation and the spreading of diseases, an image that may have inspired Count Dracula's ability to transmogrify into mists and bats. The other illustration, "TE DEUM," further associates the czar with bats.

Countless journalists similarly raised the clarion call against Russia. One of the earliest to sound the alarm was David Urquhart, a former assistant ambassador to Turkey. In 1834 he published the pamphlet *England, France, Russia, and Turkey*, wherein he contended that Russian designs on Turkey portended ominous possibilities for England should Turkey fall under the sway of Russia.[26] Following Urquhart's lead, Sir John McNeill published *The Progress and Present Position of Russia in the East* in 1836, another pamphlet drawing attention to the insatiable Russian appetite for imperial aggrandizement. McNeill reissued his screed in 1854 with a plea for an immediate invasion of Russia.[27] Foreign journalists weighed in as well. Karl Marx, who, while living in London, served as a foreign correspondent for the *New York Tribune*, editorialized upon the consequences

CONSULTATION ABOUT THE STATE OF TURKEY.

Figure 7.1 "Consultation about the State of Turkey,"
Punch, July–December 1853.

TE DEUM!

Figure 7.2 "Te Deum," *Punch*, January–June 1854.

of Russian mastery of Turkey. He, too, saw war with Russia as a necessity to maintain Turkey's independence, to protect British interests, and to
safeguard nascent democratic movements in the region.[28] Similarly, Louis
Kossuth, a Hungarian nationalist who immigrated to England shortly
after Austria and Russia crushed an independence movement in Hungary
in 1849, waged a press campaign against the czar in the *Sunday Times* and
the radical newspaper *The Atlas*.[29] Some twenty years later, the art world
and waves of immigrants would bring Russia to the forefront of Stoker's
consciousness yet again.

At its 1874 exhibition, the Royal Academy displayed in "a most envi-
able location" Lady Elizabeth Thompson Butler's *The Roll Call: Calling
the Roll after an Engagement, Crimea*. So popular was the painting that
the Academy had to station a policeman in front of the work to keep the
crowds at bay.[30] The artist had made extensive studies of the war, especially
the newspaper accounts of the war written by the first modern war journalist, William Howard Russell of *The Times*. Nicolas Bently attests that "it
was due to Russell's despatches from the scene more than any other single
factor that the British government's mishandling of affairs, and the gross
negligence of the War Office in particular, came to light."[31] As an engaged
member of the London art community, Stoker most likely either read the
glowing reviews of the painting in the press or perhaps joined the crowds
thronging before it. Likewise, he must have assuredly been cognizant of
Lady Butler's two other highly acclaimed Crimean paintings, *Balaclava*
(1876) and *Inkerman* (1877). The former reiterates many of the tropes
witnessed in *The Roll Call*.

Hard upon the display of these paintings, another powerful reminder
of Eastern Europe and Russia would emerge in the popular imagination. Between 1881 and 1905 more than one million Jews fled political
and racial persecution in Russia, Austria-Hungary, and Romania, most
transiting through England seeking new homes on such distant shores as
Australia and Canada. Of these, 100,000 took up residence in England,
many thousands in London's East End.[32] Not long after their arrival, these
refugees came to be associated with an assortment of deviancies, among
them sloth, decay, disease, crime, and sexual predation, leading many to
see them as a very real threat to the nation itself. Notable writers such as
Robert Sherard and Joseph Banister typified the reaction. Writing in the

Standard, Sherard described the physical characteristics of the ghetto Jews making their way to Britain in most horrific terms:

> The faces that, under matted and verminous locks, peer out into the streets are scarcely human. They are the faces of imbeciles, of idiots, ape-faces, dog faces—all that is hideous and most profoundly pitiful. These people are clad in rags and live in kennels, where they ply their trades. In the doorways and the mire of the thoroughfare little children are moving about. Their half naked bodies are black with filth and red with sores.[33]

An equally petulant attack on the Jews taking up residence in the East End appeared in Banister's *England under the Jews,* wherein he vilified the immigrants' foul odor and their "propensity to carry and spread disease."[34] In the long term, Banister and his like came to warn of "a specifically Jewish contribution to the country's social problems and to decay and decline in England."[35] Exacerbating the anti-Semitism stirred up by Sherard and Banister, the murder of prostitutes in the East End ascribed to Jack the Ripper raised fears of a dangerous immigrant Jewish population intent on ritual murder. According to Sander Gilman, media descriptions of Jack were essentially "the caricature of the Eastern Jew," especially the shochet, or kosher butcher.[36] Eventually, these anxieties about the Russian threat to the nation and the empire would find expression in Stoker's writing.

What has been conjectured to be the discarded first chapter of *Dracula,* the short tale "Dracula's Guest," provides an early signal of Stoker's wariness concerning Russia. "Dracula's Guest" opens with Jonathan Harker setting out for an afternoon carriage drive at the commencement of "Walpurgis Nacht." Despite the objections of his coachman, Jonathan sets off alone to explore a deserted village and is forced by a sudden snow storm to seek refuge in the only available shelter, "a great massive tomb of marble." As he enters this structure, a sudden flash of lightening reveals "a beautiful woman, with rounded cheeks and red lips, seemingly sleeping on a bier." Before he can investigate further, however, an unseen force hurls him back out into the storm, he loses consciousness, and, when he awakens, he discovers a giant wolf gnawing at his throat. Fortunately

Figure 7.3 *The Roll Call: Calling the Roll after an Engagement, Crimea*, Elizabeth Thompson, 1874. Printed with permission of The Royal Collection and Her Majesty, Queen Elizabeth II.

for Jonathan, he is saved by a group of mounted troopers. What makes this scene significant is that, as he enters the tomb, Jonathan notices a most unusual inscription carved on its back wall, "'*The dead travel fast*,'" a message "graven in great Russian letters."[37] This wolf and the others populating his novel *Dracula* further suggest that Stoker was cognizant of Russia's potential danger as he set about drafting his vampire narrative. Stoker's research for the novel bears this point out.

In 2008 Elizabeth Miller and Robert Eighteen-Bisang published *Bram Stoker's Notes for Dracula: A Facsimile Edition*. While compiling the facsimile, Miller and Eighteen-Bisang uncovered a previously undocu-mented notation in Stoker's own handwriting: "Spottiswoode, W. A Tarantasse Journey through Russia [ditto] Miscellany." In their annotation to this note they write:

> William Spottiswoode's *A Tarantasse Journey through Eastern Russia in the Autumn of 1856* was published in London in 1857. We do not know if Stoker used any information from this hith-erto unidentified source, but it does contain a map that shows three rivers—the Bistritza, the Sereth and the Pruth—which are mentioned in the final chapters of *Dracula*.[38]

The three rivers highlighted on the map appended to Spottiswoode's memoir illustrate how history and geopolitics merge in Stoker's fiction. Castle Dracula sits near the confluence of these rivers at a spot where the territories of Wallachia, Moldavia, and Bessarabia meet—the last of these a Russian possession wrested from Turkey in 1812. After the Crimean War Britain and France forced Russia to return Bessarabia to Turkey. Russia later reacquired Bessarabia at the conclusion of the Russo-Turkish War in 1878, the subject of George Stoker's memoir, only to lose it again when the Congress of Berlin—dominated by Britain, France, and Germany— demanded that Russia cede the province to newly independent Romania. Matthew Gibson notes that in the Treaty of Berlin of 1878, the document that formally concluded the Congress, "[o]nly Britain, from amongst the major powers, recognised the threat, and so tried to shore up a bloc for maintaining the Ottoman presence in Europe as a counterbalance to Russia (a possible threat to Britain's control of India—a fear Stoker himself may well have shared)."[39] Appropriately, then, Castle Dracula rests not only at the site of many ancient "battles,"[40] but also in a region that would prove to be a source of Turco- and Anglo-Russian frictions. As late as 1885, Stoker's friend Vambery would bitterly note that since mid-century from "the Isker in Siberia to the banks of the Pruth, all became Russian," a position of strength from which Russia could advance upon British imperial possessions.[41]

Soon after he initiates his tour of Russia, Spottiswoode observes that "in our travels we dispensed with many items which Western prejudice considers necessary to comfort, health, and cleanliness."[42] Although a specific reference to hotel accommodations, this passage aptly describes the means and course of his journey as well. For days, Spottiswoode must contend with the physical discomfort of riding in a tarantasse, an unsprung carriage, along what he ironically terms the "Great Siberian Road." Spottiswoode records that on "either side of the road is an open space, intended to give the traveler a chance of seeing his enemy before being attacked, be that enemy man or beast."[43] Among the "beasts" he most frequently encounters are bears and packs of wolves. Jonathan Harker travels a similarly primitive route on the final leg of his trip to Castle Dracula. Along the way he, too, notices the "howling ... of the wolves" (D 15, 16). He soon learns of Dracula's fondness for wolves—"the children of the night. What music they make!" (D 21). When Dracula eventually descends on Britain, he does so as "an immense dog," a cognate of the wolf, who "jumped from the bow" (D 76) of his vessel as it runs aground in Whitby. And, later, to attack Lucy Westenra, Dracula employs "a great gaunt grey wolf" (D 134).

Dracula fairly bristles with such direct and indirect allusions to Russia. Over fifty years ago, during the height of the Cold War between the West and the Soviet Union, Richard Wasson in "The Politics of *Dracula*" argued that "the novel represents those forces in Eastern Europe which seek to overthrow, through violence and subversion, the more progressive democratic civilization of the West."[44] It is fitting, therefore, that Dracula, a representative of Eastern autocracy and violence, should travel to Britain on a Russian vessel, the *Demeter*. Although Devendra Varma contends that Stoker chose the name because of "the goddess Demeter's connection, by her daughter's marriage, with the King of the Underworld,"[45] Barbara Belford offers a more compelling explanation for the name of the ship.

Noting that "Stoker loved codes," an interest made evident in his 1902 novel *The Mystery of the Sea*, Belford is convinced that Stoker took the name from an actual ship that washed ashore in Whitby in October 1885 during a terrible storm. The ship was the Russian schooner *Dimitry*, which sailed from Narva on the Baltic carrying a load of silver sand. Belford further contends that Varna, the port from which the *Demeter* sailed, is really an "anagram of Narva."[46] If true, Belford's assertion is doubly significant. First, Stoker might quite consciously have linked Narva with Varna because both are important places in Russian history. Varna figured prominently in the Crimean War and the Russo-Turkish War of 1877–78, serving in the former instance as a major staging area for British forces and the site of a hospital treating British casualties. Narva, on the other hand, is the scene of the famous defeat suffered by Peter the Great at the hands of Sweden's Charles XI; it is worth noting here that Peter experienced a similar military reversal at the Pruth in 1710.[47] Appropriately, the "Russian consul" takes "formal possession" (*D* 78) of the *Demeter* once British authorities have concluded their investigation.

Further aligning Dracula with the Russian menace, the Count bears distinct attributes of the prejudicial stereotypes of the Russian and Eastern European Jews who emigrated to Britain in the 1880s and 1890s. Joseph Banister made much of their filth and "propensity to carry and spread disease and thereby infect and weaken other elements of the population":

> If the gentle reader desires to know what kind of blood it is that flows in the Chosen Peoples veins, he cannot do better than take a gentle stroll through Hatton Garden, Maida Vale, Petticoat Lane, or any other London "nosery." I do not hesitate to say that in the course of an hour's peregrinations he will see more cases of lupus, trachoma, favus, eczema, and scurvy than he would come across in a week's wanderings in any quarter of the Metropolis.[48]

Dracula's residences at Carfax, in Purfleet near the Whitechapel district, and in Piccadilly call to mind the taint associated with London's immigrant Jews by the indigenous population. At Carfax, a "nosery" in its own right, the foulness of the place leads the laborer who delivers Dracula's boxes to remark that one "might 'ave smelled ole Jerusalem in it" (*D* 212).

When Jonathan and colleagues subsequently enter the estate to destroy the Count's boxes of soil, they encounter a "malodorous air" (*D* 233). Even in Dracula's upscale Piccadilly digs, Arthur cannot help but notice that "'[t]he place smells so vilely'" (*D* 279).

The Count himself also bears the marks of a stereotypical Jewish appearance. Describing Dracula's "very marked physiognomy," Harker records in his diary that the Count's

> face was a strong—a very strong—aquiline, with high bridge of the thin nose and peculiarly arched nostrils: with lofty domed forehead, and hair growing scantily round the temples, but profusely elsewhere. His eyebrows were very massive, almost meeting over the nose, and with bushy hair that seemed to curl in its own profusion. The mouth [...] was fixed and rather cruel-looking, with peculiarly sharp white teeth; these protruded over the lips .... (*D* 20)

David Glover has shown that Stoker subscribed to the nineteenth-century theory of "'ethnological physiognomies,'" which posited that "social identities were ... plainly readable from appearances," in this instance facial features popularly ascribed to Jews.[49] Jonathan is also struck by the fact that the Count's "breath was rank" (*D* 20); glancing at Dracula's hands, Jonathan "could not but notice ... there were hairs in the centre of the palm" (*D* 20). Leonard Wolf suggests in a footnote to this passage that Dracula's hairy palms affiliate him "with the standard nineteenth-century image of the masturbator." This figure, argues Holocaust scholar George Mosse, was thought to be akin to "those infected with venereal disease," people who were "pale, hollow-eyed, weak of body and spirit," common signifiers of the presumed pestilential Jew in the popular imagination.[50]

Aside from Dracula's physical proximity to the loathed Jewish immigrant, his apparent hoarding of wealth ties him to the despised aristocracy as well. Zanger has suggested that to the Victorian conception of the "Jew as Ritual Murderer or Anti-Christ" the image of "the Jew as Usurer, as Miser" should be added.[51] In *Dracula*, as Judith Halberstam contends, the various facets of anti-Semitism coalesce in a notion of the Jew as a "blood-sucker [who] drains health and wealth, [and] feeds on lives and labor."[52] And, as such a figure, Dracula moreover "fits in with the popularly received image of the Jew as the friend to aristocracy,"[53] the group that lost prestige and favor as a consequence of their failings exposed fully during the Crimean War. Many critics have seen Dracula as the quintessence of the aristocrat. Malcolm Smith writes that "*Dracula* pits Eastern Europe, tyranny, and aristocracy against England, democracy and the middle class."[54] Anne Cranny-Francis further deems the Count "an ancient, East European aristocrat."[55] Undoubtedly, then, Dracula is both socially and, as Burton Hatlen believes, "culturally" challenging to the Victorian middle class "values of technology, rationality, and progress."[56] As an aristocrat, Dracula threatens the liberal reforms enacted first by the Reform Bill of 1832, which allowed the middle class ever greater political and economic leverage. Dracula militates against this emerging social and economic force, attempting to re-establish the political and economic power of the privileged landed gentry of the past. For Victorian readers, he also would have symbolized the formidable Russian aristocracy, whose hold over the populace was historically many times more brutal and comprehensive than any exercised by the British aristocracy since the Middle Ages.

It is only appropriate that a group made up almost exclusively of bourgeois professionals should drive Dracula from England and eventually extirpate him on his native soil. Consisting of Dutch and English physicians, a lawyer, an American frontiersman, a teacher, and a single aristocrat, who does little more than provide the financial support for their crusade, the group fights to secure "the values of the English professional middle class."[57] Employing the latest available technology and intelligence, they set out to destroy the Count, who retreats from Britain on a ship named the "Czarina Catherine," bound for, where else, Varna (*D* 294). At the behest of Quincey, they arm themselves "with Winchesters." The American member knows from experience the need for modern weapons when taking on an archaic foe, for he and Holmwood had previously confronted a Russian enemy in "Tobolsk," a city in western Siberia (*D* 301), without the benefit of modern weapons. As the Crew follows the Count's route of retreat, they virtually retrace the path taken by British forces in their advance on and withdrawal from the Crimea, a course similar to that George Stoker also followed in 1877. Thus, as in the

Crimean campaign, their assault begins in Varna, where they take rooms at the hotel "Odessus," named for the port of Odessa in the Crimean. From thence they move on to Galatz, modern-day Galati, a Romanian Black Sea port situated near the confluence of the Seret and Pruth rivers in the disputed region of Bessarabia (*D* 313). At Galatz, a group that evokes images of Russia comes to the Count's assistance. One Immanuel Hildesheim, "a Hebrew of rather the Adelphi Theatre type," and a party of "Slovaks" take possession of Dracula's boxes for transhipment up the Seret to the Castle (*D* 324). As Dracula and his pursuers approach the castle, a heavy snow begins to fall, prompting Seward to worry that they may be forced to find sledges and proceed "Russian fashion" (*D* 333). While Holmwood and Seward hold off Dracula's Slovaks with their Winchesters, Quincey plunges a bowie knife into the Count's heart, and Jonathan severs his head with his Kukri knife. Thus, Dracula dies from wounds inflicted by men aligned with the British empire wielding what Arata terms "weapons of empire."[58] Imperial warriors and weapons would likewise play a pivotal role when Stoker wrote again of vampires in *The Lady of the Shroud* in 1909, but against a background of a wholly new threat to Britain's empire, in this instance Germany.

A series of events occurring at the end of the nineteenth and beginning of the twentieth centuries radically altered European great power relations. In 1888 Turkey granted a German syndicate a contract to build a railway from Constantinople to Ankara. Known as the Baghdad Railway, the project made evident Germany's increasing economic influence in the Near East and raised apprehensions in Britain that the empire's commercial interests might suffer from German competition. When another German firm received a concession to extend the railway to the Persian Gulf, anti-German sentiments began to appear in the press and among members of parliament. When Germany supplied arms and diplomatic assistance to the Boer rebels in 1900, she transmogrified in the public's mind from what had once seemed Britain's "most likely friend" in Europe to her most "potent threat."[59] Furthermore, Germany's support of Austro-Hungarian incursions in the Balkans in the early 1900s eventuated in a great power realignment that would have seemed impossible twenty years earlier. Subsequently, after resolutions reached in 1904 and 1907, two alliances stood bitterly opposed over the fate of the Balkans: the Triple

Alliance, composed of Austria-Hungary, Germany, and Italy, and the Triple Entente, consisting of Britain, France, and Russia.[60]

Ever cognizant of threats to British imperial dominion, Stoker addresses the challenge posed by Germany in *The Lady of the Shroud*, which Victor Sage sees as a fictional effort to restore "Britain's Imperial presence in Europe through creating a buffer-state ... which would deter German ambitions in the south and the east."[61] Nevertheless, although Stoker's narrative accommodates the new political alliances evolving after the turn of the century, it also illustrates that, despite improvements in relations between London and St. Petersburg, vestiges of Russophobia and anti-Slavic sentiments prevailed in Britain. Stoking this ongoing distrust, an incident in October 1904 "raised Russophobia to fever pitch and very nearly led to war between the two powers."[62] Later, in 1907, notable Russophobes Lord Curzon, viceroy of India, and the seemingly ever-present Arminius Vambery raised alarms about the recently concluded Anglo-Russian agreement over the disposition of Tibet, an arrangement that effectively endorsed Russian hegemony in Persia. Both men were fearful that the pact would damage British prestige in Asia and give Russia another base of operations from which to threaten India.[63] Stoker notes this prevailing wariness toward Russia and his own ongoing antipathy toward Britain's rival when he dedicates *The Lady of the Shroud* to Genevieve Ward, a wealthy American expatriate with every reason to detest Russians. Genevieve had been cruelly betrayed by a Russian suitor, Count de Gerbel, whom the czar himself later forced to marry her to dissolve this dishonor, only for them to part forever "at the church door."[64]

Although Germany looms as a threat in this novel, Russia is clearly still a force to be reckoned with in the Land of the Blue Mountains, the fictitious Balkan country where events play out in the novel. The country has had to fight off successive incursions by Russia's client states in the region, most notably the Slavs of "Albania, Dalmatia, Herzegovina, Servia, Bulgaria"; Russia, which had been "often hurled back," always awaited "an opportunity to attack" (*TLS* 33). Toward the end of the novel, during the deliberations surrounding the creation of Balka, a federation of Balkan states resembling the former Yugoslavia but aligned with Britain, Russia once more reveals her duplicitous intentions. When the "Czar of Russia" is asked to be "the referee in the 'Balkan Settlement," he declines "on the ground that he was himself by inference an interested party" (*TLS* 245). The threat of continued interference in Balkan affairs by Russia, who "historically enjoyed imperial and diplomatic interests in the Balkans, and claimed racial connection with ethnic groups, particularly in Serbia,"[65] could not be more apparent. No matter, the principal villain is Turkey, Germany's ally and at this time Britain's foe, who is "preparing for a war of offence" as the novel opens (*TLS* 34).

Reflecting the new political realities of the day and Britain's desire for a base of operations in the Balkans to forestall "German expansionism to the south,"[66] the people of the Land of the Blue Mountains turn to "mighty Britain" (*TLS* 81) in their "hour of need" (*TLS* 145), willingly accepting British intervention in their internal and external affairs. By doing so, they invite their eventual absorption into the empire itself as British colonists come to assume control of their military and government. Further cementing the ties that bind them to Britain, their crown princess, Voivodin Teuta, marries Britain's imperial representative, Rupert Sent Leger, who, as with Stoker himself, is not English by birth but nonetheless staunchly loyal to the crown. He is the scion of a mixed English–Irish marriage, born to an Irish father serving in Her Majesty's service and an English mother of affluent middle-class origins. Though poor, his father's family distinguished itself in the imperial wars of the 1890s and 1900s. A "Captain in the Lancers," his father won the "Victoria Cross" at the "Battle of Amoaful" during the Ashanti Revolt of 1900 in Uganda. Moreover, a paternal great uncle died in the "Indian Mutiny at Meerut in 1857," while a paternal uncle, a "subaltern," perished at "Maiwand" in the Second Afghan War (*TLS* 4, 5). On his mother's side, Rupert is related to another imperial warrior, the Scotsman "Major-General Sir Colin Alexander MacKelpie, Baronet, holder of the Victoria Cross, Knight Commander of the Order of the Bath" (*TLS* 20).

To rescue Voivode Peter Vassarion, the dynastic ruler of the Land of the Blue Mountains, and his daughter, Voivodin Teuta, from Turkish forces and ultimately prevent Turkey from conquering the nation, Rupert introduces British military expertise, a phalanx of British soldiers and sailors, and an arsenal made up of the most advanced weapons to be had, including "a torpedo yacht. A small cruiser with turbines up to date, oil-fuelled, and fully armed with the latest and most perfect weapons and explosives of all kinds" (*TLS* 116). But the jewel of the arsenal Rupert assembles is an "aeroplane," a machine apparently combining the features of both a fixed-wing aircraft and a dirigible (*TLS* 139–40). To assemble a fighting force, Rupert enlists Major-General MacKelpie to reorganize the native militia (*TLS* 99). As was the case with the British colonial army in India, this force will be led by officers recruited from England (*TLS* 209) and organized around a core of two hundred Scots troops hand-picked and trained by General MacKelpie. Rupert himself takes command of what Harry Ludlam terms the "royal air force" of the Land of the Blue Mountains.[67] Although these moves are apparently meant to ensure the independence and sovereignty of the nation, Major-General MacKelpie articulates an underlying foreign policy agenda when, in an aside to Rupert, he says that his ultimate goal is to help form "a new 'nation'—an ally of Britain, who will stand at least as an outpost of our own nation, and a guardian of our eastern road" (*TLS* 209).

Rupert fulfills his imperial mission when crowned as king at the behest of Voivode Peter Vissarion, his coronation reinforcing the close ties established with Britain. Although the ceremony takes place in the church of St. Sava, which was "built in the manner of old Greek churches," the building has been reconfigured "after the fashion of Westminster Abbey for the coronation of King Edward VII" (*TLS* 227, 228). During the subsequent festivities, Edward VII arrives on the "King's yacht" at the head of a squadron of "fifty of the finest ships in the world; the very latest expression of naval giants, each seemingly typical of its class—Dreadnoughts, cruisers, destroyers." When Edward joins Rupert and Teuta, now husband and wife as well as king and queen, Teuta "kneeled before him with the gracious obeisance of a Blue Mountain hostess, and kissed his hand" (*TLS* 252, 255). Clearly, this act signifies Britain's absolute dominion over the Land of the Blue Mountains, an authority deriving, in no small measure, from Teuta's willing submission to both Rupert and the King. Teuta, therefore, may be seen as a representation of what the Land of the Blue Mountains becomes by the novel's end, a compliant subject of the British empire. Thus, in *The Lady of the Shroud*, Stoker may be said to have completed the project of imperial Gothic desire he initiated in *Dracula*. In that novel, an Eastern, Russian menace is driven from English shores, pursued to his fortress, and eradicated. His castle and Balkan homeland are subsequently appropriated into the Baedeker world of British tourism. With *The Lady of the Shroud*, a permanent British colony is established in the Balkans to frustrate German economic and military ambitions by blocking Turkish expansion in the region.

In the intervening years between the publication of *Dracula* in 1897 and *The Lady of the Shroud* in 1909 Stoker produced two more novels that respond to contemporary geopolitical events affecting the empire. The first of these, *The Mystery of the Sea*, published in 1902, opens a window onto Stoker's unbounded admiration for the United States of America and suggests that he understood full well that Britain's position on the world stage would come to depend more and more on strong cultural and political ties to America. Stoker's fascination with America had been evident since his student days at Trinity, where he was introduced to the works of Walt Whitman.[68] Stoker eventually established a life-long friendship with the poet. After reading Whitman's "Memoranda During the War," Stoker was inspired to pen a lecture lionizing Abraham Lincoln, "Abraham Lincoln: How the Statesman of the People Saved the Union and Abolished Slavery," which he declaimed to American and British audiences from 1888.[69] Some three years prior to his first lecture, Stoker proffered yet another proof of his unbound admiration for Britain's former colony and contemporary ally. On December 28, 1885, he gave a lecture titled *A Glimpse of America* at the London Institution. Recounting this incident, Barbara Belford writes that the lecture revealed that Stoker "reveled in America's freedom and openness, a welcome antidote to the strictness of Victorian England."[70]

One form of freedom permitted in America that he found to be "the most marked characteristic of American life is the high regard in which woman is held." So much leniency are women given in America, as opposed to their British sisters, that in the United States "a young woman is, almost if not quite, as free to think and act for herself as a young man is."[71] Marjory Anita Drake, the focus of the action in *The Mystery of the Sea*, is just such a high-minded and independent woman.[72] Saved from drowning by the protagonist of the novel, the barrister Archibald Hunter, who besides prodigious size and strength is blessed with preternatural "Second Sight," Marjory quickly acknowledges her free spirit. When Archie quips, "'all you American girls are so independent!'" Marjory readily responds, "Yes! We are as a rule brought up to be independent. It seems to be a part of what our people call the 'genius' of the country" (*TMS* 109). Marjory demonstrates in the course of the novel that she is, indeed, a prototypical American woman with a mind of her own. However, in her eventual salvation by and marriage to Archie, she also proves to be an apt metaphor for what Stoker perceived as America's place in a grand trans-Atlantic partnership with Britain.

The novel is set in Cruden Bay, Scotland, which Stoker had first visited in 1893 and would return to many times hence, completing the "last pages of *Dracula*" there in 1896.[73] The plot follows Archie and Marjory's efforts to discover a treasure of gold and jewels hidden in the vicinity by Don Bernardino De Escoban, a Spanish "Grandee" who had sailed with the Armada against England in 1588. When his personally commissioned flagship, the *San Cristobal*, is damaged, he takes refuge at Cruden Bay and buries his load of treasure in a cave (*TMS* 94–95). In the course of uncovering the whereabouts of this treasure trove, Archie and Marjory encounter the Don's descendant, "Don Bernardino Yglesias Palealogue y Santordo y Castlenuova de Escoban," who is likewise seeking the treasure. The presence of Spanish treasure and an erstwhile Spanish antagonist helps to explain the novel's connection to contemporary geopolitical events. Stoker sets the novel in the summer of 1898, almost 310 years after the Spanish Armada but also in the very midst of the Spanish–American War, a conflict in which Marjory is intimately involved. Soon after the three meet, Marjory reveals that Sir Francis Drake is her "great uncle" and that she, like Don Bernardino, has commissioned a battle ship (*TMS* 117, 207). Marjory's natural antipathy toward the Spanish—earlier in the novel she tells Archie "'I hate them! Nasty, cruel, treacherous wretches!'"—has been compounded in this instance by the plight of the "*reconcentrados*," Cuban peasants forced into concentration camps by the Spanish so as to pacify rural guerilla strongholds (*TMS* 68, 117). Moreover, Archie soon comprehends that the treasure, if returned to Spain by Don Escoban, would "be used to harm America" and, by implication, Britain:

> This great treasure, piled up by the Latin for the conquering of the Anglo-Saxon, and rescued from its burial of three centuries, would come in the nick of time to fulfill its racial mission; though

that mission might be against a new branch of the ancient foe of Spain, whose roots only had been laid when the great Armada swept out in all its pride and glory on its conquering essay. (*TMS* 253–54)

Although Don Escabon's intent in seeking the treasure is to fulfill a familial obligation laid down by his ancestor, what comes to be perceived by Archie as a noble, if not justifiable, cause for the Don's actions, the Spanish government's actions are wholeheartedly malicious. Marjory has taken refuge in Cruden Bay to avoid mercenaries hired by the Spanish government to kidnap her. When they eventually do, what follows illustrates the role that Stoker deemed appropriate for America in her alliance to Britain.

Carol Senf has conjectured that Stoker has Quincey Morris die in *Dracula* because "he is too primitive to exist in a Europe dominated by modern professionals like Harker, Seward, and Van Helsing." Senf further contends that Quincey "seems bent on bringing his uncouth frontier behavior to old Europe," defying Victorian social conventions to the point of "introducing Lucy to American slang, shooting off guns and thereby endangering his fellow vampire hunters, and generally misbehaving in ways that sometimes baffle his companions."[74] The kidnappers, predominantly Americans, who spirit away Marjory, inject a similar primitive violence and discord into the narrative of *The Mystery of the Sea*. A loathsome collection in the eyes of the American and British lawmen pursuing them, the group includes Featherstone and Whiskey Tommy, who had previously stolen the body of a wealthy American and demanded ransom; Dago, "'a half-bred Spaniard that comes from somewheres over here';" Max, "'a Dutchman';" "'two Chicago bums from the Levee, way-down politicians and heelers';" Sailor Ben, "'a man from Frisco';" and, rounding out the gang, "'a buck nigger from Noo Orleans. A real bad 'un he is.'" The last of these is singled out for particular derision by the chief of the American Secret Service detectives working with Archie to rescue Marjory:

"What hasn't he done that's vile, is what I'd like to know. They're a hard crowd in the darkey side of Noo Orleans; a man doesn't get a bad name there easily, I tell you. There are dens there that'd make

God Almighty blush, or the Devil either; a darkey that is bred in them and gets to the top of the push, doesn't stick at no trifles!" (*TMS* 285–87)

His potential for brutality and savagery emerge as the chase unfolds. At one point, Archie finds Don Escabon bloodied and beaten at the entrance to the cave where the treasure had been hidden. From the Don, Archie learns that the kidnappers had carted off the loot and that one of their number, "with grey lips of terrific thickness, and whose hands were black, was for knifing [Don Escabon] at once or cutting his throat," but was over-ruled by the gang leader. Later, Archie admits that he "had come to think of this miscreant as in some way the active principle of whatever evil might be" (*TMS* 292, 302). In a vision which comes to him as he keeps watch on the ship upon which Marjory is held, Archie recoils from the image of this "huge coal-black negro, hideous, and of repulsive aspect. A glimpse of him made my blood run cold, and filled my mind at once with hate and fear." And, just as his vision is fading, Archie imagines the possibility of what at the time would be considered the most terrifying of desecrations: the rape of a white woman by a black man: "At a moment, when all others were engaged and did not much notice him, I saw the great negro, his face overmuch distorted with an evil smile, steal towards the after hatchway" (*TMS* 320), where Marjory lay bound. Archie makes evident the depth of his animosity toward this figure when they eventually clash:

> He was callous to everything, and there was such a wicked, devilish purpose in his look that my heart hardened grimly in the antagonism of man to man. Nay more, it was not a man that I loathed; I would have killed this beast with less compunction than I would kill a rat or a snake. Never in my life did I behold such a wicked face. In features and expression there was every trace and potentiality of evil; and these superimposed on a racial brutality which made my gorge rise. (*TMS* 328–29)

Unsurprisingly, Archie relishes dispatching his foe, noting that although "It may have been that between the man and myself was all the antagonism that came from race, and fear, and wrongdoing; but the act of his killing was to me a joy unspeakable. It will rest with me as a wild pleasure till I die" (*TMS* 329).

In describing the role of this African-American character in the novel, Andrew Smith contends that he "stands in for the Cubans, for whom American support largely disappeared when they feared the formation of a Negro Republic;" moreover, Smith views him as also "the common enemy of Don Escoban."[75] This shift in American public perception of the war with Spain goes far to explain the ambiguous role of Don Escoban in the novel. When Archie and Marjory first confront the Don, Archie notes "his high aquiline nose and black eyes of eagle keenness, his proud bearing and the very swarthiness which told of Moorish descent" (*TMS* 204–05). Unmistakably, as this description makes plain, the Don in both his physical features and mannerisms shares similarities with Count Dracula, another old-world aristocrat out of place in the modern twentieth century. Complicating matters further is the Don's "Moorish" blood, which ties him to the African-American kidnapper. But what eventually rehabilitates the Don in the eyes of Archie is his sense of honor. William Hughes asserts that "Stoker's writings consistently embody [a] conception of acceptable masculinity," a conception "drawn from a nineteenth-century appropriation of medieval chivalry," and nowhere is this notion of masculinity more pronounced than where Stoker's fictions "address the relations between the sexes." When the Don willingly joins Archie in the hunt for Marjory, "the Spaniard effectively privileges the common standard of the gentleman above race, religion and romance."[76] In a sense, the Don takes on the character of American men as described by Stoker in *A Glimpse of America*:

> It seems, now and then, as if a page of an old book of chivalry had been taken as the text of a social law. Everywhere there is the greatest deference, everywhere a protective spirit. Such a thing as a woman suffering molestation or affront, save at the hands of the criminal classes—which are the same all the world over—is almost unknown, and would be promptly resented by the first man coming along.[77]

Consequently, as the novel ends, Don Escoban is afforded a hero's death and burial. But others who cannot live up to this standard of "acceptable masculinity" are not accorded such sympathy. Among them, insists Hughes, are "women as well as criminals;" the men who dominate "white, Anglo-Saxon America," however, are "doubly attractive" to Stoker.[78]

Likewise, Marjory's fate reveals that women, even strong-willed, independent American women, must give way to the authority of white Anglo-Saxon men. Lisa Hopkins has shown that Marjory "like Mina Harker in *Dracula*, is uneasily poised between New Woman and proper wife." Even though she bears the name "of a male bird" and "disavows any sympathy with the most prominent of the New Woman's aims," Marjory and the other women in the novel "in general get short shrift."[79] It is not surprising, then, that, despite all her athletic bicycling, courageous spelunking, ciphering, and material independence, Marjory is beholden to men to survive the ordeal of her kidnapping. Just as her marriage to Archie protects her from social slander, her alignment with a "gifted" English barrister saves her first from drowning and later kidnap and rape. Thus *The Mystery of the Sea* constructs an instance of what Carol Senf terms the "transatlantic marriage," whose "diplomatic and economic relationships signify the future as both nations move into the twentieth century."[80] Working with American Secret Service agents and naval forces, Archie rescues Marjory. However, although Americans play a significant role in her rescue, they would not have been successful without the guidance of Archie, a British subject. In *The Lady of the Shroud*, the marriage of Teuta and Rupert signals that the Land of the Blue Mountains has entrusted her fate to Britain, but that of Marjory and Archie shows, according to Carol Senf, that Britain's "once colony" is now viewed as a "potential ally," albeit one still in need of the mature stewardship only Britain could provide as her former colony takes its place "on the world stage."[81]

Appearing a year after *The Mystery of the Sea* in 1903 and set amidst a purely Eurocentric political conflict, *The Jewel of Seven Stars* further attests to Stoker's abiding interest in geopolitics and the conflicts that emerged from them. This work, according to Ailise Bulfin, should be read as a manifestation of British imperial paranoia about the Suez Canal, a paranoia engendered, no less, by Russian meddling in Egyptian affairs.[82] Russia, and by implication other threats to Britain and her empire, would weigh on Stoker throughout his adult life. The latest biography of Stoker to appear, David Skal's *Something in the Blood*, published in 2016, provides tantalizing evidence to support this assertion. Among Skal's findings is a "recently unearthed" fragment of an unfinished novel found among Stoker's library holdings sold by his wife shortly after Stoker's death. The title of this work in progress is *The Russian Professor*.[83] Undoubtedly, until his death in 1912, Stoker would find narrative material in the politics and military adventures of his time. And readers should not be surprised that the Russian menace would haunt him to his final days.

CHAPTER EIGHT

Black Eyes, White Skin

An Aristocratic or Royal Type in Bram Stoker's Writings

Damian Shaw

Important issues raised by Bram Stoker's writings, such as the "new woman," Liberalism, the Egyptian Gothic, and anxieties relating to contemporary social and scientific theories have received cogent critical attention.[1] Apart from analyses of *Dracula*, however, the issue of Stoker's treatment of the aristocracy or royalty in his writing has received scant attention, though David Glover does note, in passing, that Stoker's texts typically show "extreme ambivalence concerning those of noble birth."[2] This chapter will first briefly situate Stoker in a political context and then present a chronological survey of a particular character type, a woman or man with black eyes and white skin, in order to assess Stoker's presentation of aristocracy and royalty. Even though this character occurs in several novels, I agree with William Hughes when he says that Stoker is not simply repetitive. Hughes notes that when we see recurrences in Stoker these are "in essence, *reworkings* rather than simply replications. Each fresh occurrence, as it were, is modified by its contiguity to other issues, other signifiers and other texts."[3] This tendency in Stoker's fiction renders focusing on a particular character type as it recurs over time particularly instructive.

Bram Stoker in a Liberal Party context

Bram Stoker was born into the Irish Protestant middle class. Paul Murray proves conclusively that Stoker was not from an "Anglo-Irish" background, with its "aristocratic connotations," as so many modern Stoker critics have contended.[4] He was a life-long advocate for Irish Home Rule[5] and a firm supporter of the Liberal Party and follower of Gladstone. The party itself, however, was a broad church, and deeply divided on the issue of the aristocracy, ravaged by "splits and divisions," especially from the 1880s to the 1920s, with Radical anti-aristocratic elements as well as more moderate ones.[6] Radical anti-royalist feeling often accompanied anti-aristocratic sentiment, though anti-royalism "remained a stance detached from the Liberal party, expressing a refusal [by the radicals] to accept the compromises of the existing party system."[7] Even so, as historian Antony Taylor argues, "anti-monarchism 'had a very real meaning for many subjects of the throne.'"[8] As such, the party provided scope for debate or consideration of these issues in a way that the Tory party did not, and we see this made manifest in Stoker's fiction.

David Glover notes the influence of one of John Bright's (a radical Liberal) speeches on Stoker as a young man, a speech that envisions the Tory party as "a reactionary formation founded upon privilege and aristocracy."[9] Yet Stoker's fiction does not show profound antipathy to the institution of the aristocracy as such, as many of his heroes and heroines are or become either aristocratic or royal. The Liberal party often needed radical support for its coalitions to survive, which, over time, led to the formulation of an image of the ideal aristocrat that could appease both pro and anti-aristocratic factions. As Jonathan Parry has it:

> the emphasis on manliness after 1850 allowed the Liberal aristocracy a new lease of life. Liberal party leaders until the 1890s took care to give prominent political roles to earnest public-spirited peers: Spencer, Ripon, Kimberly (and a duke's son, Harrington). These men were not typical of the aristocracy as a class, but they presented a Liberal ideal of aristocratic leadership: hard-working, plain-spoken, of good character.[10]

This emphasis on manly simplicity describes many of Stoker's male and female characters perfectly. After the 1890s, however, the Liberal party felt increasing pressure to support anti-aristocratic sentiment, up to the point where, by 1910, the party "used traditional opposition to the aristocracy to attack the Lords," which resulted in the 1911 Parliament Act, which "drastically and permanently reduced the power of the House of Lords."[11] Stoker was keenly aware of contemporary debates, and his fiction repeatedly touches on the issue of aristocracy, but my contention is that his writings, especially in the Edwardian era, attempt to validate a potentially fading and unfashionable view of "Liberal ideal aristocratic leadership" from within his own Liberal perspective. This accounts for the portrayal of both positive and negative aristocratic types, rather than any distinct criticism of the idea of aristocracy itself.[12]

The aristocratic or royal characters with a combination of black eyes and white skin first emerge in Stoker's *The Jewel of Seven Stars* (1903). Several prototypes of these characters, however, occur in earlier writings, so a short consideration of portrayals of the aristocracy or royalty in these writings, as they relate to my theme, will be instructive.

Early Fiction

Carol Senf notes that in the early *A Glimpse of America* (1885) Stoker "consistently praises Americans for … their lack of class distinctions."[13] In the same piece, however, Stoker's writing frequently uses the rhetoric of nobility and aristocracy. On America, he speaks of "joy that England's first-born child has arrived at so *noble* a stature," and maintains that "Columbia is strong enough in her knowledge of her own beauty and power to sail, unruffled and unawed, into the salon of old Time amidst the *queens of the world*" (my italics).[14] This note, written more than a decade before *Dracula*, implies that the European aristocratic and royal coterie is something worth joining, and that the aristocracy as such should be a social hierarchy that concerns itself with character and merit, rather than mere accidents of birth. Americans have the "beauty and power" to enter the European aristocratic club of their own volition, and their innate nobility qualifies them to join. The idea that the aristocracy should be open to outsiders is a theme repeated frequently in Stoker's novels, as we shall see, even though, in this case, Americans are portrayed as genetic offspring.[15]

In *The Snakes's Pass* (1890), the wealthy Englishman Arthur Severn travels to Ireland. Though not an aristocrat, he is portrayed as being of a higher social class than the other protagonists. In Ireland he falls in love with Norah Joyce, even though "she was only a peasant girl, manifestly and unmistakably, and had no pretence of being anything else" (*SP* 75). She is described as a "perfect beauty of the Spanish type" (traces of "Spanish blood" being found, according to the novel, on the west coast of Ireland [*SP* 75]),[16] and, by implication, of a darker skin color than most of the Irish. They eventually marry, after she has spent two years being educated in Paris. Her class status is, therefore, not an impediment towards her upward mobility, specifically because of her innate nobility: As Arthur replies to Norah's claim that she is a peasant, "'Peasant!' I laughed. 'Norah, you are the best lady I have ever seen! Why, you are like a queen—what a queen ought to be!'" (*SP* 225). Norah Joyce also has "black-blue eyes" (*SP* 75). Like America, Norah is a "noble" outsider who is accepted into a higher class.

This paradigmatic love relationship is reversed sexually in *The Shoulder of Shasta* (1895), in which a wealthy English heiress, Esse Elstree, is sent to America to relieve her "anaemic" condition (*SoS* 1).[17] Esse, who has "dark" eyes which "flash," falls for a rugged American hunter named Grizzly Dick, a man "away outside the class [she had] been reared in" (*SoS* 98). Though she is weak, she saves Dick's life by shooting a grizzly bear and dragging him to safety, showing that she has "true grit" (*SoS* 75). When men and women act heroically, as Esse does here, "they bring out all that is *royal* (my italics) in their natures, from physical strength to highest nerve and psychic power" (*SoS* 75). Dick is a "generous and chivalrous" soul (*SoS* 76). Even though Esse eventually becomes engaged to a young English painter with the regal name of Reginald Hampden, San Franciscan society, after first attempting to shame Dick, embrace him when they recognize his innate nobility: "[t]here was something about him so fresh, and wild, and free – so noble a simplicity and manhood" that women did not wonder why Esse had invited him to be with her in San Francisco (*SoS* 128). The implication here, as in the case of Norah Jones, is that innate nobility, for Stoker, qualifies characters to enter a social hierarchy that would have excluded them, traditionally, on the basis of birth.

The Mystery of the Sea (1902), written just before *The Jewel of Seven Stars*, concerns the Spanish–American war. The heroine, a very wealthy American heiress, Marjory Drake (distantly related to Sir Francis Drake), has "dark" eyes, which seem to "blaze" and "flash." Though Marjory does not have a royal bloodline, she is pictured in royal terms. Her future husband, the British man Archibald Hunter, sees their meeting as "an up-to-date story of the Princess in disguise." Jokingly, while searching for treasure in a cave, she refers to herself and Archie as queen and king, before changing into the "vernacular:" "Her Majesty is pleased with the ready understanding of her Royal Consort, ... and oh! Archie, isn't this simply too lovely for anything?" While at times girlishly naive, she is also a patriot, a fighter, and a generous woman who understands the "responsibility of great wealth" (*TMS* 66, 118, 215, 136). The first encounter between Marjory and her adversary, the Spanish aristocrat Don Bernardino, is depicted as a struggle between aristocratic "types of the two races" then at war, the "Latin" and the "Anglo-Saxon" (*TMS* 204–05).[18] Don Bernardino, with his "high aquiline nose and black eyes of eagle keenness, his proud bearing and the very swarthiness which told of Moorish descent," addresses her with "hauteur" (*TMS* 204–05). Marjory has "courage," "self belief," and "noble beauty" (*TMS* 205).

The Don, for historical, cultural, and even racial reasons, presents a major threat in the novel. Yet, because he is innately a gentleman, he eventually sacrifices his own life in order to help in the rescue of Marjory from kidnappers. As William Hughes shows at length, the Don is finally found to be acceptable because of his behavior, which is found to be "noble," "as a knight of old" (*TMS* 147).[19] As Hughes has it, his inscription in an order of "chivalric manliness" ultimately "purges the negative associations, political and religious as well as physical, with which the text has burdened him. The Don is 'Other' no more."[20] The threat of his racial (Moorish) otherness, as well as the potential danger represented by his non-British aristocratic lineage, are equally purged by his behavior.[21] Though racial "impurity" and aristocratic descent may trouble Stoker's text, it is made clear that they are ultimately not insurmountable obstacles to acceptance in society, as long as particular codes of conduct are adhered to.

In the above three novels we see that dark or black-eyed types may be male or female, and from a variety of social classes and nationalities, yet they are all heroic characters who are connected in differing ways to the idea of aristocracy or royalty and find eventual approval (even if they have weaknesses) as a result of their innate nobility and codes of conduct. Through these prototypical characters, Stoker is suggesting that the aristocracy as well as royalty is much more than a matter of blood, which argues against traditional notions of the aristocracy based simply on hereditary privilege. Before considering later works, however, I will briefly consider the possible significance of eye and skin color.

Black Eyes and White Skin

White skin has obvious racial and aristocratic connotations, as well as representing a particular western ideal of beauty. As we have seen above, however, white skin color is not necessarily an indicator of positive aristocratic qualities in Stoker's writings. Miss Esse is pale and anaemic, but her skin color is naturally brown, a trait which reasserts itself under the healthy influences of Grizzly Dick and the American wilderness. Don Bernardino is swarthy, and has a trace of Moorish blood, yet is revealed to be a truly noble character. In subsequent novels, however, characters with black eyes and white skin who are connected to aristocracy or royalty become particularly important.

Concerning female characters with black eyes and white skin, one is reminded of several famous literary antecedents, as Baumbach points out: namely, Shakespeare's "Dark Lady," Sidney's "Stella," and Petrarch's "Laura."[22] In Petrarch's sonnets, Laura has both a bright and a dark side, the dark side being associated with Medusa, a point to which I will return.[23] The contrasting blackness and brightness of Stella's eyes are explored in Sidney's sonnet 7 in *Astrophil and Stella*, where they are associated with both beauty and death. Shakespeare's "Dark Lady," though her skin might be "dun," has "raven black" eyes, which can "kill," albeit metaphorically.[24] These aristocratic characters are, therefore, beautiful, mysterious, and potentially dangerous: ideas which could well be informing Stoker's own literary creations. Furthermore, Graeme Tytler maintains that in the European novel "dark eyes (brown or black) frequently belong to the physically or morally strong."[25] This is true of most of Stoker's characters with this trait. Another probable influence on Stoker is physiognomy. Glover rightly points out the "foundational status" of Lavatar's work on physiognomy in Stoker's writing, so we should turn to this text.[26] Though Lavatar does not have much to say on eye color, he quotes Paracelsus, who claims that "blackness in the eyes generally denotes health, a firm mind, not wavering but courageous, true and honourable."[27] Lavatar makes the point, however, following Buffon, that black eyes actually do not exist. They only appear to be so from a distance, or turned to the light, in contrast with the iris.[28] In effect, therefore, black eyes function as a cipher, opening up a range of possible characteristics. In the literary and physiognomical tradition, blazing black eyes contrasted with white skin tend to denote physical or moral strength, but also, a potentially dualistic nature, both positive and negative.[29] Stoker has also used the type to hint at occult power, in the case of Gormala, and oriental racial otherness, as in the case of Don Bernardino. The combination, therefore, seems ideally suited to exploring the question of what makes for an acceptable aristocrat, or, in the case of *The Jewel of Seven Stars*, an ideal queen. In this novel the character Margaret Trelawney has eyes which blaze "like black suns" and white skin "as pale as snow" (*JSS* 240, 23).

The Jewel of Seven Stars and Beyond

The Jewel of Seven Stars (1903) tells the tale of a group of people who try to resurrect the mummy of the ancient Egyptian queen Tera, while the soul of Tera progressively struggles to possess her modern doppelgänger. Given that the novel was published shortly after the death of Queen Victoria and involves a conflict between an ancient and a modern queen, one of the key questions of the novel seems to be: "what type of character would make a good modern queen?" The coterie in the novel consists of a youthful barrister (the narrator) named Malcom Ross; a professional Egyptologist and scientist, Eugene Corbeck; a Doctor Winchester; the renowned Egyptologist Abel Trelawney; and his daughter Margaret. Ross falls deeply in love with Margaret, but is ultimately disappointed as all members of the group besides himself and Tera (who is revived at the end of the book) are killed, at least in the original version of the novel.

This group is similar in composition to the "crew of light" in *Dracula* (1897), even though it does not contain a titled aristocrat.[30] Nevertheless, Abel Trelawney is an extremely wealthy member of the gentry who still owns property that has been in the family since Jacobean times. He is, "from his physiognomy," "a man of iron will and determined purpose." His large household in London contains different "classes" of servants, and in his behavior and demeanor he is an aristocrat in all but name (*JSS* 196, 70). As a master, however, Abel Trelawny is "stern and cold," as Clive Leatherdale puts it.[31]

His daughter, Margaret, who is essentially a double of queen Tera, is continually portrayed in regal terms. In the opening dream sequence of the novel Hebblethwaite notes that Ross's vision of the boat trip with her is "reminiscent of Enobarbus' description of Cleopatra's barge in Act II Scene 2 of Shakespeare's *Antony and Cleopatra*."[32] Margaret's appearance, from the outset, appears to be naturally royal: "She seemed to rule all around her with a sort of high-bred dominance." Her bearing and movements are both "high-bred" and "dignified." When she gazes at Ross in chapter two, he states that he "would not have changed places with a king," though, ironically, he might have hoped to become a princely consort, metaphorically, if they were married. Margaret seems to exemplify the best qualities of royalty (*JSS* 11, 47, 26).[33]

She has "[t]he pride that has faith; the pride that is born of conscious purity; the pride of a veritable queen of Old Time, when to be royal was to be the first and greatest and bravest in all high things" (*JSS* 160). Unlike her father, however, when most of the servants of the household scatter in fear, she responds with a "haughty dignity" characterised by great "generosity." She increases the salaries of the remaining servants, causing the faithful Mrs Grant to remark: "No wonder the house is like a King's house, when the mistress is a Princess!" Ross continues:

> "A Princess!" That was it. The idea seemed to satisfy my mind, and to bring back in a wave of light the first moment when she swept across my vision at the ball in Belgrave Square. A queenly figure! tall and slim, bending, swaying, undulating as the lily or lotos [*sic*]. (*JSS* 73)

On their second meeting Ross feels a "thrill" when he takes her hand, as he feels her "unconscious self-surrender" (*JSS* 63, 64, 11). Since Margaret later returns his love, she seems like the perfect, obedient prize in a (Stoker-esque) fairy tale, where the non-aristocratic hero would be ennobled by marriage to a queen in all but name.[34]

Physically, the features constantly associated with Margaret are her white skin and black eyes, a combination that reoccurs in several of Stoker's other novels. In Margaret's case, although she initially fits the description by Paracelsus, she gradually comes under the influence (or possession) of Queen Tera's "Double" soul, which leads to a distancing and "intellectual aloofness" from Ross that causes him to "doubt" her (*JSS* 206, 204). Her "self-surrender" to Ross, is, therefore, challenged by a similar demand from Tera. As this alienation is caused by Queen Tera, it is appropriate to investigate Tera's character here.

The figure of Queen Tera is largely based on the historical Queen Hatshepsut (1508–1458 BCE), whose name means "Foremost of Noble Ladies," a veritable queen of the "Old Time."[35] As Jasmine Day points out, "[s]ince the nineteenth century" mummies have been overwhelmingly presented in "popular" Western literature in terms of "curse" narratives.[36] In the nineteenth century, however, "romantic visions of mummies" competed with curse narratives and the well-established European notions of Egypt's leaders as "decadent and cruel,"[37] hence opening readers up to potentially conflicting interpretations of Pharaonic culture. Whether historically accurate or not, Stoker's text initially portrays Tera in very positive terms, as a person of "extraordinary character as well as ability" (*JSS* 128). She has been taught both statecraft and the "lore of the very priests themselves," and uses this to secure her power as pharaoh, in a male guise, against the priests who are intent on "transferring the governing power from a Kingship to a Hierarchy." As such, she is a successful monarch. Abel Trelawney praises her as a woman "skilled in all the science of her time" (*JSS* 167), and is convinced that she wishes to be resurrected as a "new woman" in the North. Her *stele* remembers her as "Protector of the Arts." Margaret, possibly under the influence of Tera, believes that she is chiefly motivated by the "love that is the dream of every woman's life," regardless of "rank or calling," and a desire to come to life in a land where there is "no scheming and malignant priesthood," a place where the "sweet and lovely Queen" might meet a "kindred spirit" as she herself has met in the form of Ross (*JSS* 128, 167, 170, 177–78).

These seem to be overwhelmingly positive attributes, but Ross has his doubts. All would be fine if Tera were "just and kind and clean … . But if not! … ." Counting against her is the fact that she has "waded to [her resurrection] through blood," even though Margaret maintains that this was mere self-preservation. Does she really intend to return as a "humble individual," as Margaret believes? Ross stresses that they actually do not know Tera's motivations at all: "as to what her after intentions were we had no clue" (*JSS* 209, 210, 214, 210). Queen Tera is a mystery. Though she is not portrayed as a figure of sexual deviancy or criminality, like Dracula, she does have negative attributes.[38] The reader notices that Tera, unlike Margaret, has seven fingers and seven toes on one hand and one foot – besides the mystical significance, this is surely a sign of inbreeding and racial degeneracy, as incest was commonly practiced by the pharaohs. Crucially, she has also been taught the arts of "white" as well as "black" magic, which Corbeck sees as "real" magic, as opposed to "harmless" white magic. The implication here is that Tera could be harmful. When Corbeck first sees Tera's jewel of seven stars, he is shocked into "momentary paralysis," as if "it were that fabled head of the Gorgon Medusa" (*JSS* 114).[39] Tera does, indeed, prove dangerous, as she kills everyone except Ross when she is resurrected in the original version.

We can presume that Margaret is the image of Tera as Ross mistakes Tera for Margaret at the end of the novel. She certainly has white skin (a fact often repeated), but the reader is not given a glimpse of her eyes.[40] Her eyes, one assumes, by implication, are black, but, unlike Margaret's, may represent evil. When Ross finds Margaret's corpse, he sees that she "had put her hands before her face, but the glassy stare of her eyes through the fingers was more terrible than an open glare." It seems that she has been petrified, perhaps after seeing the true nature of the gorgon's eyes and attempting to ward herself against them. Though Tera is a complex and generally positive character, two forces are ultimately opposed to her. The "Great Experiment" to resurrect her seems to be going well, producing a "cascade of brilliant points—a miracle of light!" but a storm (nature) actively intervenes ("I almost fancied that the storm was a living thing, and animated with the wrath of the quick!"), and disrupts the experiment, which then produces a "black, impenetrable smoke" (*JSS* 244, 242). The nuance here is that Tera's use of black magic is ultimately unnatural.[41] Secondly, Ross, who is the only character with religious sensibilities, makes the following comment earlier in the novel: "The Recording Angel writes in the Great Book in no rainbow tints; his pen is dipped in no colours but light and darkness. For the eye of infinite wisdom there is no need of shading." Complexity is resolved into (Manichean) "direct opposites," and it seems that Tera is ultimately found wanting from the perspective of the Recording Angel, and also Ross, who sees himself as "the guardian of the light!" even though the light he is guarding is only electric (*JSS* 203, 243).

In Ross's view, therefore, Tera does constitute a potential threat, but the denouement of the novel does not imply any anti-royal sentiment. Margaret can be seen to represent the possibility of an ideal modern queen who is simply unable to overcome a more powerful ancient one, though she does attempt to resist by shielding herself at the final moment.[42] Stoker also does not seem averse to the idea of ancient (female) royalty *per se*, though the character of the person is all-important. Of Queen Elizabeth I he writes: "The world at that crisis wanted just such an one as Elizabeth. All honour to her whosoever she may have been, boy or girl matters not."[43]

Some critics have seen connections between Tera and Ayesha in Rider Haggard's *She* (1887).[44] Certainly they are both powerful queens in Africa (who are also sorceresses)[45] and whose coming or intended coming to England is seen as a threat, but Ayesha's threat to Queen Victoria is direct, whereas the danger posed by Tera to British society is ambiguous and discounted by Margaret.[46] *She* might be read as an "extended fantasy" on Victoria's monarchy, and readers might well have drawn connections between Ayesha, Tera, and Victoria, but the links between Tera and Victoria are implied, rather than obvious.[47] Tera, as mentioned above, was remembered as "Protector of the Arts." The goddess Minerva was frequently portrayed as "protector of the arts," and there was a strong iconic link between Victoria and Minerva in the public mind, most clearly exemplified by the 1887 Jubilee coin issue, but found as early as 1837.[48] This is surely a positive rather than a negative association.[49] Contemporary readers of Stoker's 1903 novel would also have been acutely aware of Victoria's recent death in 1901, as is the narrator, Ross: "I was made a Q.C. in the last year of the Queen's reign" (*JSS* 150). Even if this link is tenuous,

Stoker might simply have thought it in poor taste to kill off a newly resurrected powerful white queen so shortly after Victoria's death, and what
Tera would go on to do in England is not answered by the novel.

Hebblethwaite opines that the novel remains "persistently evasive
of definitive critical analysis" (JSS xi). If we accept that a key concern of
the novel is the question of what would constitute an ideal queen, then
the conclusion would seem easier to resolve. Abel Trelawney, who is not
generous with his wealth, is punished. The ancient queen survives, perhaps
owing to her many admirable qualities, yet is a threat to modern England,
as she remains largely mysterious and has connections to both good and
evil magic. The generous, ideal, modern queen, Margaret, dies tragically,
as she comes too much under the influence of the ancient queen, leaving
Ross in a state of despair. Even considering this gloomy state of affairs,
however, the novel implies that a generous woman who did not have
either aristocratic or royal blood could well become a queen in England,
if only she were capable of resisting the malign and "unknowable"[50] influences of archaic (Pharaonic) female power, for all its positive attributes.[51]

The Man and *Lady Athlyne*

In Stoker's next novel, *The Man* (1905), a wealthy British squire names
his daughter "Stephen Norman."[52] She inherits his estates. Much of the
novel revolves around the issue of female dominance. Certainly, her
physiognomy, extensively described, suggests that "[p]ride, self-reli-
ance, dominance and masterdom were all marked in every feature." Her
ancestry is traced through Saxon and Norman lines, as well as "some
Eastern blood of the far-back wife of the Crusader," which gives her
"black eyes, deep blue-black, or rather purple-black." The "lightning of
the black eyes" is reminiscent of a submissive "Saracen maid who cheer-
fully left her glowing sunlight for the chilly north to be with her lord,"
similar to Tera, who, we are told, wishes to come to England for love (*GoL*
7, 73).[53] She has skin as white as ivory and looks like a statue by "a greater
Praxiteles." (When Tera's body is unwrapped in *Jewel*, in a rather sexually lurid scene, she looks like a "statue carven in ivory by the hand of a
Praxiteles" (JSS 235)). Stephen can, thus, be seen as a continued embodiment of the Margaret/Tera duality. Tellingly, Stephen's mother is called

Margaret.[54] At the end of the text Stephen is reunited with Harold, who has learned the merits of heroic masculine dominance in America and Alaska, and they live happily ever after, as Stephen has learned the value of female submission: "Nature, sweet and simple and true, reigned alone. Instinctively she rose and came towards him. In the simple nobility of her *self-surrender* (my italics) and her purpose, which were at one with the grandeur of nature around her, to be negative was to be false." What is important for my purpose is that Stephen has just succeeded to "the Earldom de Lannoy." She has become "Lady de Lannoy," and has earned the nickname of "Lady Bountiful" because of her generosity, one of Margaret Trelawney's virtues in *Jewel*. When Harold is brought to her castle, not knowing she is there, he is placed in the queen's room, the "Royal Chamber where Queen Elizabeth had lain" (*GoL* 332, 248, 289). The couple is rewarded with not only elevation to the aristocracy—they have virtually become royalty. This romantic ending affirms once again that a character without aristocratic or royal blood can rise to the ranks of the aristocracy, or even be viewed as royal, if that character shows various positive traits, such as generosity, and, in the case of a female, is capable of "self-surrender" to her male lover.

In the following novel, *Lady Athlyne* (1908), the wealthy (non-aristocratic) American Joy Ogilvie marries the heroic "Scotch and Irish" Lord Athlyne after a series of adventures.[55] According to her aunt Judy, Joy has skin "like ivory" and "patrician hands," and her physiognomy betokens the "making ... of a noble life." Joy's eyes are grey (a union of black and white),[56] "great gray eyes as deep as the sky or sea," but they share some of the qualities of Margaret's and, later, Teuta's eyes. They "shone like stars," or "like two great gray suns." They flash with "gray lightning."[57] The color is not accidental. The final chapter is titled "A Harmony in Gray," and we are told by the narrator that "the whole colour scheme of the couple had been built around Joy's eyes." Joy, as a variation on a theme, might represent, therefore, a compromise in terms of sexual politics that Margaret/Tera was not able to reach, and which Stephen achieved only at the end of *The Man*.

Lady Athlyne, as Glover rightly shows, continues Stoker's "search for a new national hybrid" (which can be cross-class, cross-national, and even cross-racial) that is a "defining characteristic of Stoker's writing."[58] Heroic figures with black eyes often represent a potentially troubling otherness, but they are rewarded if they adhere to Stoker's moralistic and gendered vision, vilified if they do not. Furthermore, there is almost always the "reward" of an aristocratic title or position for those considered worthy, usually a heroic man from the Celtic world and a woman who submits to him. There are several characters in Stoker's fiction (most notably Dracula) who are plainly unworthy aristocrats, but there is most often a place within the aristocracy for those who deserve it in Stoker's terms.[59] This pattern is especially plain in Stoker's next (utopian) novel, *The Lady of the Shroud* (1909), which was dedicated by Stoker to his "dear old friend the Comtesse de Guerbel."[60]

The Lady of the Shroud

In *The Lady of the Shroud* Rupert Saint Leger, a larger-than-life adventurer, inherits massive wealth, including a castle in the "Land of the Blue Mountains" in the Balkans. Once there, he encounters a mysterious, shrouded woman whom he at first (along with the local population) thinks is a vampire. It turns out that she is actually the hereditary queen of the country who has adopted the disguise to protect herself from Turkish infiltrators. Her name is Teuta, and she can, thus, be read as an avatar or reincarnation of the third-century BCE queen Teuta who reigned in Illyria (now Dalmatia) and whom Rupert calls "a great Queen" (*TLS* 191). Like queen Tera in *Jewel* she has skin "whiter than the snow" and "eyes black as the sea at night," but there are always "stars in them" (*TLS* 138, 135). Her eyes "sent through their stars fiery gleams" (*TLS* 74). Unlike Tera, however, she is an embodiment of "true and perfect womanhood" according to Saint Leger, marked by "hereditary dignity," generosity, self-sacrifice, and obedience: "[l]ike a good wife she obeyed" (*TLS* 126, 72, 170). She renounces power in favor of her husband, as she says: "[w]hat an example such would be in an age when self-seeking women of other nations seek to forget their womanhood in the struggle to vie in equality with men!" (*TLS* 224). She is, therefore, an idealized version of what Margaret or Tera could have become and realizes the fantasy of *Jewel* (1903) that ended in despair. Crucially, this Stokerian male fantasy requires the existence of a benign monarchy.

Because of his efforts on behalf of the country, Rupert is elected as King Rupert and a constitutional monarchy is established following the British model (*TLS* 221–22). The country is co-defended by Rupert's brave Scottish relatives and their highland followers, who join the local leaders in the formation of a new ruling class, who are, nevertheless, still men of the people. The intensely snobbish aristocrat Ernest Melton, Rupert's cousin, is a man who desires social elevation but treats the people of the Blue Mountains with contempt and is ridiculed throughout the novel. He is an example of an outdated notion of aristocracy, which befits a "hooligan of the Saurian stage of development" (*TLS* 207).

The plot of *The Lady of the Shroud* is, no doubt, inspired by Anthony Hope's *The Prisoner of Zenda* (1894) and its sequels *Rupert of Hentzau* (1898) and *Sophy of Kravonia* (1906). *Zenda* commences with a conversation in which Lady Rose Burlesdon urges her brother-in-law, Rudolf Rassendyll, to behave more like his brother (her husband) Lord Robert Burlesdon. She accuses Rudolf of being an "idle scamp" and says that the difference between them is that Robert "recognizes the duties of his position, and you see the opportunities of yours."[61] When the chips are down, however, Rudolf proves himself to be a man of the finest qualities and highest sense of duty, fit to become king of Zenda, even though he is assassinated in *Rupert of Hentzau* just before this potentiality becomes a reality. He is remembered in Ruritania as the "noblest [of] gentlemen."[62] The British aristocrats in the two novels are thus ultimately portrayed in a positive light. On the contrary, Rudolf's doppelgänger in Ruritania, King Rudolf Elphberg, is an ineffectual, craven drinker, and his aristocratic rivals, Prince Michael (his brother) and Count Rupert von Hentzau, are ruthlessly ambitious murderers. Though Rupert is manly, he is ultimately shown to be lacking in any gentlemanly qualities, as is Michael, who "doesn't understand a gentleman."[63] With the exception of the Ruritanian Queen Flavia, who acts impeccably, therefore, there is a clear opposition in Hope's two novels between an enlightened and ultimately heroic British aristocracy and their degenerate or Machiavellian European counterparts. Stoker's vision in *The Lady of the Shroud*, however, admits to weaknesses on the British side, in the shape of Ernest Melton. The character Rupert Saint Leger (an anti-type of Rupert of Hentzau) becomes a perfect and popular king because he has all the manly qualities of the latter, but all the noble qualities embodied by Rudolf Rassendyll, and he is far from idle.[64] Furthermore, his background is only marginally aristocratic—his mother came from an "old and somewhat good family" but his father was "only a subaltern" (*TLS* 4, 5). Stoker therefore moves a step beyond Hope's early novels by suggesting, once again, that an aristocratic or royal background is not required to become an admirable king.[65] Finally, Stoker's novel supports the maintenance of an aristocratic system as long as the aristocrats themselves and those who become aristocrats behave according to a strict chivalric and gentlemanly (or ladylike) code.

The Lair of the White Worm

Although his final novel, *The Lair of the White Worm* (1911), is notoriously incoherent, the same pattern is followed. Unusually for Stoker, the novel is set in the past, in Derbyshire in 1860. The evil characters could be said to embody, therefore, the type of nobility that Stoker has attempted to replace in the previous novels. The first is the demented Edgar Caswell, the heir to "Castra Regis," who belongs to a line of domineering (and mostly absentee) aristocrats: "cold, selfish, dominant, reckless of consequences in pursuit of their own will." Their salient characteristic is their eyes: "[b]lack, piercing, almost unendurable" (*LWW* 9, 11). The eyes here are linked directly to the devil. The female side is represented by Lady Arabella Marsh, who is "cold and distant," and characterised by cruelty and disdain for the lower classes. She is white-skinned, but her eyes glint the green of emeralds, a color associated with the worm that is possibly a saurian monster (*LWW* 11, 12, 19, 43, 82).[66] In opposition are Adam Salton, his uncle Richard, and Sir Nathaniel de Salis, members of the local landed gentry.[67] Adam (the first man, biblically speaking) returns to inherit in Derbyshire, but is a self-made man who has made an independent fortune in Australia. Fighting with him is the woman he will marry, Mimi Watford. She is half Burmese, and the "trace" of her race is shown in "black eyes," which can glow when she is upset (*LWW* 23). If this novel is a kind of thematic prequel to *Jewel*, given its earlier historical setting, then Mimi can be seen as a precursor of the Margaret type. Though the wicked Edgar's castle is destroyed and the novel ends with Mimi and her "stalwart" Adam departing on honeymoon, we can assume that they will return as local worthies, aristocrats in all but name.[68]

Discussion

Certainly, many critics have read the character Dracula as being a strong indictment of the aristocracy. For example, Jimmie E. Cain opines that: "Dracula manifests an aristocratic hauteur out of place in a thoroughly middle-class Victorian England."[69] As Clive Leatherdale puts it: "Dracula is the embodiment of the anachronistic land-owning class, seeking to sequestrate the newly-earned privileges of the *nouveaux riches* and reopen the historic struggle between the aristocracy and the bourgeoisie."[70] David Punter sees the count as "the final aristocrat," who, in seeking the survival of his house, is seeking "the survival of the dead."[71] One common thread in these views is that the days of aristocrats like Dracula in England were over, and this was essentially true. As David Cannadine details, the British aristocracy began a terminal decline in the 1880s as far as its economic, political, and social power was concerned, and there was little chance that an *ancien regime* in its previous form would return.[72] So, even though the count may represent a threat on this level, it was not a pronounced threat in the real world of the late 1890s and early 1900s, when Stoker was at his most active as a writer. We should remember that Lord Godalming serves as a useful manly foil to Count Dracula in the novel. Even though Carol A. Senf describes him as a little "out of touch with the modern world" and a "dim bulb," he eventually "shows himself perfectly willing to accept the direction that the modern world is taking, and, unlike Dracula, he is willing to share his wealth and his power with representatives of the middle class."[73] These qualities are shared by many of Stoker's other aristocratic or would-be aristocratic heroes and heroines.

Concerning Stoker's attitudes, Leatherdale maintains in an annotation to *Jewel* that "Stoker's well-to-do are portrayed as generous, caring and paternalistic. His fiction is politically conservative, offering no challenge to the social hierarchy, or relations between people in it."[74] I would take issue with this. Firstly, one only needs to consider, for example, the cases of Count Dracula, Margaret's father Abel Trelawny, Lady Arabella Farmer, Ernest Melton, Edgar Caswell, and possibly Tera: wealthy aristocratic or royal types who are anything but caring or generous. Secondly, there are a host of other characters, as I have shown, who are portrayed as models for an aristocratic or royal ideal, such as Stephen Norman, Don Bernardino, Margaret, and Teuta. This ideal is conservative, to some extent, but Stoker's imaginings also present a vision of a new English aristocracy for both men and women from traditionally aristocratic as well as middle-class backgrounds, different nationalities (especially from the Celtic world), and even those with slightly mixed racial backgrounds, as long as they adhere to a chivalric and sexually conservative code. In summary, if we consider Stoker's characters with black, blazing eyes and white skin, we see that they come from a variety of social backgrounds, are either male or female, at times have infusions of Oriental or African "otherness," and are either good or evil. What unites them is that they are all pivotal, powerful characters and are almost always linked to the aristocracy or royalty, whether by inheritance or eventual marriage, which leads to social elevation or even coronation, as is the case with Rupert St. Leger. This survey suggests, therefore, that even though the issue of aristocracy and royalty was not always foregrounded by Stoker it is an essential concern of his fiction. Stoker uses the conventions of the romance to rework, repeatedly, possible aristocratic and royal role models infused with his own values. Indeed, though debate concerning the aristocracy and the monarchy continues in the United Kingdom to this day, Stoker's model of generous chivalric aristocrats and royalty had great appeal, which only seems to be increasing over time, as their political power declines. The overall popularity of a potential future monarch, Prince William, who has recently married a commoner (a possibility denied to King Edward VIII, who had to abdicate in favor of his American lover), and the royal endorsement enjoyed by Prince Harry's wife Meghan Markle, suggests that Stoker's recipe for a British aristocracy and monarchy based on merit rather than blood was ahead of its time, however conservative his other views on gender, empire, and race may have been by today's standards.

CHAPTER NINE

Bram Stoker's Ambivalent Response to the Frontier and the American Frontiersman

Carol Senf

A man who was born in one cosmopolitan center, Dublin, and spent the second half of his life in another, London, Bram Stoker was nonetheless fascinated with the American frontier, which he wrote about in both his fictional works and his nonfiction, sometimes enthusiastically, sometimes with a degree of apprehension, and occasionally with a mixture of the two responses. Stoker's first mention of America came early in his career, when on November 13, 1872 he delivered a lecture entitled "The Necessity for Political Honesty" at the first meeting of the Trinity College Historical Society. This early lecture was followed by *A Glimpse of America* (delivered at the London Institution on December 28, 1885 and published in early 1886) and a series of lectures on Abraham Lincoln delivered in the United States in 1886 and 1887,[1] and in England until at least 1893. While the lectures reveal his enthusiasm for American culture, many of his fictional works—perhaps most obviously *Dracula* (1897), which features both the American frontiersman Quincey Morris and Dracula, the Old World opponent who nonetheless resembles him in some ways—reveal his ambivalence about the frontier and the people who inhabit it. Among the other fictional works that examine the American frontier are *The Shoulder of Shasta* (1895) and *The Man* (1905), as well as shorter works such as "The Squaw"

(1893) and two stories in *Snowbound* (1908)—"Mick the Devil" and "Chin Music." In addition, Stoker occasionally uses frontier experience to reinforce certain character traits, as with Colonel Lucius Ogilvie in *Lady Athlyne* (1908) and a number of characters in *The Mystery of the Sea* (1902): the heroine Marjory Drake, her guardian Mrs. Jack, and the criminals who kidnap Marjory to hold her for ransom. Among the traits that Stoker associates with the frontier are a willingness to stand up for oneself and one's loved ones, quick—indeed, impulsive—reactions in the face of physical challenges, and an independent spirit. Finally, toward the end of his career Stoker introduces frontiersmen from other countries, including the rugged mountaineers in *The Lady of the Shroud* and Adam Salton, an Australian frontiersman, and Oolanga, an African practitioner of voodoo, in *Lair of the White Worm* (1911).

A number of critical studies have commented on Stoker's interest in Americans: Andrew Smith[2] and James R. Simmons[3] focus on the treatment of Americans in *Dracula*; Havlik publishes Stoker's lecture on Lincoln for the first time and comments on both the lecture and Stoker's admiration for Lincoln; Louis S. Warren writes about Buffalo Bill Cody as a possible influence for "Grizzly Dick" in *The Shoulder of Shasta* and "The Squaw" and provides exhaustive treatment of the influence of the frontier on both Quincey Morris and Dracula;[4] and Andrew Garavel writes about *The Shoulder of Shasta*, the only Stoker novel set in America. Because *Dracula* and the Quincey Morris character have already received so much critical attention, the following essay will begin by examining other works by Stoker. These works often reveal the contrast between the two very different kinds of frontiersmen that Stoker presents in *Dracula* and reinforce the ambivalence about the frontier that is evident there.

Stoker learned about the United States both by reading and by taking careful notes during his eight tours with the Lyceum's traveling company between 1883 and 1904. During this period, he and the company visited every major city in the United States and also—according to biographer Paul Murray—traveled "more than 50,000 miles on American railways."[5] As is especially evident from *Personal Reminiscences of Henry Irving* (1906), Stoker also met American writers, politicians, entertainers, and thinkers during these tours, gaining a sense of the American character from these encounters.[6]

"The Necessity for Political Honesty" reveals that Stoker had opinions about the United States and its inhabitants long before he had personal experience with them. Even though almost no one does more than mention "The Necessity for Political Honesty," that forward-looking lecture reveals that Stoker associated the United States with the kinds of scientific and political progress that he celebrates in other works.[7] Beginning with *A Glimpse of America* (1886), which Henry Morton Stanley described as having "more information about America than any other book that had ever been written" and ending with the two-volume *Reminiscences*, in which he writes with enthusiasm about the Americans that he and Irving met, Stoker wove his observations about a region that was disappearing into his fictional creations. Based on the Lyceum's U.S. tour from November 1884 to April 1885 and written primarily to inform his fellow Londoners about the United States, *A Glimpse of America* touches on all aspects of life in the United States, including politics, geography, educational opportunities, and social customs. Stoker begins his lecture by pointing out similarities of "blood, religion, and social ideas, with an almost identical common law,"[8] and reinforces that commonality at the conclusion:

> We have not ... so strong an ally, so close a friend. America has got over her childhood .... There is every reason we can think of why the English on both sides of the Atlantic should hold together as one. Our history is their history—our fame is their pride—their progress is our glory. They are bound to us, and we to them, by every tie of love and sympathy .... We are bound each to each by the instinct of a common race, which makes brotherhood and the love of brothers a natural law; a law which existed at the first, and which, after the lapse of a century, still exists—whose tenets were never broken, even by the shocks of war, and whose keen perception was never dimmed in the wilderness of stormy sea between.[9]

Though Stoker refers to America's emergence from childhood, there is no explicit reference to the frontier. At the same time that he was lecturing about all aspects of American culture to people in England, Stoker was also sharing his knowledge about Abraham Lincoln with people in England

and the United States, and these lectures present Lincoln as someone shaped by the frontier, "manifestly a man of the people, born of the wilderness, self taught from the days when he followed the plough, pulled fodder or split rails."[10] Indeed, Stoker's lecture suggests that Lincoln's childhood experience on the frontier instilled in him a love of freedom and the desire that all people share in that freedom:

> A plain simple man who had taken life as he had found it and made it; and yet a suitable instrument for the working out of a great democratic idea. It was meet that in the time of the Nation's peril, when dismemberment threatened her and when anarchy and slavery combined to crush her aspirations, this type of her working people, this embodiment of her prosaic life should appear as the genius of her safety.[11]

The lecture on Lincoln demonstrates a strategy that Stoker will use in his fiction, suggesting that the frontier is far more than the place where Lincoln was born and reared but a force on the development of his character and ideology. In Lincoln's case the influence is entirely positive, but the influence of frontier life on Colonel Ogilvie and Elias P. Hutcheson is more damaging because the individuality they acquired living close to the wilderness sometimes means that they do not consider the feelings of others.

While writers including Murray have commented on the influence that the sea had on Stoker's writing, less attention has been paid to the other settings of his fiction. The omission is strange, as Stoker has a good eye for the natural world, as is evident in the following passage from Jonathan Harker's journal. Awareness of the beauty of Transylvania causes him to forget momentarily that he is a prisoner in Dracula's castle:

> The view was magnificent, and from where I stood there was every opportunity of seeing it. The castle is on the very edge of a terrible precipice .... As far as the eye can reach is a sea of green tree-tops, with occasionally a deep rift where there is a chasm. Here and there are silver threads where the rivers wind in deep gorges through the forests.
> But I am not in heart to describe beauty. (D 28)[12]

The Transylvanian frontier, which remains untouched by the progress of civilization, is a beautiful but terrifying place where Dracula and his followers, the gypsies and Szecklers, are at home, as Dracula brags to Harker: "Here I am noble; I am *boyar*; the common people know me, and I am master" (*D* 23). Stoker thus combines the wild landscape with Dracula's assertion of personal and political power to establish a unique individual who represents a past way of life. A medieval warlord, Dracula was able to dominate his opponents in the fifteenth century, but his physical dominance is less appropriate in the nineteenth century. Even though Stoker never traveled to Transylvania, he knew how to adapt for his own purpose the descriptions of its untamed landscape from people who had been there, such as Emily Gerard, Major E.C. Johnson, Charles Boner, and William Wilkinson. The beauty of the frontier serves as a contrast to London, where most of the novel takes place.

By contrast, the setting of *The Shoulder of Shasta* is based on Stoker's own observations during a trip that, according to Alan Johnson's introduction to the first American edition of the novel, Stoker made "on September 17, 1893" (*SoS* 7). The following reflection is typical:

> Beyond, in the distance, rose the mighty splendour of Shasta Mountain, its snow-covered head standing clear and stark into the sapphire sky, with its foothills a mass of billowy green, and its giant shoulders seemingly close at hand when looked at alone, but of infinite distance when compared with the foreground, or the snowy summit.
>
> There is something in great mountains which seems now and then to set at defiance all the laws of perspective. The magnitude of the quantities, the transparency of cloudless skies, the lack of regulating sense of the spectator's eye in dealing with vast dimensions, all tend to make optical science like a child's fancy. (*SoS* 25)

Because Stoker was not a well-established writer at the time he published *Shasta* in England in late 1895, there were relatively few reviews of it. Nonetheless, Johnson comments that most of the reviews "had high praise for its descriptions of natural scenery" (*SoS* 16).

In addition to Stoker's continued emphasis on the frontier's natural beauty, both *The Shoulder of Shasta* and the lecture on Lincoln reveal his realization that it is being rapidly replaced. For example, Grizzly Dick[13] relates his upbringing to the youthful heroine, explaining that he was raised by parents who kept escaping into a wilderness that is being supplanted by railroads and other developments. Stoker reveals the same process in the lecture on Lincoln:

> Before the march of the pioneer the woods fell back and in his wake were smiling fields of corn. The rivers were explored, the prairies were lined with tracks of caravans of the pioneers. These pioneers were great men, full of the daring, full of hope; of great strength and endurance, with self belief and self-reliance unequalled. Whole families of them followed the sun-set driving the wolf from the track and the bear from its lair, the Indian from the path, one continuous stream swept into that wild rich North West, Towns and cities sprung up like magic, and began to pour Eastwards the fruits of Western enterprise.[14]

The brief references to wild animals and indigenous peoples provide the merest suggestion that the frontier represents the primitive past and also hint that the onslaught of technological progress and urbanization is not only evidence of progress but is perhaps inevitable.

As should be evident, most of these descriptive passages merely reveal Stoker's awareness of many of the physical attributes of the North American frontier, many of them characteristics that he witnessed himself during his many tours of America. Elsewhere, however, he zeroes in on the impact the frontier has on people. Esse Elstree in *The Shoulder of Shasta* is prescribed a dose of wholesome mountain air as a cure for anemia, and she regains health, strength, and self-awareness as a result of her residence near Mount Shasta.

The impact of the frontier on Grizzly Dick is somewhat more nuanced, suggesting the ambivalence that comes to the forefront in Stoker's presentation of Dracula and Quincey Morris. Like William Cody, who probably served as inspiration (Warren mentions that Dick shares the long hair, buckskin clothing, and high black boots that were Cody's trademark), Dick is a guide and a hunter. Concerned for Esse's safety, he kills a female grizzly with a bowie knife, the same weapon associated with Quincey Morris in *Dracula* and an iconic American weapon, before being seriously wounded by her enraged mate. The grateful Esse then kills the male grizzly with a revolver and transports Dick back down the mountain, where she nurses him back to health and thinks she is falling in love with him. Andrew Garavel, one of the few scholars to explore *The Shoulder of Shasta* on its own terms rather than as a forerunner of *Dracula*, analyzes Dick in contrast to other residents of the frontier:

> Dick clearly is a *natural* man, indeed a kind of intermediary between the wild and civilization. And whereas he is seen as Nature ennobled, his strength and vitality at the service of the protection of the weak, the Native Americans of Mount Shasta are portrayed throughout as Nature debased.[15]

Problems arise, however, when Dick encounters the modern world. Born on the frontier to people who are comfortable there, Dick is plainly an outcast in the new, more progressive America. The frontier had nurtured him but had not prepared him for urban living. So long as he stays on the frontier, he is a gentle man, if not a gentleman in the Old World sense of the term. His frontier skills are out of place when Esse invites him to visit her in San Francisco:

> When the time for his visit to San Francisco was ripe, Dick had come as far as Sacramento, and had then prepared himself for what he considered a fashionable visit. This he did by getting himself up as like as he could to the more aristocratic-looking of the Two Macs. (*SoS* 115)

Dick, who appeared ruggedly handsome on the frontier, looks like a vaudeville clown when he attempts to replicate what he thinks of as civilized clothing. Even worse, though, he responds with anger when he understands that Esse's friends are laughing at him, plunging his bowie knife into the floor. He quickly realizes that such rash behavior is more appropriate on the frontier, where it may save lives, and he quickly apologizes to

Esse and her guests: "Let me get back to the b'ars an' the Injuns. I'm more to home with them than I am here … . I couldn't keep my blasted hands off my weppins in the midst of a crowd of women! Durn the thing! I ain't fit to go heeled inter decent kempany!" (*SoS* 124). And Stoker concludes the novel by reinforcing Dick's positive attributes: "There was something so fresh, and wild, and free—so noble a simplicity and manhood, that more than one woman present did not wonder that Esse had asked him to come down to 'Frisco" (*SoS* 128). Although an anachronism, he remains an attractive figure who represents the old-fashioned chivalric values of loyalty to the people he loves and courage in the face of physical danger.

"Chin Music," one of the short stories in *Snowbound*, also features a gentle giant. This is a story of a journey by train in which many of the travelers, angered by an inconsolable crying baby, threaten to throw it off the train before a young man steps in to help. On learning that the mother had died, he offers to comfort the child: "And all night long, up and down, up and down, in his stockinged feet, softly marched the flannel-clad young giant, with the baby asleep on his breast, whilst in his bunk the tired, sorrow-stricken father slept—and forgot" (*SnB* 95). The young man may have been raised on the frontier, but he had acquired far more than hunting, fishing, and fighting skills there.

Stoker also explores the positive impact of the frontier in *The Man*,[16] in which Harold An Wolf leaves his native England when the woman he loves rejects his marriage proposal. As the narrator summarizes, Harold, who is not a frontiersman by birth, finds renewed mental health as well as wealth in the wilderness:

> And The Man, away in the wilds of Alaska, was feeling, day by day and hour by hour, the chastening and purifying influences of the wilderness … . Hot passions cooled before the breath of the snowfield and the glacier. The moaning of a tortured spirit was lost in the roar of the avalanche and the scream of the cyclone. Pale sorrow and cold despair were warmed and quickened by the fierce sunlight which came suddenly and stayed only long enough to vitalise all nature.
>
> And as the first step to understanding, The Man forgot himself.[17]

While most of *The Man* takes place in England, Stoker points out that Harold is able to use his brief interlude on the frontier to learn about himself as well as make his fortune and regain his physical health. Stoker also emphasizes that Harold, like other positive male protagonists, is a man of the future and thus must leave the frontier behind: "But he felt strong enough by this time to look forward in life as well as backward."[18] He is also mentored by an American who represents the next stage in American and European progress, Andrew Stonehouse, "the great iron-master and contractor."[19] If the frontier represents the primitive past, then Stoker is suggesting that Stonehouse and Harold represent the future. Certainly Harold decides to leave the frontier town that he has established to return to his native England. And Stonehouse has already amassed his fortune by using his skills in manufacturing and building to industrialize America.

If *The Man* features the way of the future, one of the short stories from *Snowbound*, "Mick the Devil," also features a character who has the technological savvy that Stoker generally associates with progress, although Mick's impulsive behavior also reveals more of the brashness that Stoker associates with the frontier when he navigates a train over a trestle bridge across Bayou Pierre during the narrator's company's journey from New Orleans to Memphis. His daring maneuver is celebrated because it is successful, but the careful reader has to conclude that, if Mick's strategy hadn't worked, everyone on board the speeding train would have drowned. Paul Murray adds another dimension to readers' appreciation of this story when he explains that Stoker based it on two real events: "the Lyceum train rushing over flooded bridges in 1884, *en route* from Cincinnati to Columbus" and an incident "on 1 February 1896 as the Lyceum was on its way to play in New Orleans. When it came to a creek at Bayou Pierre the train had to pick its way slowly over a flooded bridge, not knowing if it remained intact."[20] Stoker had to know that the engineer's reckless behavior could have resulted in the deaths of the entire Lyceum Company, and describing him as a "devil" suggests something threatening about such rash behavior even if in this case it has a positive result.

Mick is a difficult character to categorize, and readers might logically argue that his rash behavior is not something acquired on the frontier. Furthermore, he is part of a scientific and technological future that Stoker

generally celebrates, even though he recognizes its tendency to malfunc-
tion. There is no doubt that the Native Americans in both *The Shoulder
of Shasta* and "The Squaw" reveal the worst of the frontier. *Shasta*, which
is essentially a comedy, presents a more light-hearted view of primitive
peoples though Esse, who gets along with the Indians around their camp,
but sees them as inferiors: "At first they amused her, and then, when she
knew them a little better, they disgusted her. In fact, she went with them
through somewhat of those phases with which one comes to regard a
monkey before its place in the scale of creation is put in perspective" (*SoS*
51–52). That contempt for beings of an entirely different species may stem
from the fact that they worship Miss Gimp's parrot, whose ability to speak
"as if he was a Christian or an Indian" (*SoS* 54) causes them to see it as a
god and to leave offerings of raw meat for it. Even though *The Shoulder of
Shasta* is comic, Stoker suggests an underlying darkness in these primitive
residents of the frontier when he has one of them consider scalping Mrs.
Estree to add her golden hair to his collection. And Dick's response is even
more complex:

> "There's times when the cruelty of that lot of ours makes me so
> mad, I want to wipe them all out; but I know all the same that
> there isn't one of them … that wouldn't stand between me and
> death … . Guess, you're about beginnin' to size up the noble red
> man without his frills!" (*SoS* 52)

And readers, including Johnson, Murray, Warren, and Garavel, are beginning to come to terms with Stoker's complex attitude to the frontier and
the cruel yet loyal people who live there.

If *The Shoulder of Shasta* glosses over the cruelty of the frontier, "The
Squaw,"[21] a short story that Stoker published in 1893 while he was working
on both *Dracula* and *The Shoulder of Shasta*, reveals an underlying cruelty
in both Native Americans and the white settlers who strive against them.
In this story three tourists meet to explore the ancient city of Nuremberg.
While two of the tourists are European newlyweds, they agree to share
their travels with an American traveler, who is presented as an anachronism—Elias P. Hutcheson from "Isthmian City, Bleeding Gulch, Maple
Tree County, Neb."[22] His unthinking behavior is underscored when,

seeing a mother cat playing with her kitten, he impulsively drops a pebble over the edge of the wall and kills the kitten. The anger of the mother cat prompts a lengthy discussion in which he compares her viciousness to that of an Apache squaw whose baby had been killed and who, in retaliation, tortures the murderer.

Hutcheson's neutral presentation of torture and murder on the frontier is horrifying enough but is made even more horrifying when he casually reveals his souvenir of the event to his horrified companions: "'Durn me, but I took a piece of his hide from one of his skinnin' posts an' had it made into a pocket-book. It's here now!' and he slapped the breast pocket of his coat."[23] That Hutcheson sees himself as a man of the frontier is made even more plain when he relays his experiences in locations associated with the frontier, the Montana Territory, a gold mine in New Mexico, and the Idaho territory, and comments on his own bravery: "Fancy a man that has fought grizzlies an' Injuns bein' careful of bein' murdered by a cat!"[24] After threatening to shoot the mother cat if she bothers them further, he accompanies the newlyweds to the torture chamber. Instead of being appalled by the medieval cruelty, it appears that its antique cruelty is arousing:

> Pears to me that we're a long way behind the times on our side of the big drink. We uster think out on the plains that the Injun could give us points in trying to make a man oncomfortable; but I guess your old mediaeval law-and-order party could raise him every time. Splinters was pretty good in his bluff on the squaw, but this here young miss [the Nurnberg Virgin] held a straight flush all high on him.[25]

Instead of being inspired by the beauty and culture of Nuremberg, Hutcheson hopes to learn more about its primitive torture technology. Not content to look at it or take notes on it, he determines to experience the thrill of being tortured by literally penetrating the Nuremberg Virgin. Shortly after stepping into it, however, Hutcheson is impaled when the cat leaps at the custodian holding the door open and causes the door to shut, trapping the impaled American inside. Lillian Nayder's "Virgin Territory and the Iron Virgin: Engendering the Empire in Bram Stoker's 'The Squaw'"[26] interprets the story as an exploration of the growing power of the United States and Stoker's anxieties over that development and the devious power of the female (Nayder focuses on the three strong women in the story: the mother cat, the Apache squaw, and the honeymooning wife who voices her disapproval of almost everything that Hutcheson does). Having learned violence through their conflict with primitive people, Americans are jaded by violence and willing to import that violence to other conflicts. Similarly, Lisa Hopkins,[27] citing Andrew Smith, reiterates that "The Squaw" reveals Stoker's "ambivalent ideas about America before writing *Dracula*."[28] Readers should be aware of the animal and primitive behavior that lies just beneath the surface of the civilized characters in this story.

Stoker turns to explore another group of Americans in *The Mystery of the Sea*, when he has his Scottish narrator fall in love with the charming and independent American heiress Marjory Anita Drake. The unflappable Marjory reveals herself as a New Woman, willing to take off on a bicycle trip or explore a cavern for hidden treasure. Though she is not a direct product of the frontier, Stoker suggests that some of her independence may come from being reared by people who did have that frontier experience. She confesses to Archie that her companion Mrs. Jack is her old nurse, whose husband was a "workman of my father's in his pioneer days" (*TMS* 133). In addition, when Archie learns of the plot to kidnap Marjorie and hold her for ransom, he also learns that she is capable of taking care of herself and that one of her skills is her ability to use a gun:

> I could see from the way that she handled the weapon that she had little to learn from its use … . "Dad always wished me to know how to use a gun. I don't believe he was ever without one himself, even in his bed, from the time he was a small boy. He used to say 'It never does any one any harm to be ready to get the drop first, in case of a scrap!'" (*TMS* 149)

She is also praised for giving a battleship to the United States Navy to help them fight the Spanish and for her ability to stay calm even in the hands of her kidnappers.

On the other hand, if Marjory Drake's independence and resourcefulness reveals much that Stoker admired in Americans, Stoker's ambivalence to Americans becomes quite clear when readers realize that most of her kidnappers are American as well. In fact, as Hopkins explains in *Bram Stoker: A Literary Life*, Stoker bases Marjory's kidnapping on the real kidnapping of the body of Alexander Turney Stewart (1803–1876), an Irish–American entrepreneur who was one of the richest men in New York at his death, having earned a fortune in the dry goods business. Hopkins ends her discussion of the kidnapping by observing that it was still unsolved when Stoker wrote *Mystery*. As a result, readers might have been inclined to respect the clever but unscrupulous gang of criminals who are described as follows by one of the detectives:

> I take it that "Feathers" is none other than Featherstone who was with Whisky Tommy—which was Tom Mason ... . If those two are in it, most likely the one they called the "Dago" is a half-bred Spaniard that comes from somewheres over here. That Max that she named ... is a Dutchman ... . Then for this game there's likely to be two Chicago bums from the Levee, way-down politicians and heelers. It's possible that there are two more; a man from Frisco that they call Sailor Ben—what they call a cosmopolite for he doesn't come from nowhere in particular; and a buck nigger from Noo Orleans. (*TMS* 285–86)

The references to Chicago, San Francisco, and New Orleans identify the gang as unscrupulous urban dwellers rather than frontiersmen, however, and at least two other members of the gang are apparently European.

If *The Mystery of the Sea* features two very different types of American, so does *Lady Athlyne* (1908),[29] which features the Ogilvies, a wealthy American family taking the grand tour for both the wife's health and the daughter's education. While the novel, which is one of Stoker's most charming romances, focuses on the daughter's love for a handsome aristocrat and the hurdles they must cross to be together, it also reveals marked differences between people who are trapped in the past and those who are oriented to the future. In contrast to his daughter Joy, who is one of Stoker's most appealing New Women characters, Colonel Ogilvie reveres the past and has taught his daughter to respect his views: "Perhaps Captain, you don't understand our part of the world. In

Kentucky we still hold with the *old laws* of Honour which we sometimes hear are *dead*—or at any rate back numbers—in other countries. My father has fought duels all his life" (*LA* 19, my emphasis). Even though she loves her father, Joy already suspects that his values may be somewhat out of step with current virtues, and Stoker may have been aware that dueling largely disappeared with the Civil War mostly as the result of public opinion rather than legislation.[30] Furthermore, if Colonel Ogilvie earned his military title during the American Civil War, Stoker would have judged him on the wrong side of history regardless of his own lack of respect for people he regarded as primitive (for which *The Shoulder of Shasta*, *The Mystery of the Sea*, and *The Lair of the White Worm* provide chilling evidence).

Lady Athlyne contrasts Lucius Ogilvie with the people of the future, including his daughter and son-in-law. Having killed his sister-in-law's suitor (presumably in a duel, though Aunt Judy does not say so) and threatened to fight the man with whom his daughter is in love because "'there are some men who want killing—want it badly!'" (*LA* 19), he is helpless when it comes to modern technology, as is made evident by the fact that both Joy and Lord Athlyne have mastered the motor car while Colonel Ogilvie depends on a chauffeur. Furthermore, Stoker demonstrates that Athlyne has already mastered the skills that Ogilvie values. A hero of the Boer War and a master horseman who meets Joy when he saves her from a runaway horse, he could be a dashing hero of the traditional type. Nonetheless, he finds these martial skills antiquated and looks forward to becoming proficient at more modern technological skills, of which the motor car is the dominant example in the novel. *Lady Athlyne* concludes with the newly married couple beginning their life together and with Aunt Judy also discovering happiness with the Scottish sheriff who intervenes to save Joy and her English lover before blood is shed. Moreover, all the problems keeping the young (and also the not-so-young) lovers apart are solved through legal means rather than through violence. The frontier is a thing of the past, and those who will dominate the twentieth century are people who understand both the law and technology. Presumably both American women will reside in the U.K. with their husbands, though the senior Ogilvies may return to the U.S.

The discussion so far suggests that, while Bram Stoker appreciated the beauty of the untamed wilderness and may even have believed that it provided the source of independence in the people who grappled with it, he was himself a product of the technologically advanced late nineteenth and early twentieth century and therefore ambivalent about the impact the frontier had on individuals. Before attempting to explain the reasons for this ambivalence, however, it is critical to look at *Dracula*, the work on which the often-harried Stoker spent almost a decade on research and revision. Certainly a number of scholars, including Joseph Valente as well as Coundouriotis, Senf, and Dittmer, have commented on Stoker's treatment of both the United States (represented by Quincey Morris, the single American in the novel and one of two characters to die at the conclusion) and the frontier (represented by both Quincey and Dracula).[31] What's interesting to me is that readers know comparatively little about either of these two frontiersmen and that what readers do know stems from what other characters record in their journals and diaries.

Elizabeth Miller and Robert Eighteen-Bisang,[32] who transcribed Stoker's notes on the novel, remind readers that the Texan (who goes by several different names in Stoker's handwritten notes), "once played a more significant part in the novel."[33] They also describe him as "a tribute to America and Americans."[34] Other scholars, notably Franco Moretti[35] and James R. Simmons, disagree with them, while Warren looks closely at *Dracula* as a "frontier myth"[36] and a "dark parable about urban Anglo-Saxons threatened by a frontier hero gone bad."[37]

Before looking at the widely divergent critical response, though, and deciding whether Stoker uses Quincey to reveal his own ambivalence about the frontier, readers should consider exactly what is known about him. Lucy's letter to Mina acknowledges that he is one of her three suitors:

> He is such a nice fellow, an American from Texas, and he looks so young and so fresh that it seems almost impossible that he has been to so many places and has had such adventures … . I must tell you beforehand that Mr Morris doesn't always speak slang—that is to say, he never does so to strangers or before them, for he is really well educated and has exquisite manners—but he

found out that it amused me to hear him talk American slang, and whenever I was present, and there was no one to be shocked he said such funny things. (*D* 56–57)

The same letter also compares Quincey to Othello because both are story-tellers and concludes by sharing Quincey's promise to be Lucy's friend even though she had just rejected his marriage proposal.

In a novel that is told almost exclusively through letters, journals, and diaries, with the occasional newspaper clipping thrown in to provide background information, readers may find it surprising that Quincey communicates in writing only once, in a letter to Arthur:

> We've told yarns by the camp-fire in the prairies; and dressed one another's wounds after trying a landing at the Marquesas; and drunk healths on the shore of Titicaca. There are more yarns to be told, and other wounds to be healed, and another health to be drunk. Won't you let this be at my camp-fire tomorrow night? (*D* 60)

The brief letter serves only to reinforce Lucy's observation that Quincey is a storyteller, but other diary and journal entries reveal other bits and pieces of his background. Dr. Seward's diary reveals that Quincey had acquired a horror of vampire bats in South America when one of them drank the blood of his favorite horse. Seward's diary also reveals that the generally well-armed Quincey often leaves the group to patrol the grounds and that at least once he shoots at something he sees on the window, for which he apologizes profusely to Mina:

> It was an idiotic thing of me to do, and I ask your pardon, Mrs. Harker, most sincerely; I fear I must have frightened you terribly. But the fact is that whilst the Professor was talking there came a big bat and sat on the window-sill. I have got such a horror of the damned brutes from recent events that I cannot stand them, and I went out to have a shot, as I have been doing of late of evenings whenever I have seen one. (*D* 225)

He seems to realize here that his impulsive behavior may be more suitable on the frontier than it is in an urban environment, though he never abandons his impulsive behavior. Indeed, while the others are contemplating ways to track Dracula back to Transylvania, Quincey is often wandering around the grounds.

While there's no evidence that Quincey (unlike his fellow frontiersman Grizzly Dick) dresses like a frontiersman, he generally is armed like one. In addition to the handgun that he uses to shoot at the bat, Quincey also carries a bowie knife at all times, and it is this uniquely American weapon that he plunges into Dracula's heart. He also recommends other armaments when the group travels to Transylvania: "'I understand that the Count comes from a wolf country, and it may be that he shall get there before us. I propose that we add Winchesters to our armament. I have a kind of belief in a Winchester when there is any trouble of that sort around'" (D 301). In addition, Mina's journal reveals her gratitude that both Quincey and Arthur have "plenty of money" and "are willing to spend it so freely" (D 330) in the battle against Dracula. In the published version of *Dracula* Stoker provides no information about how Quincey acquired his wealth, though the *Notes* suggest that Stoker considered at one time making him an inventor. That he finally decided to associate Quincey with weapons and a kind of frontier mentality suggests that Stoker ultimately took his single American character in a different direction, eventually sacrificing him when he and Dracula meet again at another frontier, a meeting that results in the destruction of these two representatives of a bygone period. Generally imagined as a man of action rather than of thought, Quincey is given one moment of self-reflection when Mina asks them to pledge to kill her if she begins to turn into a vampire. Quincey's somber response is here recorded in the diary of his friend Seward: "'I'm only a rough fellow, who hasn't, perhaps, lived as a man should to win such a distinction,[38] but I swear to you by all that I hold sacred and dear that, should the time ever come, I shall not flinch from the duty that you have set us'" (D 307).

Finally, Stoker provides one additional insight into Quincey and the United States when Renfield identifies Quincey with his home state, Texas, and also refers to the Monroe Doctrine:

"Mr Morris, you should be proud of your great state. Its reception into the Union was a precedent which may have far–reaching effects hereafter, when the Pole and Tropics may hold allegiance to the Stars and Stripes. The power of Treaty may yet prove a vast engine of enlargement, when the Monroe doctrine takes its true place as a political fable." (*D* 227)

The policy that later became known as the Monroe Doctrine was written by John Quincey Adams, who was Secretary of State to President James Monroe, and issued on December 2, 1823 to warn European nations against further colonization of the North American continent. In essence, it declares the newly created United States independent of European intervention.[39] During the early part of the nineteenth century the doctrine was used to defend westward movement and expansion (Manifest Destiny). However, by the end of the century, the United States also used it to claim a right to influence activities in Latin America.

Both Leatherdale and Murray comment on the passage that refers to the doctrine, with Leatherdale referring primarily to the fact that the United States lacked the military power to enforce the doctrine. Murray is more insightful:

Morris has aroused a good deal of critical interest, with some seeing him as representative of an expansionist America, an ambiguous threat to British interests who had to be killed off and who may even have been in league with the Count. Another view is that he represents the enterprising spirit of the English race, reinvigorated by transplantation to the United States. Yet others hold that, through Quincey Morris, Stoker may have been trying to advocate an end to American isolationist policies or that Renfield's reference to the Monroe Doctrine may represent a longing on Stoker's part for American intervention in European affairs ... . As well as embodying Stoker's admiration for the United States and its people, Quincey may reflect Stoker's own ambiguous position in London society, well integrated but differentiated by his Irish brogue.[40]

None of these explanations helps readers to understand why the two fron-tiersmen, Quincey and Dracula, are the only two characters who are killed off at the end of *Dracula*.

Unlike Grizzly Dick, who returns comfortably to life on the frontier, Quincey and Dracula have come too far, with both of them attempting to integrate into or, in Dracula's case, conquer modern Europe. And Stoker suggests that neither is suited for the task. Dracula, like Colonel Ogilvie, cannot master modern technology. When faced with a powerful adversary, he resorts to the skills he had depended on during his lifetime. Neither he nor his supporters are able to protect themselves against the communication technology, the faster transportation, or the collaboration of the modern world. As Warren succinctly puts it, Dracula "is a constant atavism, a return to the most basic and crude of beings, substances, and appetites that mocks the advances of modern civilization."[41] Quincey is presented as more adaptable, having learned how to use modern trans-portation and weaponry; however, he cannot rid himself of the frontier skills that cause him to act impulsively and put others at risk, though he does wind up sacrificing only himself at the end of *Dracula*. When his former companions return seven years later to the site of their victory over the vampire they reminisce about their friend and about the Harker child who shares all their names but who is called Quincey. Ironically, while Jonathan notes that Mina believes that "some of our brave friend's spirit has passed into him" (*D* 351), little Quincey Harker actually shares the blood of all the characters *but* Quincey since Lucy died before Dracula could drink Quincey's blood that was transfused into her. Thus the child who represents the future is European through and through.

To summarize, Bram Stoker, during the course of his lengthy writing career, reveals a fascination with the American frontier as well as with the men and women who are influenced by it. Nonetheless, almost every-thing he writes also reveals a profound ambivalence about this frontier experience, which can create both strong and independent people such as Lincoln but, more often, people whose behavior is brash, impulsive, and even cruel. So long as these individuals are willing to remain on the frontier, this behavior allows them to thrive and to conquer the wilderness through sheer brute strength. It is not sufficient to allow them to interact successfully with sophisticated residents of the modern world, and it may even be counterproductive. Indeed, Stoker suggests that the future will be dominated by individuals who can wield the power of technology to conquer the frontier and transform it into something productive instead of merely lovely.

An Unpublished Letter
from Bram Stoker to Laurence Hutton

edited by Matthew Gibson and William Hughes

The travel writer and theater critic Laurence Hutton (1843–1904) was one of the few people to retain Bram Stoker's correspondence to him, just as Stoker himself kept Hutton's letters. Hutton, who was closely associated with another correspondent of Stoker's, the American academic Brander Matthews (1852–1929), was a quixotic character, traveling inexorably every summer and acting as literary editor for *Harper's Magazine* from 1886 to 1898.

Hutton's correspondence with Stoker shows a sense of great bonhomie, despite being about the usual business with which Stoker dealt on a daily basis: arranging tickets, introducing on one occasion an artist to Stoker to provide an illustration of Henry Irving, and so on. In 1884 the Lyceum Theatre Company traveled extensively within the States, and they performed in New York in both April and November of that year, prompting dinner invitations from Hutton to Stoker at his home at 229 West 34th Street in New York. One letter dated April 3, 1884 invites him to dinner there the following Sunday, while another, dated April 22, 1884, asks Stoker to send autographed pictures of Henry Irving and Ellen Terry. In both letters Hutton makes reference to "carving," punning in the first case on the idea of carving a roast, but presumably intending the idea of playfully attacking people through satirical banter, which is certainly how the term is used in the second. When Stoker replies to another dinner invitation at Hutton's home, he happily refers back to this phrase, while showing off his knowledge of both Shakespeare and various humorists.

14 Novr 1884
Star Theatre

My dear Hutton
on lunch at 1.30 "I shall
have a banquet with certain politic
worms" at 229 West 34th
Hamlet reasimalized[1]

"I shall go to carve a sheeps head"
Benedick (recollections of)[2]

"I shall walk with you talk with you
eat with you drink with you swear
at you." Shylock in his later days, at the
"Daft house". (no 229 W. 34.)[3]

[New page – verso]
"Fate cannot harm me I shall have
lunched that day".[4]
old writer – name of no
consequence
"It takes a surgical (or carving) operation
to get a joke into the head of a
Scotchman" – Lamb[5]

"They carved in a way that all
admired"
John Hay[6]
I am at present practising as a nunte[7] in the
morning & working in a dissecting room at night
as I can stand either extreme – a joke whilst carving

or a carve whilst joking – at any rate I
shall be there Ha! Ha!! Ha!!!
yours ever
Bram Stoker

Notes

Notes to Preface

1 Lisa Hopkins, *Bram Stoker: A Literary Life* (Basingstoke: Palgrave Macmillan, 2007).
2 Bram Stoker, *Personal Reminiscences of Henry Irving* [1906], rev. ed. (London: Heinemann, 1907), 233.
3 Paul Murray, *From the Shadow of Dracula: A Life of Bram Stoker*, 2nd ed. (London: Pimlico, 2005), 103–04.
4 David J. Skal, *"Something in the Blood": the Untold Story of Bram Stoker, the Man Who Wrote Dracula* (New York, London: Liveright, 2016), 193.

Notes to Chapter 1: Bram Stoker, *Dracula*, and the English Common Law   *Terry Hale*

1 With the notable exception of two papers by Anne McGillivray: "'What sort of grim adventure was it on which I had embarked?': Lawyers, Vampires, and the Melancholy of Law," *Gothic Studies* 4, no. 2 (2002), 116–32 and "He Would Have Made a Wonderful Solicitor: Law, Modernity, and Professionalism in Bram Stoker's *Dracula*," in W. Wesley Pue and David Sugarman, eds., *Lawyers and Vampires: Cultural Histories of Legal Professions* (Oxford and Portland: Hart Publishing, 2003), 225–67.
2 Graham Robb, *Balzac: A Biography* (London: Picador, 2000), 44.
3 See "Forged Ticket Sales," *South Wales Daily News*, September 2, 1885; "Alleged Fraud on Theatre Manager," *South Wales Echo*, April 20, 1895.
4 First published in *Snowbound: The Record of a Theatrical Touring Party*, ed. Bruce Wightman (London: Collier, 1908); rept. Westcliff-on-Sea:

Desert Island Books, 2000. Wightman's annotations to the 2000 edition provide some useful background information about the story's setting.

5   Barbara Belford, *Bram Stoker: A Biography of the Author of Dracula* (London: Weidenfeld and Nicolson, 1996), 151–54.

6   Belford, *Stoker*, 181.

7   John Henry Wigmore, "A List of One Hundred Legal Novels," *Illinois Law Review* 2 (April 1908), 574–93, at 574.

8   Paul Murray, *From the Shadow of Dracula: A Life of Bram Stoker*, 2nd ed. (London: Pimlico, 2005), 44–49.

9   Murray, *Shadow*, 45.

10   McGillivray, "Grim Adventure," 264.

11   David Ormerod and Karl Laird, *Smith and Hogan's Criminal Law* (Oxford: Oxford University Press, 2015), 166–67. Successive editions of this textbook have been standard reading for lawyers, whether students or practitioners, for more than fifty years.

12   First published in the *Pall Mall Magazine*, February 1894, 656–69.

13   For a good example of this, see Renfield's confession to Seward and Van Helsing as to how Dracula inveigled him to inviting him into the asylum (*D* Ch. XXI, 259–60).

14   For a useful discussion of the nature of the "pupillage" arrangement, see Ernest Bowen-Rowlands, *In the Light of the Law* (London: Grant Richards, 1931), 50–51. The pupil's 100 guineas allows him to "use" his "master's" chambers and "see work" for one year. "No tuition is given," though sometimes a "kindly disposed" master may give advice about "how not to do a set of pleadings." Bowen-Rowland, who served his pupillage around the same time as Stoker, claims that most masters were too busy to more than nod to their pupils in the corridor. The pupil was allowed to follow his master into court and would be allowed to read such documents and papers as the clerk "thought were suitable for one of his condition." Presumably, since Stoker and Inderwick were already at least social acquaintances, if not on more intimate terms, these rules would have been considerably relaxed. Elsewhere, the same author describes the long hours spent in the library, the sort of lectures and other activities, including "moots," arranged by the Council for Legal Education, and even the manner in which those barristers who combined a legal career with parliamentary duties managed to juggle their timetable (Bowen-Rowlands, *Light*, 58–72).

15   Daniel Duman, *The English and Colonial Bars in the Nineteenth Century* (Beckenham: Croom Helm, 1983), 81.

16   I am grateful to Celia Pilkington, Archivist of *The Honourable Society of the Inner Temple*, and James Lloyd, of the same organization, for their kind assistance with regard to identifying Frederick Inderwick (1836–1904) as the barrister whose chambers Stoker shared in his pupillage. Mr.

Lloyd was also able to provide me with scans of Stoker's admission form and papers issued on his call to the Bar. At the time of Stoker's pupillage Inderwick was a Bencher of the Inner Temple—i.e., a senior member of the Inn who, once elected, holds the post for life. From 1880 to 1885 he was Liberal M.P. for Rye, where he later served two terms as mayor. He also served as a Commissioner in Lunacy (1903–04). It is believed that Inderwick would have attained high legal office had not his career been so closely associated with the Divorce Court. On this subject, see, for example, Henry Edwin Fenn, *Thirty-Five Years in the Divorce Courts* (London: T. Werner Laurie, 1910), 59–63. Stoker's pupillage coincided with that of Charles Waterfield Hayward (1867–1934), who subsequently returned to his native Australia after his call to the Bar. A fulsome obituary ('Death of Mr. C. W. Hayward') can be found in the *Advertiser* (Adelaide) of February 3, 1934.

17 G. H. Fleming, *Lady Colin Campbell: Victorian 'Sex' Goddess* (Moreton-in-Marsh: The Windrush Press, 1989), 15.

18 John Juxon, *Lewis and Lewis: The Life and Times of a Victorian Solicitor* (London: Collins, 1983), 19–20.

19 Juxon, *Lewis*, 91–100.

20 Madeleine Bingham, *Henry Irving and the Victorian Theatre* (London: George Allen & Unwin, 1978), 67–71.

21 Bingham, *Irving*, 73. Though of Cornish yeoman stock, Irving's father, Samuel Brodribb, is described by Bingham as a failed commercial traveler barely one step away from a peddler.

22 Bingham, *Irving*, 89.

23 Anne Jordan, *Love Well the Hour: The Life of Lady Colin Campbell (1857–1911)* (Kibworth Beauchamp: Matador, 2010), 135–36.

24 Jordan, *Love Well*, 88–89.

25 Jordan, *Love Well*, 102–03. See also Fleming, *Lady*, for a detailed account of the trial itself, including Frederick Inderwick's contribution.

26 Robert Eighteen-Bisang and Elizabeth Miller, eds., *Bram Stoker's Notes for Dracula: A Facsimilie Edition* (Jefferson and London: McFarland, 2008), 15, 283, and 318.

27 Of that 26 percent, moreover, some 8 percent came from families with estates worth more than £10,000 a year, 37 percent were from families with estates worth between £3,000 and £10,000 a year, 42 percent from families with estates worth between £1,000 and £3,000 a year, and only 13 percent from families with estates worth less than £1,000 a year. The other occupational groups from whom the bar recruited heavily were the offspring of barristers themselves (8 percent), solicitors (6 percent), the clergy (8 percent), those in business (14 percent), and the urban gentry (17 percent). See Duman, *English*, 17–18.

28 Duman, *English*, 24.

29 Murray, *Shadow*, 19.

30 Belford, *Stoker*, 148.

31 Belford, *Stoker*, 165, 174–75. For an alternative view that the rivalry was not so "poisonous" as has sometimes been described, see Murray, *Shadow*, 104.

32 Duman, *English*, 18.

33 Duman, *English*, 13.

34 Duman, *English*, 23.

35 Murray, *Shadow*, 115.

36 Belford, *Stoker*, 194.

37 Murray, *Shadow*, 115.

38 Belford, *Stoker*, 194.

39 Murray, *Shadow*, 115; Belford, *Stoker*, 194.

40 On this point, it is worth noting that, in 1911, the making of false statements relating to the registrations of births or deaths became a statutory offense punishable by up to seven years' imprisonment under s.4(1) of the Perjury Act.

41 On this subject see two papers by Guyora Binder: "The Culpability of Felony Murder," *Notre Dame Law Review* 8 (2008): 965–1060 and "The Meaning of Killing," in *Modern Histories of Crime and Punishment*, ed. Marcus Dubber and Lindsay Farmer (Stanford: Stanford University Press, 2007), 88–114. According to Binder, English juries, unlike American ones, would seem to have been reluctant to return convictions for murder involving constructive malice. Given his familiarity with North America, Stoker may well have been aware of this. Prosecutors in both countries have always been keen to bring such cases to trial, however.

42 Stoker's numerous sojourns in North America with the Lyceum would have perhaps drawn his attention to this aspect of the common law. It is unlikely that other European legal systems operated in the same manner. See also my earlier remarks concerning a traveler's common law rights to accommodation and the folkloric tradition of first-footing.

43 Ormerod and Laird, *Smith etc*, 111.

44 This area of law was reinvigorated by a succession of cases in the 1980s. See Alexander Busuttil and Alexander McCall Smith, "Fright, Stress and Homicide," *Journal of Criminal Law* 54, no. 2 (1990): 257–70.

45 A. W. Brian Simpson, *Cannibalism and the Common Law: A Victorian Yachting Tragedy* (London and Rio Grande: The Hambledon Press, 1994), 218–25.

46 For more detailed discussion see Simpson, *Cannibalism*. This study is particularly recommended with regard to its legal analysis. For additional information concerning the maritime background see Neil Hanson's *The Custom of the Sea* (London: Doubleday, 1999).

47 Simpson, *Cannibalism*, 68.

48 As Brian Simpson notes, the topic of cannibalism was legitimated by the custom of the sea in such situations, complete with its code of conduct involving the drawing of lots (Simpson, *Cannibalism*, 144). This remains true to the present day, as attested by the success of works such as Piers Paul Read's 1974 bestseller *Alive*, an account of how survivors of an air crash in the Andes managed to keep themselves alive by eating the bodies of those who had perished, or the various stage versions of *Sweeney Todd* (Simpson, *Cannibalism*, 110–11).

49 Simpson, *Cannibalism*, 195.

50 Simpson, *Cannibalism*, 204.

51 This case was superseded by the Abortion Act 1967.

52 For a discussion of some recent successful uses of the defense of Necessity in other common law jurisdictions see Richard Small, "Necessity as a Criminal Defence, Some Practical Pointers," Jamaican Bar Association Seminar Papers, n.d. (circa 2006); H. Tremblay, "Eco-terrorists Facing Armageddon: The Defence of Necessity on Law's Normative Rigidity in a Context of Environmental Crisis," *McGill Law Journal* 58 no. 2 (2012): 321–64.

53 Curiously, when Van Helsing and Seward break into Lucy's tomb (*D*, Ch. XV) or, later, drive the stake through her heart (*D* Ch. XVI), it is quite possible (providing that she is dead) that they are doing nothing illegal. For though there are numerous laws regulating the burial of bodies in Britain, not least the Burial Act 1857, which makes it an offense to disturb or remove a body without lawful authority, there is no specific offense of corpse desecration with regard to a body, such as that of Lucy Westenra, which has not been buried. This led to some confusion with regard to a 1984 case in which various charges of "criminal damage to a corpse" (a crime unknown to English law) and "public nuisance" (which requires witnesses) were later substituted with a no less specious charge of "mutilating a corpse." See Imogen Jones, "A Grave Offence: Corpse Desecration and the Criminal Law," *Legal Studies* 37, no. 4 (2017): 599–620, at 603. In the case of Van Helsing and Seward, I suggest that the only viable charges the two men might face would be of criminal damage to the tomb itself. The absence of any members of the public precludes a public nuisance charge, as it should have done in the 1984 case.

54 Vivien Allen, *Hall Caine: Portrait of a Victorian Romancer* (Sheffield: Continuum, 1997), 38–39; Richard Storer, "'Beyond 'Hommy-Beg': Hall Caine's Place in *Dracula*," in *Bram Stoker and the Gothic: Formations to Transformations*, ed. Catherine Wynne (Basingstoke: Palgrave Macmillan), 172–84.

55 R. E. Ferner and Sarah E. McDowell, "Doctors Charged with Manslaughter in the Course of Medical Practice, 1795–2005: A Literature Review," *Journal of the Royal Society of Medicine* 99, no. 6 (2006), 309–14, at 310–11.

56 Ferner and McDowell, "Doctors," 312.

Notes to Chapter 2: "Receptive Emotion"? Stoker and Irving—
Collaboration, Hagiography, Self-fashioning   *Rui Carvalho Homem*

Research for this chapter was supported by CETAPS, funded by Fundacão para a Ciência e a Tecnologia(Ref.UID/ELT/04097/2013).

1   Bram Stoker, *Personal Reminiscences of Henry Irving* [1906], rev. ed. (London: Heinemann, 1907), 389.
2   David J. Skal, *Something in the Blood: The Untold Story of Bram Stoker, the Man Who Wrote* Dracula (New York and London: Liveright, 2016), 67.
3   My use of "hagiography" and "hagiographic" in the course of this paper draws on that extended sense of these words that sees them used in connection with "any biography that idealizes or idolizes its subject" (*Collins English Dictionary*)—an extrapolation, of course, of their primary and etymological sense as involving "the writing of the lives of saints" (*Oxford English Dictionary*). This extension, however, is not dismissive or ironical; it acknowledges rather the reverential import of a discourse (Stoker's on Irving) that construes its object as revealing sublime and quasi-supernatural conditions in the deployment of his artistic skills.
4   Stoker, *Reminiscences*, 233.
5   Kevin Corstorphine, "Stoker, Poe, and American Gothic in 'The Squaw'," in *Bram Stoker and the Gothic: Formations to Transformations*, ed. Catherine Wynne (Houndmills: Palgrave Macmillan, 2016), 48–62, at 53.
6   As pointed out by Paul Murray, this wish did not fail to attract the attention of Stoker's contemporaries when the *Reminiscences* were published, as suggested by a review in the *Times Literary Supplement* that was "critical of Stoker's intrusion of his own personality and his 'Grand Ducal' manner"—Paul Murray, *From the Shadow of Dracula: A Life of Bram Stoker*, 2nd ed. (London: Pimlico, 2005), 236. Stoker's aspirations have been rendered largely ironical also by the extent to which posterity has tended to make him secondary to his best-known character: as pointed out by Jarlath Killeen, "Together, Irving and Dracula have continued to edge Stoker out of the picture and have attracted more attention than him in the subsequent century [i.e. following his death]"—Jarlath Killeen, ed., *Bram Stoker: Centenary Essays* (Dublin: Four Courts Press, 2014), 15.
7   Katharine Cockin, "Bram Stoker, Ellen Terry, Pamela Colman Smith and the Art of Devilry," in *Bram Stoker and the Gothic*, ed. Wynne, 159–71, at 163.
8   Adrian Poole, *Shakespeare and the Victorians* (London: Thomson Learning, 2004), 4.
9   Lisa Hopkins, *Bram Stoker: A Literary Life* (Houndmills: Palgrave Macmillan, 2007), 66.
10 Stoker, *Reminiscences*, 215, 217.
11 Stoker, *Reminiscences*, 209.

12   Stoker, *Reminiscences*, 213–14.

13   Stoker, *Reminiscences*, 217.

14   For a recent assessment of the overall significance of Comte's project for a secular religion, see Andrew Wernick, *Auguste Comte and the Religion of Humanity: the Post-Theistic Program of French Social Theory* (Cambridge: Cambridge University Press, 2001), *passim*. For English developments of his intellectual and sociological project, see also Michel Bourdeau, "Auguste Comte," in *The Stanford Encyclopedia of Philosophy*, ed. Edward N. Zalta (Winter 2015 edition), https://plato.stanford.edu/archives/win2015/entries/comte/.

15   Cf. Terence Hawkes, "Swisser-Swatter: making a man of English letters," in *Alternative Shakespeares*, ed. John Drakakis (London: Methuen, 1985), 26–47, at 30–32 and *passim*.

16   Murray, *Shadow*, 88.

17   Stoker, *Reminiscences*, 248.

18   Stoker, *Reminiscences*, 53.

19   Stoker, *Reminiscences*, 67.

20   Stoker, *Reminiscences*, 60.

21   Cited in Richard Foulkes, "The Staging of the Trial Scene in Irving's 'The Merchant of Venice,'" *Educational Theatre Journal* 28, no. 3 (1976): 312–17, at 313; see also Sybil Rosenfeld, *A Short History of Scene Design in Great Britain* (Oxford: Blackwell, 1973), 133–36.

22   Stoker, *Reminiscences*, viii, 113, 245.

23   Stoker, *Reminiscences*, 248.

24   Stoker, *Reminiscences*, 369.

25   Cf. Poole, *Shakespeare and the Victorians*, 27–30.

26   Stoker, *Reminiscences*, 369.

27   Murray, *Shadow*, 56.

28   Catherine Wynne, ed., *Bram Stoker and the Stage: Reviews, Reminiscences, Essays and Fiction*, 2 vols (London: Pickering & Chatto, 2012), I xvii.

29   Poole, *Shakespeare and the Victorians*, 233.

30   Wynne, *Stoker and the Stage*, I 143.

31   I am indebted to Matthew Gibson for kindly sharing transcripts of letters from Dowden to Stoker (with dates ranging from 1879 to 1905), a correspondence that reveals complicity and a pervasive sense of humor.

32   Poole, *Shakespeare and the Victorians*, 207.

33   Edward Dowden, *Shakspere: A Critical Study of His Mind and Art* [London: Henry S. King & Co., 1875] (Cambridge: Cambridge University Press, 2009), 7.

34   Dowden, *Shakspere*, 8.

35   Dowden, *Shakspere*, 23.

36   Dowden, *Shakspere*, 24.

37 Dowden, *Shakspere*, 35.
38 Dowden, *Shakspere*, 40.
39 Skal, *Something in the Blood*, 7.
40 I employ the term in full awareness of its original use by Stephen Greenblatt to characterize the crafting of identities and public personae under the particular historical conditions of early modern aristocratic cultures—Stephen Greenblatt, *Renaissance Self-Fashioning: From More to Shakespeare* (Chicago, Ill: The Univ. of Chicago Press, 1980); but I am also drawing on the considerable conceptual and contextual latitude with which the notion has been critically deployed in more recent years.
41 Skal, *Something in the Blood*, 193.
42 Murray, *Shadow*, 93.
43 A signal example of this comes with the moment when Irving had to make an instant decision, indicative of how "the manager of a theatre must have 'nerve' to do the work entailed by his high responsibility," to interrupt a performance when he noticed that an actor was unfit to perform that evening (apparently—Stoker is not explicit—because he was drunk). The performance was resumed minutes later with an understudy—Stoker, *Reminiscences*, 50–51.
44 In Jonathan Bate, ed., *The Romantics on Shakespeare* (London: Penguin, 1992), 130.
45 Stoker, *Reminiscences*, 244.
46 Stoker, *Reminiscences*, 48.
47 Stoker, *Reminiscences*, 246.
48 Stoker, *Reminiscences*, 252.
49 Stoker, *Reminiscences*, 246, 366.
50 The views expressed by Stoker, arguably prevalent in most nineteenth-century theatrical environments and certainly at the *Lyceum*, reflect an utterly un-Aristotelian (but predominantly Romantic) understanding of the hierarchy of tragic elements. This involves reversing Aristotle's dictum in the *Poetics* that "The plot (…) is the first principle, and, as it were, the soul of a tragedy; Character holds the second place"—but retaining and enhancing, from Aristotle's disquisition, an important stress on the role of "pain" or "suffering" as a component of the plot and a factor towards catharsis—cf. S. H. Butcher, ed., trans., *Aristotle's Theory of Poetry and Fine Art: with a critical text and a translation of the* Poetics (London: Macmillan, 1895), *passim*.
51 Stoker, *Reminiscences*, 49–50. Not all of Stoker's contemporaries shared his enthusiasm for the "passion" with which Irving played Hamlet. As noted by Adrian Poole, it "prompted George Belmore to write a burlesque entitled *Hamlet the Hysterical*"—Poole, *Shakespeare and the Victorians*, 14.
52 Stoker, *Reminiscences*, 49.

53 Wynne, *Stoker and the Stage*, I 233.
54 Wynne, *Stoker and the Stage*, I 258.
55 Wynne, *Stoker and the Stage*, I 271–72.
56 Stoker, *Reminiscences*, 90.
57 Wynne, *Stoker and the Stage*, I x; II ix.
58 Cf. Carol A. Senf, *Bram Stoker* (Cardiff: University of Wales Press, 2010), *passim*; Catherine Wynne, *Bram Stoker, Dracula and the Victorian Gothic Stage* (Houndmills: Palgrave Macmillan, 2013), *passim*; Catherine Wynne, ed., *Bram Stoker and the Gothic: Formations to Transformations* (Houndmills: Palgrave Macmillan, 2016), *passim*.
59 Stoker, *Reminiscences*, 341, 244–59.
60 Stoker, *Reminiscences*, 342.
61 Poole, *Shakespeare and the Victorians*, 20, 40; Hopkins, *Bram Stoker*, 73.
62 Cf. Adam Putz, *The Celtic Revival in Shakespeare's Wake: Appropriation and Cultural Politics in Ireland, 1867-1922* (Houndmills: Palgrave Macmillan, 2013), 123.
63 Stoker, *Reminiscences*, 245 (italics in the original).
64 Stoker, *Reminiscences*, 244.
65 Stoker, *Reminiscences*, 244.
66 Stoker, *Reminiscences*, 245–46.
67 Stoker, *Reminiscences*, 249.
68 Stoker, *Reminiscences*, 247.
69 Stoker, *Reminiscences*, 328.
70 Wynne, *Stoker and the Stage*, I ix.
71 Stoker, *Reminiscences*, 198.
72 Stoker, *Reminiscences*, 179.
73 Bram Stoker, "Dramatic Criticism," *The North American Review* 158, no. 448 (1894): 325–31, at 328.
74 Stoker, *Reminiscences*, 250.
75 Thomas Hood's ballad *The Dream of Eugene Aram* (1831). Irving had also played the central role in W.G. Wills's play *Eugene Aram*, produced at the Lyceum three years earlier (1873). Paul Murray cites Irving's grandson to suggest that the actor's decision to treat Stoker to that particular reading, part of his emotionalistic "stock in trade," would have been "calculated" to make the listener "fall under his spell"—Murray, *Shadow*, 73.
76 Stoker, *Reminiscences*, 20.
77 Stoker, *Reminiscences*, 20. Stoker's pride in his athleticism was probably enhanced by the extent to which it contrasted with his sickly childhood, when he was (under conditions that remain rather enigmatic) virtually confined to bed for several years—cf. Murray, *Shadow*, 24.
78 Cf. William Hughes, "The Un-Death of the Author: The Fictional Afterlife of Bram Stoker," in Wynne, *Bram Stoker and the Gothic*, 207–21, at 209.
79 Stoker, *Reminiscences*, 20–21.

80   Stoker, *Reminiscences*, 17—my emphasis.

81   Stoker, *Reminiscences*, 17.

Notes to Chapter 3: The Impress of the Visual and Scenic Arts on the Fiction of Bram Stoker   *Matthew Gibson*

1   Unpublished letter from J. B. Yeats, dated September 23, 1879. In Brotherton Collection, Leeds.

2   Lisa Hopkins, *Bram Stoker: A Literary Life* (Basingstoke: Palgrave Macmillan, 2007), 58–59.

3   Catherine Wynne, *Bram Stoker, Dracula and the Victorian Gothic Stage* (Basingstoke: Palgrave Macmillan, 2013), 135–37.

4   Stephanie Moss, "Bram Stoker and the London Stage," *Journal of the Fantastic in the Arts* 10 (1999): 124–32, at 128.

5   Bastian Lepage. Two undated letters held at the Brotherton Collection, Leeds.

6   Bram Stoker Archive, Brotherton Collection, Leeds.

7   Bram Stoker, *Reminiscences of Henry Irving* [1906] rev. ed. (New York: Macmillan and Company, 1907), 165.

8   Stoker, *Reminiscences*, 165.

9   Cited in Richard Foulkes, "The Staging of the Trial Scene in Irving's 'The Merchant of Venice," *Educational Theatre Journal* 28, no. 3 (1976): 312–17, at 313. See also Sybil Rosenfeld, *A Short History of Scene Design in Great Britain* (Oxford: Blackwell, 1973), 133–36.

10   Catherine Wynne, ed., *Bram Stoker and the Stage: Reviews, Essays, Reminiscences and Fiction*: I Theatrical Reviews (London: Pickering and Chatto, 2012), I 11 "The Pantomime, Dresses etc"—*Dublin Evening Mail*, 6th January 1872, 3.

11   Wynne, *Stoker and the Stage*, I 44, "Theatre Royal—Pygmalion & Galatea"—*Dublin Evening Mail*, 27th July 1972, 3.

12   Wynne, *Stoker and the Stage*, I 75. "Theatre Royal—Leah"—*Dublin Evening Mail*, 22nd October 1872, 4.

13   Wynne, *Stoker and the Stage*, I 135. "Theatre Royal"—*Dublin Evening Mail*, 13th October 1873, 3.

14   Stoker, *Reminiscences*, 133.

15   W. L. Telbin, "Art in the Theatre," *The Magazine of Arts* 12 (New York, London, Paris: Cassells and Co, 1888–89), 92–97, at 94.

16   Sybil Rosenfeld, *A Short History of British Theatre Design* (London: Rowman and Littlefield, 1973), 122.

17   Wynne, *Stoker and the Stage*, I 35, "Theatre Royal—*The Woman in White*," *Dublin Evening Mail*—8th May 1872, 3.

18   Wolfgang Iser, *The Act of Reading: a Theory of Aesthetic Response* (Baltimore and London: The Johns Hopkins Press, 1978), 21.

19   David Glover, *Vampires, Mummies and Liberals: Bram Stoker and the Politics of Popular Fiction* (Durham, NC, and London: Duke University Press, 1996), 110.

20   John Beddoe, *The Races of Britain: A Contribution to the Anthropology of Western Europe*, with a New Introduction by D. E. Allen [1885] (London: Hutchison, 1971), 102.

21   Bram Stoker, *Famous Impostors* (London: Sturgis and Walton, 1910), 162.

22   Literally "*Solaris et Lunaris est (Matrimonio perpetuo) copulando*"— *Monas Hieroglyphica Ioannis Dee, Londiniensis* (1564), 7.

23   Later in *Famous Impostors* Stoker describes how when Cagliostro "was at work he brought to bear the influence of all his 'properties,' amongst them a tablecloth embroidered with cabalistic signs in scarlet and the symbols of the Rosy Cross of high degree; the same mysterious emblems marked the globe without which no wizard's atelier is complete." Stoker, *Famous Impostors* (London: Sturgis and Walton, 1910), 87.

24   Roger Luckhurst, *The Mummy's Curse: The True Story of a Dark Fantasy* (Oxford: Oxford University Press, 2012), 174.

25   Glover, *Vampires, Mummies and Liberals*, 85.

26   Stoker praises the accuracy of the Assyrian set, based, he presumes, on records from the British Museum. Wynne, *Stoker and the Stage*, I 209–13, at 211. "Theatre Royal—*Sardanapalus*," *Dublin Evening Mail*—25th October 1875, 3.

27   Stoker, *Famous Impostors*, 155–62.

28   *Hegel's Introduction to Aesthetics, being the Introduction to the Berlin Aesthetic Lectures of the 1820s*, trans T. M. Knox (Oxford: Clarendon, 1979), 84.

29   *Hegel's Aesthetics: Lectures on Fine Art*, trans. T. M. Knox, 2 vols (Oxford: Clarendon Press, 1975), II 761–64. It is unlikely that Stoker read Hegel in any great depth, although his ideas, thanks to the likes of Bosanquet and Walter Pater, were beginning to be popularized at this time.

30   Joseph Harker, *Studio and Stage* (London: Nisbet and Co., 1924), Chapter 12, 185–201.

31   Stoker, *Reminiscences*, 171.

32   http://bramstoker.org/pdf/stories/01sunset/06lilies.pdf, accessed November 15, 2017.

33   Carol A. Senf, "Bram Stoker: Ireland and Beyond," in *Bram Stoker: Centenary Essays*, ed. Jarlath Killeen (Dublin: Four Courts Press, 2014), 87–102, at 98.

34   Cf. in *Arcana Coelestia*, Swedenborg's encyclopedia of the correspondences between Holy "Dinners" and "suppers" in the bible and the "consociation by love." *Miscellaneous Theological Works of Emanuel Swedenborg*, trans. Rev. John Whitehead (New York: Swedenborg Foundation, 1951), 142.

35 S. T. Coleridge, *Lectures 1795 on Politics and Religion*, ed. Lewis Patton and Peter Mann (London: Routledge & Kegan Paul; Princeton, NJ: Princeton University Press, 1971), 216–19.

36 The exact language used by Coleridge in Chapter 13 to describe the imagination is "The counteraction then of two assumed forces ... the power which acts in them is indestructible ... the result of these two forces, both alike infinite ... the product must be a *tertium aliquid*, or finite generation."—*Coleridge's Biographia Literaria*, ed. J. Shawcross, repr. (Oxford: Oxford University Press, 1968), I 198. He does not define whether this "*tertium aliquid*" is the primary or secondary imagination in his later rephrasing in this chapter, but it is probably both, as the "Primary IMAGINATION" is "A repetition in the finite mind of the eternal act of creation in the infinite I AM", meaning that the imagination is involved in the act of perception and knowledge from an *a priori* basis, while the secondary is simply the more creative activity of this "differing only in *degree*, and in the *mode* of its operation" (I 202). Debate still rages as to whether Coleridge's imagination is based on the Kantian imagination or is simply the "productive intuition" of Schelling.

37 Immanuel Kant, *Critique of Judgement*, trans. James Creed Meredith (Infomotions LLC, 2000), 55–59. Kant initially discovers this inability of the imagination to find an end in descriptions of the Pyramids and St Peters, and the effect they have on the apprehender, but moves to discussing "magnitude" in nature as well.

38 Kant, *Critique*, 59.

39 Kant, *Critique*, 51.

40 William Wordsworth, "I wandered lonely as a cloud", in *Poems: Wadsworth Handbook and Anthology*, ed. C. F. Main and Peter J. Seng, 3rd ed. (Belmont, CA: Wadsworth, 1973), 23–24, at 24; ll. 11, 20–21.

41 William Gilpin, "Essay I on Picturesque Beauty", in *Five Essays on Picturesque Subjects*, 3rd ed. (London: T. Cadell and W. Davies, 1808), 4, 6.

42 Here there is even a pictorial metaphor to describe the way in which Esse regards her own memories, namely the "nimbus" of a halo, atop the head of a saint in a painting, to show the added charm that memory gives the initial impression.

43 Andrew J. Garavel, "*The Shoulder of Shasta*: Bram Stoker's California Romance", in *Bram Stoker: Centenary Essays*, ed. Killeen, 103–12, at 110.

44 Garavel, "*Shoulder*", 105.

45 The stated aims of the Pre-Raphaelites in 1848, recorded by W. M. Rossetti, were: "1, To have genuine ideas to express; 2, to study Nature attentively, so as to know how to express them; 3, to sympathise with what is direct and serious and heartfelt in previous art, to the exclusion of what is conventional and self-parading and learned by rote; and 4, and most indispensable of all, to produce thoroughly good pictures and statues."

William Michael Rossetti, ed., *Dante Gabriel Rossetti: His Family-Letters, with a Memoir* (London: Ellis, 1895), I 135.

Notes to Chapter 4: "Sure we are all friends here!": Bram Stoker's Ideal of Friendship and Community in the Context of Nineteenth-century Bio-social Thought   *Sabine Lenore Müller*

1   Thomas Hall Caine, "Bram Stoker: The Story of a Great Friendship," *The Daily Telegraph* (April 24, 1912): 16.
2   Caine, "Stoker," 251.
3   Piers Hale, *Political Descent: Malthus, Mutualism, and the Politics of Evolution in Victorian England* (Chicago and London: University of Chicago Press, 2014), 3.
4   William Hughes, *Beyond Dracula: Bram Stoker's Fiction and Its Cultural Context* (London: Palgrave Macmillan, 2000), 1.
5   Hale, *Descent*, 108.
6   Hale, *Descent*, 5.
7   Matt Ridley, *Origins of Virtue: Human Instincts and the Evolution of Cooperation* (London: Penguin, 1998), 5.
8   Hale, *Descent*, 3.
9   Ridley, *Origins*, 4.
10   Ridley, *Origins*, 4.
11   Hale, *Descent*, 10.
12   Hale, *Descent*, 12.
13   Hale, *Descent*, 3.
14   See Carol A. Senf, "*Dracula*, *The Jewel of Seven Stars* and Stoker's 'Burden of the past,'" in *Bram Stoker's Dracula: Sucking through the Past, 1897–1997*, ed. Carole Margaret Davison (Oxford and Toronto: Dundurn Press, 1997), 77–93; Charles S. Blinderman understands Dracula as "Darwinian Superman" in "Vampurella: Darwin and Count Dracula," *The Massachusetts Review* 21, no. 2 (1980): 411–28: Barbara Creed reads Dracula as a "figure of degeneration" in *Darwin's Screens: Evolutionary Aesthetics, Time and Sexual. Display in the Cinema* (Melbourne: Melbourne University Press, 2009), 9. John Glendening reads Dracula as an instance of an evolutionary gothic narrative in that the count is seen as regressively primitive: John Glendening, *The Evolutionary Imagination in Late-Victorian Novels: An Entangled Bank* (Aldershot: Ashgate, 2007).
15   Hale, *Descent*, 12.
16   Hale, *Descent*, 20.
17   Vivien Allen, *Hall Caine. Portrait of a Victorian Romancer* (Sheffield: Sheffield Academic Press, 1997), 62.

18 Allen, *Hall Caine*, 31.

19 Bram Stoker, *Personal Reminiscences of Henry Irving*, 2 vols [1906] rev. ed. (London: William Heinemann, 1907), viii.

20 Hughes, *Beyond Dracula*, 6.

21 Stoker, *Reminiscences*, 21.

22 Hughes, *Beyond Dracula*, 8.

23 Paul Murray, *From the Shadow of Dracula: A Life of Bram Stoker* (London: Pimlico, 2005), 101.

24 Irving "at his manipulative worst." Murray, *Shadow*, 104. Irving had fostered rivalry between Stoker and Louis Frederick Austin, an informal secretary who had read a biting satire against Stoker at a Lyceum Christmas gathering: Murray, *Shadow*, 98.

25 Hall Caine, "Bram Stoker: The Story of a Great Friendship," *The Daily Telegraph*, April 24, 1912, 16.

26 Caine, "Stoker," 16.

27 Michael Kilgariff, "Henry Irving & Bram Stoker: A Working Relationship," *The Irving Society*, November 24, 2015, accessed March 17, 2018, https://www.theirvingsociety.org.uk/henry-irving-bram-stoker-a-working-relationship/.

28 The extent to which the union failed for a legally and economically disenfranchised majority rather than just for a rogue and rebellious dissatisfied few was not widely recognized, to the detriment of the union: "[r]ural poverty was supremely evident in the hundreds of thousands of miserable one-room cabins dotted across the country. Beggars were, as travellers noted consistently, omnipresent," and in absence of any effective reform or political representation the "predictable disorder" resulted in more and more organised forms of mobilization. Hilary Larkin, *A History of Ireland, 1800–1922: Theatres of Disorder?* (New York: Anthem Press, 2014), 27.

29 R. F. Foster, "Indomitable Irishry. From Daniel Maclise to Wilde, Yeats and Shaw, Irish artists and writers took Victorian London by storm – and transformed 20th-century English culture," *The Guardian*, February 26, 2005, accessed June 27, 2018, https://www.theguardian.com/books/2005/feb/26/1.

30 Neil R. Storey, *The Dracula Secrets: Jack the Ripper and the Darkest Sources of Bram Stoker* (Stroud: History Press, 2012), 33.

31 Bram Stoker, "The Necessity for Political Honesty," originally published in *Freeman's Journal and Daily Commercial Advertiser*, Dublin, Ireland, November 14, 1872, from extract, reprinted in Storey, *Dracula Secrets*, 34–37.

32 Stoker, "Necessity," 35–36.

33 Stoker, "Necessity," 37.

34 Stoker, "Necessity," 37.

35 T. R. Malthus, *An Essay on the Principle of Population*, selected and introduced by Donald Winch (Cambridge: Cambridge University Press, 1992), 42.

36 Brian Jenkins, *Fenian Problem: Insurgency and Terrorism in a Liberal State* (Montreal: McGill-Queen's University Press, 2008), 70.

37 Stoker, *Reminiscences*, 18.

38 Carol A. Senf, *Bram Stoker* (Cardiff: University of Wales Press, 2010), 46.

39 Louis S. Warren, *Buffalo Bill's America: William Cody and the Wild West Show* (New York: Alfred A. Knopf, 2005), 313.

40 Thomas H. Huxley, "The Struggle for Existence in Human Society," in *Collected Essays*, 10 vols (London, Macmillan, 1888), IX 199–200.

41 Stoker, "Necessity," 36.

42 Hughes, *Beyond Dracula*, 96.

43 Hughes, *Beyond Dracula*, 96.

44 Peter Kropotkin, *Mutual Aid, A Factor of Evolution* [1904], repr. (Cosimo: New York, 2009), 75.

45 Stephen D. Arata, "The Occidental Tourist. 'Dracula' and the Anxiety of Reverse Colonization," *Victorian Studies* 33, no. 4 (1990): 621–45, at 643.

46 See Jeanne Dubino, "Mad Dogs and Irishmen: Dogs, *Dracula*, and the Colonial Irish Other," in *Animals in Irish Literature and Culture*, ed. Kathryn Kirkpatrick and Borbála Faragó (London: Palgrave Macmillan, 2016), 199–213, for a broad scope of examples of the contradictory readings of Dracula, mentioned above.

47 Dubino, "Mad Dogs," 199.

48 Johan Höglund, "Militarizing the Vampire: Underworld and the Desire of the Military Entertainment Complex," in *Transnational and Postcolonial Vampires: Dark Blood*, ed. Tabish Khair and Johan Höglund (Basingstoke: Palgrave Macmillan, 2012), 173–87, at 178.

49 Michael J. Dennison correctly observes that Dracula is "more a great amorphous power than a character:" *Vampirism: Literary Tropes of Decadence and Entropy* (New York: Peter Lang, 2001), 84.

50 Giorgio Agamben, *Homo Sacer. Of Sovereign Power and Bare Life*, trans. Daniel Heller-Roazen (Stanford, CA: Stanford University Press, 1998).

51 Stoker, *Reminiscences*, 359.

52 Patrick Brantlinger, *Rule of Darkness. British Literature and Imperialism, 1830–1914* (Ithaca: Cornell University Press, 1988), 229.

53 Hale, *Descent*, 218.

54 Van Helsing describes the Dracula "principle" as that which is characterized not so much by any identity but by adaptation: "He learn new social life; new environment of old ways, the politic, the law, the finance, the science, the habit of a new land and a new people who have come to be since he was" (*D* 298).

55 Storey, *Dracula Secrets*, 37.

56   Kropotkin, *Mutual Aid*, 228.
57   Elizabeth Miller, *Bram Stoker's Notes for Dracula* (Jefferson, NC: McFarland, 2008), 278ff.
58   Agamben, *Homo Sacer*, 8.
59   Stoker was well acquainted with rural Ireland and its legal situation and discontents. He had worked for twelve years in the Civil Service in Ireland, and from 1876 to 1878 acted as Inspector of Petty Sessions: Murray, *Shadow*, 44–49.
60   During this time Stoker came in contact with such dysfunctional institutions as the "gombeen man," or "gombeenman" (a compound noun including an anglicisation of the Irish word for debt, "gaimbin").
61   Quoted in Grenfell Morton, *Home Rule and the Irish Question* (London and New York: Routledge, 1980), 97.
62   Allen, *Caine*, 31.
63   Allen, *Caine*, 61ff.
64   Allen, *Caine*, 154.
65   Allen, *Caine*, 160.
66   Bram Stoker, "The Ethics of Hall Caine," in *The Homiletic Review* (New York: Funk & Wagnalls Company, NY, August 1909): 98–102, at 98.
67   Stoker, "Ethics," 100.
68   Stoker, "Ethics," 99.
69   Stoker, "Ethics," 100.
70   Stoker, "Ethics," 101.
71   Not unlike the gombeen man, however, in 1908 Hall Caine had bought up most of the Isle of Man and what he didn't own he held a mortgage over, at one point finding himself in an ugly law suit with a farmer over "the value of straw and manure." Allen, *Caine*, 325.
72   Peter Haining, ed., *Bram Stoker. Midnight Tales* (London: Peter Owen, 2001), 71.
73   Richard English, *Irish Freedom: A History of Nationalism in Ireland* (London: Macmillan, 2006), 211.
74   English, *Irish Freedom*, 210.
75   Sarah J. Butler, *Britain and Its Empire in the Shadow of Rome: The Reception of Rome in Socio-Political Debate from the 1850s to the 1920s* (London and New York: Bloomsbury Academic, 2012), 82.
76   Butler, *Britain*, 83.
77   Quoted in Butler, *Britain*, 82.
78   In Robert J. Havlik, ed., "Bram Stoker's Lecture on Abraham Lincoln," *Irish Studies Review* 10, no. 1 (2002): 5–27.

Notes to Chapter 5: Communication Technologies in Bram Stoker's *Dracula*: Utopian or Dystopian? *Anne Delong*

1 Erika Gottlieb, *Dystopian Fiction East and West: Universe of Terror and Trial* (Montreal: McGill-Queen's University Press, 2001), 8.

2 D. R. Fisher and L. M. Wright, "On Utopias and Dystopias: Toward an Understanding of the Discourse Surrounding the Internet," *Journal of Computer-Mediated Communication* 6, no. 2 (2001): doi:10.1111/j.1083–6101.2001.tb00115.x.

3 Neil Postman, "The Judgment of Thamus," in *Reading Pop Culture: A Portable Anthology*, ed. Jeff Ousbourne, 2nd ed. (New York: Bedford/St. Martin's, 2016), 151–66. In weighing the relative benefits and burdens which technological innovation brings, Postman also quotes Freud's *Civilization and Its Discontents* at length:

> One would like to ask: is there, then, no positive gain in pleasure, no unequivocal increase in my feeling of happiness, if I can, as often as I please, hear the voice of a child of mine who is living hundreds of miles away or if I can learn in the shortest possible time after a friend has reached his destination that he has come through the long and difficult voyage unharmed? Does it mean nothing that medicine has succeeded in enormously reducing infant mortality and the danger of infection for women in childbirth, and, indeed, in considerably lengthening the average life of a civilized man?

Postman then shows how Freud follows up this utopian assessment of technology with some decidedly more dystopian reflections:

> If there had been no railway to conquer distances, my child would never have left his native town and I should need no telephone to hear his voice; if traveling across the ocean by ship had not been introduced, my friend would not have embarked on his sea-voyage and I should not need a cable to relieve my anxiety about him. What is the use of reducing infantile mortality when it is precisely that reduction which imposes the greatest restraint on us in the begetting of children, so that, taken all round, we nevertheless rear no more children than in the days before the reign of hygiene, while at the same time we have created difficult conditions for our sexual life in marriage … . And, finally, what good to us is a long life if it is difficult and barren of joys, and if it is so full of misery that we can only welcome death as a deliverer? (quoted in Postman, "The Judgment," 153–54).

4 Bram Stoker, *Dracula*, ed. Nina Auerbach and David J. Skal (W. W. Norton & Co., 1997), 231, n.4.

5 Isaac Pitman, *Isaac Pitman's shorthand instructor: an exposition of Isaac Pitman's system of phonography. Designed for class or self-instruction* (London: I. Pitman & Sons, 1901), x, viii.

6   Jennifer Wicke, "Vampiric Typewriting: Dracula and Its Media," *ELH* 59, no. 2 (1992): 467–93, at 471.

7   Robert Ready, "Textula," *Journal of Narrative Theory* 40, no. 3 (2010): 275–96, at 283.

8   Wicke, "Typewriting," 471.

9   Pamela Thurschwell, *Literature, Technology, and Magical Thinking, 1880–1920* [electronic resource]. (New York: Cambridge University Press, 2001), 94, 90.

10 Jill Galvan, *The Sympathetic Medium: Feminine Channeling, The Occult, and Communication Technologies, 1859–1919* (Ithaca: Cornell University Press, 2010), 106.

11 Edison's complete list of possible uses includes the following: "1. Letter writing and all kinds of dictation without the aid of a stenographer. 2. Phonographic books, which would speak to blind people without effort on their part. 3. The teaching of elocution. 4. Reproduction of music. 5. The "Family Record"—a registry of sayings, reminiscences, etc., by members of a family, in their own voices, and of the last words of dying persons. 6. Music boxes and toys. 7. Clocks that should announce in articulate speech the time for going home, going to meals, etc. 8. The preservation of languages, by exact reproduction of the manner of pronouncing. 9. Educational purposes; such as preserving the explanations made by a teacher, so that the pupil can refer to them at any moment, and spelling or other lessons placed upon the phonograph for convenience in committing to memory. 10. Connection with the telephone, so as to make that invention an auxiliary in the transmission of permanent and invaluable records, instead of being the recipient of momentary and fleeting communications." Thomas Alva Edison, "The Perfected Phonograph," *The North American Review* 146, no. 379 (1888): 641–50, at 646.

12 Edison, "Phonograph," 649–50.

13 John M. Picker, "The Victorian Aura of the Recorded Voice," *New Literary History* 32, no. 3, (2001): 769–86, at 769.

14 Wicke, "Typewriting," 470–71.

15 Thurschwell, "Literature," 33.

16 Thurschwell, "Literature," 34.

17 Other instances of children being casually sacrificed include the bagged baby that Dracula tosses to his "wives" and the random children that Van Helsing and Seward leave for the police to find.

18 Leah Richards, "Mass Production and the Spread of Information in Dracula: 'Proofs of so Wild a Story,'" *English Literature in Transition 1880–1920* 52, no. 4 (2009): 440–57, at 441.

19 Galvan, *Sympathetic Medium*, 82–83.

20 Wicke, "Typewriting," 476.

21 *Belfast News-Letter*, July 1, 1897, in Bram Stoker, *Dracula* (New York: Longman, 2011), 393.
22 *The Bookman* (London), August 1897: "Novel Notes: 'Dracula,'" in Stoker, *Dracula*, 394.
23 *Pall Mall Gazette* (London), June 1, 1897: "For Midnight Reading" in Stoker, *Dracula*, 402.
24 Richards "Mass Production," 440.
25 Richards, "Mass Production," 443, 442.
26 Gottlieb, *Dystopian*, 12.
27 Christine Ferguson, "Nonstandard Language and the Cultural Stakes of Stoker's 'Dracula,'" *ELH* 71, no. 1 (2004): 229–49, at 243.
28 The excised description of the implosion of Castle Dracula reads as follows:

As we looked there came a terrible convulsion of the earth so that we seemed to rock to and fro and fell to our knees. At the same moment, with a roar which seemed to shake the very heavens, the whole castle and the rock and even the hill on which it stood seemed to rise into the air and scatter in fragments while a mighty cloud of black and yellow smoke volume on volume in rolling grandeur was shot upwards with inconceivable rapidity. Then there was a stillness in nature as the echoes of that thunderous report seemed to come as with the hollow boom of a thunder clap—the long reverberating roll which seems as though the floors of heaven shook. Then down in a mighty ruin falling whence they rose [shot?] the fragments that had been tossed skywards in the cataclysm.

From where we stood it seemed as though the one fierce volcano burst had satisfied the need of nature and that the castle and the structure of the hill had sank again into the void. We were so appalled with the suddenness and the grandeur that we forgot to think of ourselves. (quoted in Stoker, *Dracula*, ed. Auerbach and Skal, 325, n.5)

Notes to Chapter 6: Tracking the Unruly Cadaver: *Dracula* and Victorian Coroners' Reports   *Rebecca E. May*

1 I follow in the footsteps of Carol A. Senf and Christopher Craft in using Crew of Light as shorthand for the group of vampire-fighters including Harker, Seward, Van Helsing, Morris, Holmwood, and to a lesser extent Mina, Lucy early on, and Renfield. Carol A. Senf, "Gothic Monster versus Modern Science," in *Science and Social Science in Bram Stoker's Fiction* (Westport, CT: Greenwood, 2002), 18 and Christopher Craft, "Gender and Inversion in *Dracula*," in *Dracula: The Vampire and the Critics*, ed. Margaret L. Carter (Ann Arbor: University of Michigan Research Press, 1988).

2   Ian Burney, *Bodies of Evidence: Medicine and the Politics of the English Inquest, 1830–1926* (Baltimore, MD: Johns Hopkins University Press, 2000). Burney exhaustively tracks inquest reform efforts and the increasing self-contained medicalization and institutionalization of deaths "to secure the integrity of the nation's vital statistics" (69). In the last quarter of the nineteenth century lax certification creates an anxiety that the nation, as it were, does not really know what is killing its citizens. This lack of knowledge is incompatible with public health movements and sanitarian agendas. Thus, there is a shift in the period from the inquest as a local moral lesson to the inquest as contributing to a set of national statistics. Early on, "[t]he corpse was ideally an object lesson, decoded and delivered to the public who, in turn, were to subject themselves to the knowledge inherent in the lesson. According to this model of death inquiry, inquests were valuable not merely (or indeed even mainly) at the level of literal policing. Instead, the inquest's proper remit was at the same time to enact a searching investigation in public to deter would-be criminals, to translate death into a public lesson in mortality, and to defuse anxieties that a death was something other than natural" (59). Above all, Burney isolates a handful of persistent issues: what should be done with uncertified deaths; how should deaths be both certified and registered; how can officials navigate "the tension between the body as scientific and as public object" (79) and respect a deceased's family's privacy; how to shelter remains to prevent the spread of infection and to promote decency; and where to hold inquests, as the local pub continued to be a common place where inquests were held well into the twentieth century. Dedicated mortuaries and inquest courts were being built across America and the United Kingdom, but this was an ongoing project.
3   Frederick W. Lowndes, *Reasons why the office of coroner should be held by a member of the medical profession* (London, 1892), 8–9.
4   Lowndes, *Reasons*, 9–10.
5   John B. Carey, *The Oddities of Short-Hand, or the coroner and his friends* (New York: Excelsior, 1891), 15.
6   Carey, *Oddities*, 15.
7   Jennifer Wicke argues that mass media is vampiric in her essay, pointing out that Lucy circulates in the public's bloodstream via the popular press as the Bloofer Lady, vamping them through narrative. Jennifer Wicke, "Vampiric Typewriting: *Dracula* and Its Media," *ELH* 59, no. 2 (1992): 467–93.
8   Allegheny County, Pa. Coroner's Office Records, 1884–1976, AIS.1982.07, Archives and Special Collections, University of Pittsburgh Library System. All references are included with kind permission from the staff of the Archives and Special Collections.

9   Contents of case files vary widely, yet in reviewing files from the United
     Kingdom and America it is clear that the kinds of document found
     in files are the same, thus enabling the transatlantic archival approach
     I employ here. In the United Kingdom, Rudolph Melsheimer, esq.
     writes that an inquisition "may be written or printed, or partly written
     or printed, and may be in the form contained in the Second Schedule
     to this Act, or to the like effect, or in such other form as the Lord
     Chancellor from time to time prescribes ... . It is not imperative that
     this form be followed exactly." Rudolph E. Melsheimer, *The Coroners
     Acts, 1887 and 1892, with Forms and Precedents* (London: Sweet and
     Maxwell, 1898), 81–82. Stateside, in an archive in Mahoning County,
     Ohio, I noted more use of preprinted forms in the case files, though
     they were still by no means standard or regular. Guy St-Denis further
     affirms the variability of documents in his essay "The London District
     and Middlesex County, Ontario, Coroner's Inquests 1831–1900," *Studies
     in Documents Archivaria* 31 (1990–91): 142–53. He writes, "[w]hile
     there can be a great variance in the number of papers in each inquest
     file, there are three basic types which are usually found to be extant:
     the witness' information or depositions, the *postmortem* report, and the
     verdict. The witnesses' information are transcripts of verbal evidence
     presented to the jury, which were written down by the coroner during
     the inquest." Guy St-Denis, "London," 144. His essay also includes
     photographs of representative documents. I also noted the prevalence
     of witness reports, postmortem reports, and verdicts in the Allegheny
     County and Mahoning County files.
10   Elizabeth T. Hurren, "Remaking the Medico-Legal Scene: A Social
     History of the Late-Victorian Coroner in Oxford," *Journal of the History
     of Medicine and Allied Sciences* 65, no. 2 (2010): 207–52.
11   Hurren, "Remaking," 237–38.
12   Burney, *Bodies*, 70.
13   Allegheny County, PA, Coroner's Office Records.
14   Allegheny County, PA, Coroner's Office Records.
15   John G. Lee, M.D., *Handbook for Coroners* (Philadelphia, 1881), 44.
16   Allegheny County, PA, Coroner's Office Records.
17   Allegheny County, PA, Coroner's Office Records.
18   Lee, *Handbook*, 60.
19   Henry O. Marcy, M.D., "The Coroner System in the US," *The Journal of
     the American Medical Association* 27, no. 8 (1891): 382.
20   Marcy, "Coroner," 384.
21   Ian Burney, "Viewing Bodies: Medicine, Public Order, and English
     Inquest Practice," *Configurations* 2, no. 1 (1994): 41.
22   Burney, *Viewing*, 42.

23   See Terry Hale's essay in this collection. Hale helpfully assesses the Crew of Light's suspect behaviors in relation to contemporary law and cases with which Stoker would have been familiar.

24   Wicke, "Vampiric Typewriting."

25   Carol A. Senf, "*Dracula*: The Unseen Face in the Mirror," *The Journal of Narrative Technique* 9, no. 3 (1979): 160–70; Stephen Arata, "The Occidental Tourist: *Dracula* and the Anxiety of Reverse Colonization," *Victorian Studies* 33, no. 4 (1990): 627–34; Nicholas Daly, "Incorporated Bodies: *Dracula* and the Rise of Professionalism," *Texas Studies in Literature and Language* 39, no. 2 (1997): 181–203.

26   Caroline Levine, "Strategic Formalism: Toward a New Method in Cultural Studies," *Victorian Studies* 48, no. 4 (2006): 626–57, at 632.

27   Levine, "Strategic Formalism," 635.

Notes to Chapter 7: Bram Stoker, Geopolitics, and War   *Jimmie E. Cain*

1   Stuart Murray, *Rudyard Kipling in Vermont: Birthplace of the Jungle Books* (Bennington, VT: Images from the Past, 1997), 7; Martin Seymour-Smith, *Rudyard Kipling* (New York: St. Martin's Press, 1989), 226.

2   Paul Murray, *From the Shadow of Dracula: A Life of Bram Stoker*, 2nd ed. (London: Pimlico, 2005), 127, 129.

3   Harry Ludlam, *A Biography of Dracula: The Life of Bram Stoker* (London: Fireside Press, 1962), 90.

4   Murray, *Shadow*, 190.

5   Barbara Belford, *Bram Stoker: A Biography of the Author of* Dracula (New York: Alfred A. Knopf, 1996), 178, 203, and 275.

6   David Gilmour, *The Long Recessional: The Imperial Life of Rudyard Kipling* (London: Pimlico, 2003), 11.

7   Angus Wilson, *The Strange Ride of Rudyard Kipling* (New York: Viking Press, 1978), 43.

8   Karl E. Meyer and Shareen Blair Brysac, *Tournament of Shadows: The Great Game and the Race for Empire in Central Asia* (Washington, D.C.: Counterpoint, 1999), xxiii.

9   Stoker, "The Necessity for Political Honesty," in *Bram Stoker's A Glimpse of America and Other Lectures, Interviews and Essays*, ed. Richard Dalby (Westcliff-on-Sea: Desert Island Books Limited, 2002), 39.

10   Stephen D. Arata, "The Occidental Tourist: Dracula and the Anxiety of Reverse Colonization," *Victorian Studies* 33, no. 4 (1990): 621–45, at 625.

11   Patrick Brantlinger, *Rule of Darkness: British Literature and Imperialism, 1830–1914* (Ithaca, NY: Cornell University Press, 1988), 229.

12 Belford, *Stoker*, 16.

13 Murray, *Shadow*, 10–11.

14 Ludlam, *Biography*, 48.

15 Belford, *Stoker*, 83–84.

16 Belford, *Stoker*, 130–31.

17 Belford, *Stoker*, 232.

18 Bram Stoker, *Personal Reminiscences of Henry Irving* [1906], rev. ed. (London: William Heinemann, 1907), 143.

19 Stoker, *Reminiscences*, 61.

20 Belford, *Stoker*, 128.

21 John Howes Gleason, *The Genesis of Russophobia in Great Britain: A Study of the Interaction of Policy and Opinion* (New York: Octagon, 1972), 1.

22 Stoker, *Reminiscences*, 238.

23 Stoker, *Reminiscences*, 238.

24 Stoker, *Reminiscences*, 276.

25 Stoker, *Reminiscences*, 277–78.

26 Gleason, *Genesis*, 174.

27 Hugh Small, *Florence Nightingale: Avenging Angel* (New York: St. Martin's, 1998), 45–46.

28 Karl Marx, *The Eastern Question: A Reprint of Letters Written 1853–1856 Dealing with Events of the Crimean War*, ed. Eleanor Marx Aveling and Edward Aveling (New York: Burt Franklin, 1968), 19.

29 Eva H. Haraszti, *Kossuth as an English Journalist* (Boulder, CO: Social Science Monographs, 1990), 11.

30 Matthew Paul Lalumia, *Realism and Politics in Victorian Art of the Crimean War* (Ann Arbor, MI: UMI Research Press, 1984), 136.

31 Nicholas Bentley, *Russell's Despatches from the Crimean War* (New York: Hill and Wang, 1966), 11.

32 Colin Holmes, *Anti-Semitism in British Society, 1876–1939* (New York: Holmes & Meier, 1979), 3–6.

33 Quoted in Holmes, *Anti-Semitism*, 38.

34 Quoted in Holmes, *Anti-Semitism*, 40.

35 Quoted in Holmes, *Anti-Semitism*, 47.

36 Sander Gilman, "'I'm Down on Whores': Race and Gender in Victorian London," in *Anatomy of Racism*, ed. David Theo Goldberg (Minneapolis, MN: University of Minnesota Press, 1990), 150.

37 Bram Stoker, "Dracula's Guest," (*D* 352–62).

38 Elizabeth Miller and Robert Eighteen-Bisang, *Bram Stoker's Notes for Dracula: A Facsimile Edition* (Jefferson, NC: McFarland, 2008), 175.

39 Matthew Gibson, *Dracula and the Eastern Question: British and French Vampire Narratives of the Nineteenth-Century Near East* (New York: Palgrave MacMillan, 2006), 71.

40 Bram Stoker, *Dracula. The Essential Dracula: The Definitive Annotated Edition of Bram Stoker's Classic Novel*, ed. Leonard Wolf (New York: Plume, 1993), 38.

41 Aminius Vambery, *The Coming Struggle for India* (London: Cassell, 1885), 4–5.

42 William Spottiswoode, *A Tarantasse Journey through Eastern Russia in the Autumn of 1856* (London: Longman, Brown, Green, Longmans, & Roberts, 1857), 23.

43 Spottiswoode, *Tarantasse*, 30.

44 Richard Wasson, "The Politics of *Dracula*," in *Dracula: The Vampire and the Critics*, ed. Margaret L. Carter (Ann Arbor, MI: UMI Research Press, 1988), 19.

45 Devendra P. Varma, "Dracula's Voyage: From Pontus to Hellespontus," in *Dracula: The Vampire and the Critics*, ed. Carter, 208.

46 Belford, *Stoker*, 223–24.

47 Bernard Pares, *A History of Russia*, rev. ed. (London: Jonathan Cape, 1947), 234.

48 Quoted in Holmes, *Anti-Semitism*, 40.

49 David Glover, "Bram Stoker and the Crisis of the Liberal Subject," *New Literary History* 23, no. 4 (1992): 983–1002, at 990.

50 George L. Mosse, *Nationalism and Sexuality: Respectability and Abnormal Sexuality in Modern Europe* (New York: Howard Fertig, 1985), 11.

51 Jules Zanger, "A Sympathetic Vibration: Dracula and the Jews," *English Literature in Transition* 34, no. 1 (1991): 32–44, at 40.

52 Judith Halberstam, "Parasites and Perverts: Anti-Semitism and Sexuality in Nineteenth Century Gothic Fiction" (PhD diss., University of Minnesota, 1991), 132.

53 Halberstam, "Parasites," 122.

54 Malcolm Smith, "*Dracula* and the Victorian Frame of Mind," in *Empire, Politics and Popular Culture: Essays in Eighteenth and Nineteenth Century British History*, ed. C. C. Eldridge, Trivium 24 (Lampeter, 1989): 77–97, at 93.

55 Anne Cranny-Francis, "Sexual Politics and Political Repression in Bram Stoker's *Dracula*," in *Nineteenth-Century Suspense*, ed. Clive Bloom, Brian Docherty, Jane Gibb, and Keith Shand (New York: St. Martin's, 1988), 76.

56 Burton Hatlen, "The Return of the Repressed/Oppressed in Bram Stoker's *Dracula*," in *Dracula: The Vampire and the Critics*, ed. Carter, 125.

57 Smith, *Dracula*, 93.

58 Arata, *Anxiety*, 641.

59 H. C. G. Matthew, "The Liberal Age (1851–1914)," in *The Oxford Illustrated History of Britain*, ed. Kenneth O. Morgan (Oxford: Oxford UP, 1989), 518–19.

60 Barbara Jelavich, *History of the Balkans: Eighteenth and Nineteenth Centuries*, 2 vols (Cambridge: Cambridge University Press, 1995), II 95–97.

61 Victor Sage, "Exchanging Fantasies: Sex and the Serbian Crisis in *The Lady of the Shroud*," in *Bram Stoker: History, Psychoanalysis, and the Gothic*, ed. William Hughes and Andrew Smith (London: Macmillan Press, 1998), 132.

62 Peter Hopkirk, *The Great Game: The Struggle for Empire in Central Asia* (New York: Kodansha International, 1994), 514.

63 Hopkirk, *Great Game*, 521–22.

64 Stoker, *Reminiscences*, 349.

65 William Hughes, ed., *The Lady of the Shroud* (Westcliff-on-Sea: Desert Island Books, 2001), 336.

66 Sage, "Exchanging Fantasies," 130.

67 Sage, "Exchanging Fantasies," 142.

68 Belford, *Stoker*, 40.

69 Murray, *Shadow*, 148. Of additional interest, Elizabeth Miller has suggested that Stoker might well have based Dr. Seward in *Dracula* after William H. Seward, Lincoln's secretary of state. Miller writes: "considering that Stoker was working on early drafts of *Dracula* during the 1890s while he was still delivering his Lincoln lecture, maybe this Seward (mentioned three times in the lecture) gave Stoker the idea for the name of Dr. John." Elizabeth Miller, "Obama, Lincoln, and—Bram Stoker," *Dracula's Homepage* (blog), January 17, 2009, accessed February 28, 2014, http://www.mun.ca/~emiller.

70 Belford, *Stoker*, 190.

71 Stoker, *A Glimpse of America*, 19.

72 Belford, *Stoker*, 296.

73 Belford, *Stoker*, 255.

74 Carol Senf, "Reflections on the American Character," *English Literature in Transition, 1880–1920* 59, no. 3 (2016): 303–19, at 305.

75 Andrew Smith, "Bram Stoker's *The Mystery of the Sea*: Ireland and the Spanish-Cuban-American War," *Irish Studies Review* 6, no. 2 (1998), 131–38, at 136, 137.

76 William Hughes, *Beyond Dracula: Bram Stoker's Fiction and Its Cultural Context* (New York: Palgrave, 2000), 55 and 76.

77 Stoker, *A Glimpse of America*, 19.

78 Hughes, *Beyond Dracula*, 56.

79 Lisa Hopkins, *Bram Stoker: A Literary Life* (Basingstoke: Palgrave Macmillan, 2007), 126, 104.

80 Senf, "Reflections," 314.

81 Senf, "Reflections," 315, 316.

82 Ailise Bulfin, "The Fiction of Gothic Egypt and British Imperial Paranoia: The Curse of the Suez Canal," *English Literature in Translation, 1880-1920* 54, no. 4 (2011): 413 and 415.

83 David J. Skal, *Something in the Blood* (New York: Liveright Publishing Company, 2016), xvi, 495.

Notes to Chapter 8: Black Eyes, White Skin: An Aristocratic or Royal Type in Bram Stoker's Writings   *Damian Shaw*

1 For comprehensive exploration of the Egyptian Gothic, see Roger Luckhurst, *The Mummy's Curse: The True History of a Dark Fantasy* (Oxford: Oxford University Press, 2012), and Ailise Bulfin, "The Fiction of Gothic Egypt and British Imperial Paranoia: The Curse of the Suez Canal," *English Literature in Transition* 54, no. 4 (2011): 411-43.

2 David Glover, *Vampires, Mummies and Liberals: Bram Stoker and the Politics of Popular Fiction* (Durham, NC, and London: Duke University Press, 1996), 98.

3 William Hughes, *Beyond Dracula: Bram Stoker's Fiction and its Cultural Context* (Basingstoke: Palgrave Macmillan, 2000), 178.

4 Paul Murray, *From the Shadow of Dracula: A Life of Bram Stoker*, 2nd ed. (London: Pimlico, 2005), 20.

5 See Glover, *Vampires*, 11, 23.

6 See Glover, *Vampires*, 5.

7 Andrzej Olechnowicz, "Historians and the modern British Monarchy," in *The Monarchy and the British Nation, 1780 to the Present*, ed. Andrzej Olechnowicz (Cambridge: Cambridge University Press, 2007), 6-44, at 40.

8 Quoted in Olechnowicz, "Historians," 40.

9 Glover, *Vampires*, 27.

10 Jonathan Parry, *The Politics of Patriotism: English Liberalism, National Identity and Europe, 1830-1886* (Cambridge: Cambridge University Press, 2006), 70.

11 Susie L. Steinbach, *Understanding the Victorians: Politics, Culture and Society in Nineteenth-Century Britain*, repr. (Oxford: Routledge, 2017), 61. See Antony Taylor, *Lords of Misrule: Hostility to Aristocracy in Late-Nineteenth and Early-Twentieth Century Britain* (Basingstoke: Palgrave Macmillan, 2005), for further background.

12 Clearly, Stoker describes the scores of Henry Irving's aristocratic and royal acquaintances in glowing terms in *Personal Reminiscences of Henry Irving* [1906], rev. ed. (London: Heinemann, 1907).

13 Carol A. Senf, *Science and Social Science in Bram Stoker's Fiction* (Westport, CT: Greenwood Press, 2000), 27.

14 Bram Stoker, *A Glimpse of America: A Lecture Given at the London Institution, 29ᵗʰ December, 1855* (London: Sampson Low, Marston & Co., 1886), 47–48.

15 Stoker's elder brother Sir William Thornley received a baronetcy in 1911. See Glover, *Vampires*, 10. Paul Murray comments how "Thornley recreated himself as an eighteenth-century grandee on the basis of his self-made, middle-class income." Murray, *From the Shadow of Dracula: a Life of Bram Stoker* (London: Pimlico, 2004), 143. This pattern, as we will see, is copied by many of Stoker's heroes.

16 For More on John Beddoe's conceptualisation of the "black Irish," see Theodore Koditschek, *Liberalism, Imperialism and the Historical Imagination: Nineteenth-Century Visions of a Greater Britain* (Cambridge: Cambridge University Press, 2011), 327.

17 Naturally, Miss Esse has "brown skin" (*SoS* 109).

18 Marjory is also contrasted with the eldritch, seer-witch Gormala, a Gaelic speaker whose great eyes "blaze" (*TMS* 18) and who is "aquiline-featured" (*TMS* 11). When Gormala eventually comes to Marjory's assistance, however, her inner nobility is shown, and she is described as the "type of noble old womanhood" (*TMS* 312).

19 The phrases are taken from Stoker (*TMS* 147).

20 Hughes, *Beyond Dracula*, 80. In *Reminiscences*, Stoker describes his idol Henry Irving as "a patrician figure" (vol. I, 3), and claims that his "real" character as a gentleman was one of "gallantry" and "chivalry" (vol. I, 5).

21 Don Bernardino himself says that "the noblest of the old families [in Spain] had some black blood in them," but that this was not seen as a "taint" (*TMS* 247).

22 Sibylle Baumbach, *Shakespeare and the art of Physiognomy* (Penrith: Humanities-Ebooks, LLP, 2008), 77–78. Compare the "raven black" eyes in Shakespeare's sonnet 127.

23 "Medusa, … might be termed Laura's death aspect." Mark Musa and Barbara Manfredi, "Introduction," in *Petrarch: Canzone or Rerum Bulgarium Fragmentum*, translated with notes by Mark Musa (Bloomington: Indiana University Press, 1996), xi–xxxvii, xx.

24 See Shakespeare, Sonnets 127, line 9, 130, line 2, and 139, line 14.

25 Graeme Tytler, *Physiognomy in the European Novel. Faces and Fortunes* (Princeton: Princeton University Press, 1982), 212.

26 Glover, *Vampires*, 72. There is documented evidence that Stoker owned a copy of Lavatar's work. See Senf, *Science*, 6. The physiognomists Lombroso and Ferrero claimed in *The Female Offender* that "dark colour of the eye" was most commonly found in female "prostitutes and thieves," yet Stoker's black-eyed women are most often chaste and virtuous. C. Lombroso and W. Ferrero, *The Female Offender* (New York: D. Appleton and Company, 1898), 71.

27 J. C. Lavatar, *Physiognomy; or, The Corresponding Analogy Between The Conformation Of The Features And The Ruling Passions Of The Mind* (London: T. Tegg, 1827), 66. Stoker extols both Paracelsus and Dr Dee in *Famous Imposters*. See Senf, *Science*, 69.

28 Lavatar, *Physiognomy*, 62–63.

29 With reference to occult power and eyes, see Luckhurst, *Mummy's Curse*, 209–14.

30 Roger Luckhurst, ed., *Dracula* (1897), (Oxford: Oxford World's Classics, Oxford, 2011).

31 Clive Leatherdale, ed., *The Jewel of Seven Stars* (Westcliff-on-Sea: Desert Island Books, 1996), 12, n. 4.

32 Kate Hebblethwaite, "Introduction" (*JSS*, xi–xxxviii, xx).

33 In *Famous Imposters*, Stoker says that John Dee, whom he praises, was descended from royalty, such as Roderick the Great, Prince of Wales. But "[t]he world cared then about such things almost as little as it does now; or, allowing for the weakness of human beings in the way of their own self-importance, it might be better to say as it professes to do now," (New York: Sturgis & Walton Company, 1910), 156. The implication is that strong human beings who are not self-important might value the aristocracy.

34 In the *Lady of the Shroud*, the hero is, indeed, made king after marrying a real queen, but I shall return to this later.

35 Her tomb was discovered in 1902. See Luckhurst, *Mummy's Curse*, 173–75.

36 Jasmine Day, *The Mummy's Curse: Mummymania in the English-speaking World* (Oxford: Routledge, 2006), 4. Roger Luckhurst also explores these narratives at length in his book *The Mummy's Curse*.

37 Day, *Mummy's Curse*, 8, 20.

38 Concerning "Dracula's" deviancy, see Matthew Gibson, *Dracula and the Eastern Question: British and French Vampire Narratives of the Nineteenth-Century Near East* (London: Palgrave-Macmillan, 2006), 95.

39 Lucy Westenra, as a vampire, is compared to Medusa in Stoker, *Dracula*, 86. For a discussion of Shakespeare's Cleopatra as "a new gorgon," see Baumbach, *Shakespeare and Physiognomy*, 137–43.

40 Tera, for instance, is described as "a white still figure, which looked like an ivory statue" (*JSS* 239).

41 In an alternative reading, Byron asserts that the storm might possibly be "working for, not against Tera." Glennis Byron, "Bram Stoker's Gothic and the Resources of Science," *Critical Survey* 19, no. 2 (2007): 48–62, 59.

42 Glover maintains that Margaret is "sacrificed so that the queen might live," *Vampires*, 88.

43 Bram Stoker, *Famous Imposters* (New York: Sturgis & Walton Company, 1910), 345. The context is the story of "The Bisley Boy," a local tradition which holds that Elizabeth I may have been a man.

44 For instance Hebblethwaite, "Introduction," xxv, and Glover, *Vampires*, 85 and footnote 62.

45 In this case, Ross might be read as an inappropriate Kallikrates, perhaps unwilling to bend to female power.

46 For the threat posed by Ayesha see Gail Turley Houston, *Royalties: The Queen and Victorian Writers* (Charlottesville: University of Virginia Press, 1999), 75, and Luckhurst, *Mummy's Curse*, 189.

47 The view of *She* as an "extended fantasy" is proposed by Thomas Richards, *The Commodity Culture of Victorian England: Advertising and Spectacle, 1851–1914* (Stanford: Stanford University Press, 1990), 117.

48 The coin reads: "Victoria Reg Dei Gra," and on the reverse: "Britt Minerva Victrix Fid Def," or "Victoria, queen by the grace of God" and "Brittania, Minerva, Conqueror, defender of the faith."

49 Stoker praises Queen Victoria in *Reminiscences* as "the great Queen," 340.

50 See Luckhurst, *Mummy's Curse*, 175.

51 In the 1912 version of the novel, which may or may not have been written by Stoker, the storm is not mentioned, Tera vanishes, and all that remains of the mummy is "impalpable dust" (*Appendix*, 250). Ross says that he "was sorry she could not have waked into a new life in a new world" (ibid.), which shows positive support for her. Ross and Margaret are happily married, as in a fairy tale. In this version, therefore, Margaret is ultimately able to resist the influence of Tera, though Tera is ultimately portrayed as a positive, if tragic, character.

52 *The Man* was republished in America in 1908 as Bram Stoker, *The Gates of Life* (New York: Couples and Leon Company), 1908. I quote from this text.

53 In the novel, Stephen's eyes are also described as "black diamonds" (*GoL* 294), perhaps anticipating the stars in Teuta's eyes in *The Lady of the Shroud*. Henry Irving's eyes could "flash like lurid fire," Stoker, *Reminiscences*, 90.

54 And Marjory Drake in *The Mystery of the Sea* prefigures these characters.

55 Bram Stoker, *Lady Athlyne* (New York: Paul R. Reynolds, 1908), chapter 10. Lord Athlyne's noble family can be traced back to twelfth-century Ireland, but is threatened with extinction as all his potential partners in England have become married while he was fighting at the front. See Glover, *Vampires*, 133 (my paraphrase).

56 For the sexual signification, see Hughes, *Beyond Dracula*, 121.

57 Stoker, *Lady Athlyne*, chapters 2, 12, 14.

58 Glover, *Vampires*, 134.

59 In *Lady Athlyne*, the "undeserving" upstarts are a "new order of 'South African Millionaires' … who by their wealth and extravagance had set at defiance the old order of social caste" and change "the whole scheme of existing values." See Glover, *Vampires*, 133.

60   The countess, Genevieve Ward, was an American-born artiste who married a European aristocrat. In 1906 Stoker described her as possessing "a rich dark beauty" with "great eyes that now and again flashed fire" (See Catherine Wynne, *Bram Stoker, Dracula and the Victorian Stage* (Hound-smills: Palgrave Macmillan, 2013), 109). Stoker notes that he had only seen two other people with this gift apart from Ward: "a great stage gift which is not given to many: her eyes can blaze." Stoker, *Reminiscences*, 352.

61   Anthony Hope, *The Prisoner of Zenda* (Bristol: J. W. Arrowsmith, 1894), 4, 3.

62   Anthony Hope, *Rupert of Hentzau* (Bristol & London: J. W. Arrowsmith, 1898), 228.

63   See Hope, *Zenda*, 83–84.

64   Edward VII was similarly popular, though he had a reputation as a "good-humoured playboy and philanderer" (Nalini Ghuman, *Resonances of the Raj: India in the English Musical Imagination, 1897–1947* (Oxford: Oxford University Press, 2014), 185), whereas Rupert Saint Leger (and Rudolf Rassendyll) behave with the utmost sexual propriety.

65   In Anthony Hope's novel *Sophy of Kravonia* (London: Harper & Brothers, 1905), the unassuming Sophy Grouch, daughter of an insignificant English farmer, Enoch Grouch, is, indeed, elevated to the throne of Kravonia and is shown to have great nobility of spirit.

66   In Senf's words, the novel shows the triumph of Western civilization: "white men over black men, dynamite over dinosaurs, the scientific middle class over remnants of the aristocracy, men's women over women alone," *Science*, 120.

67   I think this is a more accurate characterization than Senf's, who claims that Salton is "definitely middle class," *Science*, 120.

68   Senf notes how this elimination of "traditional forms of family power … opens up England to the positive contributions of the colonies, at least where Adam and Mimi are concerned." Carol Senf, "Bram Stoker's *The Lair of the White Worm*: Supernatural Representations and Nineteenth-Century Paleontology," *Supernatural Studies* 2, no. 2 (2015): 48–58, at 54.

69   Jimmie E. Cain Jr, *Bram Stoker and Russophobia: Evidence of the British Fear of Russia in* Dracula *and* The Lady of the Shroud (Jefferson: McFarland & Company, 2006), 129.

70   Clive Leatherdale, *Dracula: The Novel & the Legend: a Study of Bram Stoker's Gothic Masterpiece* (Wellingborough: Aquarian Press, 1985), 217. Qtd in Cain, *Russophobia*, 128.

71   David Punter, *The Literature of Terror. A History of Gothic Fictions from 1765 to the Present Day. Volume 2. The Modern Gothic* (London: Routledge, 2013), 17.

72 David Cannadine, *The Decline and Fall of the British Aristocracy* (New York: Vintage Books, 1999), 1.
73 Senf, *Science*, 25.
74 Leatherdale, *Jewel of Seven Stars*, 72, n. 2.

Notes to Chapter 9: Bram Stoker's Ambivalent Response to the Frontier and the American Frontiersman   Carol Senf

1 Robert J. Havlik comments on these lectures in Robert J. Havlik, "Bram Stoker's Lecture on Abraham Lincoln," *Irish Studies Review* 10, no. 1 (2002): 5–27.

   Later on the tour, through several acquaintances of Irving, Stoker and Irving were able to subscribe to a new edition of the Volk life casts of Lincoln's face and hands made by Augustus Saint-Gaudens. Marginal notes in the manuscript indicate that Stoker subsequently took these casts with him during his lectures.

   Stoker continued to present his lectures in America during the tours of 1886 and 1887. By the end of 1887, however, the American lecture series had run its course. (7)

   That Stoker valued these life casts is evident in the fact that they remained in Stoker's possession even when he and Florence began to downsize their household. They were sold by Sotheby's after Stoker's death.

2 Andrew Smith, "Demonising the Americans: Bram Stoker's Postcolonial Gothic," *Gothic Studies* 5, no. 2 (2003): 20–31.

3 James R. Simmons, "'If America Goes on Breeding Men Like That'": *Dracula*'s Quincey Morris Problematized," *Journal of the Fantastic in the Arts* 12, no. 4 (48) (2002): 425–36.

4 Louis S. Warren, "Buffalo Bill Meets Dracula: William F. Cody, Bram Stoker, and the Frontiers of Racial Decay," *American Historical Review* 107 (2002): 1124–57 and Louis S. Warren, *Buffalo Bill's America: William Cody and the Wild West Show* (New York: Knopf, 2005). Warren's full-length study is one of the most thorough treatments of the American frontier currently available.

5 Paul Murray, *From the Shadow of Dracula: A Life of Bram Stoker* (London: Jonathan Cape, 2005), 105.

6 Bram Stoker, *Personal Reminiscences of Henry Irving* [1906], rev. ed. (London: William Heinemann, 1907). While *Reminiscences* focuses primarily on Irving's friendships with Americans, Stoker was also friendly with Americans, as is evident from the books by American authors that were put on sale after his death. Among them are a two-volume set of William T. Sherman's memoirs and inscribed volumes by Samuel Clemens (Mark Twain), Bret Harte, Eugene Field, and James

Whitcomb Riley. A complete list of the items sold at Stoker's death is available in John Browning, *The Forgotten Writings of Bram Stoker* (New York: Palgrave Macmillan, 2012), 221–41.

7   I explore Stoker's interest in science and technology in Carol A. Senf, *Science and Social Science in Bram Stoker's Fiction* (Westport, CT: Greenwood Press, 2002).

8   Bram Stoker, "A Glimpse of America," in *A Glimpse of America and other Lectures, Interviews and Essays*, ed. Richard Dalby (Westcliff-on-Sea: Desert Island Books Limited, 2002), 11. Future references to this work will be included parenthetically in the text.

9   Stoker, "Glimpse," 30.

10   Havlik, "Lincoln," 15.

11   Havlik, "Lincoln," 15.

12   Bram Stoker, *Dracula*, ed. Clive Leatherdale (Westcliff-on-Sea: Desert Island Books, 1998), 63.

13   Johnson (Introduction to *SOS*), Murray (*Shadow*), and Warren (*Buffalo Bill's America*) all write about the influence of William Cody (Buffalo Bill) on Stoker's portrayal of Grizzly Dick. Johnson's introduction explains that Stoker had attended his Wild West Show in 1887 and 1892 (11), while Murray refers to correspondence between Stoker and Cody. Of the three, Warren provides the most thorough analysis of Cody's influence on Stoker.

14   Havlik, "Lincoln," 12.

15   Andrew S. J. Garavel, "*The Shoulder of Shasta*: Bram Stoker's California romance," in *Bram Stoker: Centenary Essays*, ed. Jarlath Killeen (Dublin: Four Courts Press, 2014), 103–13, at 105.

16   Bram Stoker, *The Man* (Charleston, SC: BiblioBazaar, 2007).

17   Stoker, *The Man*, 202–03.

18   Stoker, *The Man*, 220.

19   Stoker, *The Man*, 175.

20   Murray, *Shadow*, 239–40.

21   Bram Stoker, "The Squaw," in *Best Ghost and Horror Stories*, ed. Richard Dalby, Stefan Dziemianowicz, and S. T. Joshi (Mineola, NY: Dover Publications, 1997).

22   Stoker, "The Squaw," 163.

23   Stoker, "The Squaw," 166.

24   Stoker, "The Squaw," 167.

25   Stoker, "The Squaw," 171.

26   Lillian Nayder, "Virgin Territory and the Iron Virgin: Engendering the Empire in Bram Stoker's 'The Squaw,'" in *Maternal Instincts: Visions of Motherhood and Sexuality in Britain 1875–1925*, ed. Claudia Nelson and Ann Sumner Holmes (London: Macmillan, 1997), 75–97.

27   Lisa Hopkins, *Bram Stoker: A Literary Life* (New York: Palgrave Macmillan, 2007). Andrew Maunder, on the other hand, looks more at

female usurpation of male power in *Bram Stoker* (Horndon, UK: North-cote House Publishers Ltd, 2006).

28 Hopkins, *Stoker*, 93.

29 *Bram Stoker's Lady Athlyne*, annotated and introduced by Carol Senf (Southend-on-Sea, Essex: Desert Island Books, 2007).

30 The following publications discuss the practice of dueling: Kenneth S. Greenberg, "The Nose, the Lie, and the Duel in the Antebellum South," *The American Historical Review* 95, no. 1 (1990): 57–74; Christopher G. Kingston and Robert E. Wright. "The Deadliest of Games: The Institution of Dueling," *Southern Economic Journal* 76, no. 4 (2010): 1094–106; R. E. Nisbett and D. Cohen, *Culture of Honor: The Psychology of Violence in the South* (Boulder, CO: Westview Press, 1996).

31 Joseph Valente, *Dracula's Crypt: Bram Stoker, Irishness, and the Question of Blood* (Chicago: University of Illinois, 2002). Eleni Coundouriotis, "*Dracula* and the Idea of Europe," *Connotations* 9, no. 2 (1999/2000): 143–59; Carol Senf, "A Response to *Dracula* and the Idea of Europe," *Connotations* 10, no. 1 (2000/01): 47–58; Jason Dittmer, "*Dracula* and the Cultural Construction of Europe," *Connotations* 12, nos 2–3 (2002/03): 233–48. None of these works looks at the connection between Dracula and the American frontier, though the connection is made in several video games and board games, including "Dracula's America: Shadows of the West," which is set in 1875 with Count Dracula as President of the United States.

32 Elizabeth Miller and Robert Eighteen-Bisang, *Bram Stoker's Notes for Dracula: A Facsimile Edition* (Jefferson, NC: McFarland and Company, Inc., 2008).

33 Miller and Eighteen-Bisang, *Stoker's Notes*, 29, n.91.

34 Miller and Eighteen-Bisang, *Stoker's Notes*, 28.

35 Franco Moretti, "The Dialectic of Fear," *New Left Review* 136 (1983): 67–85.

36 Warren, "Buffalo Bill," 1127.

37 Warren, "Buffalo Bill," 1129.

38 Leatherdale's footnote observes that "Quincey hints at a shadowy, not to say sinful past. One wonders momentarily if he is referring to past links with Dracula, hinted at in early drafts of the Novel." Leatherdale, *Dracula*, 450, n.15.

39 Additional information on the Monroe Doctrine can be found in the following sources: Magdalena Alagna, *The Monroe Doctrine: An End to European Colonies in America* (New York: Rosen Publishing Group, 2003); Ernest R. May, *The Making of the Monroe Doctrine* (Cambridge, MA: Harvard University Press, 1975); Gretchen Murphy, *Hemispheric Imaginings: The Monroe Doctrine and Narratives of U.S. Empire* (Durham, NC: Duke University Press, 2005); Edward J. Renehan, Jr., *The Monroe*

Doctrine: The Cornerstone of American Foreign Policy (Langhorne, PA: Chelsea House Publications, 2007); Jay Sexton, *The Monroe Doctrine: Empire and Nation in 19th-century America* (New York: Hill & Wang, 2011); Gaddis Smith, *The Last Years of the Monroe Doctrine, 1945–1993* (New York: Hill & Wang, 1995).

40 Murray, *Shadow*, 207.

41 Warren, "Buffalo Bill," 1152.

Notes to Coda: An Unpublished Letter from Bram Stoker to Laurence Hutton
edited by Matthew Gibson and William Hughes

1   This is, of course, a metalepsis of the lines from *Hamlet*, after the Prince has killed Polonius and Claudius wants to know where he is. Hamlet replies that he is at supper:

"KING: At Supper where?
HAMLET: Not where he eats, but where 'a is eaten. A certain convocation of politic worms are e'en at him. Your worm is your only emperor for diet."

(Shakespeare, *Hamlet*, ed. Ann Thompson and Neil Taylor (London: Arden Shakespeare [Imprint of Cenage Learning], 2006), 362–63, IV, 3. ll. 18–21). The implication here is that Stoker is attempting to grasp at the term "reassimilated," and that he thus means that Hamlet would be happy to himself attend a banquet with "politic worms" were he less rebellious. Thus, it would appear, that there may have been some tension between himself, Hutton, and the (unknown) others invited to lunch at 229 West 24th Street.

2   This appears to be a metalepsis and conflation of two speeches by Benedick in *Much Ado About Nothing*. The first is when Benedick, talking of Claudio's sudden change from warrior to lover, ponders over the changes:

I have known when he would have walked ten mile a-foot to see a good armour; and now will he lie ten nights awake, carving the fashion of a new doublet. He was wont to speak plain and to the purpose, like an honest man and a soldier, and now is he turned orthography; his words are a very fantastical banquet, just so many strange dishes.

(Shakespeare, *Much Ado About Nothing*, ed. Claire McEachern (London: Arden Shakespeare [Imprint of Cenage Learning], 2006), 205–06, II, 3; ll. 15–21).

The second is later in the scene, when he describes the strange effects of musical strings on a man's heart, when hearing an air played:

> Now, divine air! now is his soul ravished! Is it not strange that sheeps' guts should hale souls out of men's bodies? Well, a horn for my money, when all's done. (209, II, 3; ll. 56–59)

3 The phrase is again a turn on Shakespeare, this time from *The Merchant of Venice*, with Shylock announcing the limits of his own tolerance to Bassanio:

> I will buy with you, sell with you, talk with you, walk with you, and so following. But I will not eat with you, drink with you, nor pray with you.

(Shakespeare, *The Merchant of Venice*, ed. Leah S. Marcus (London, New York: W.W. Norton, 2006), 13, I, 3; ll. 30–33). The change again indicates the idea that the luncheon will bring opposites together.

4 The original quotation is the last line from the poem "Recipe for a Salad" by the famously witty Anglican Cleric Sydney Smith (1777–1845), sent in a letter of 1839 to his daughter Lady Saba Holland, and is in fact as follows: "Serenely full, the epicure would say, / 'Fate cannot harm me, I have dined to-day.'" –(*The Letters of Sydney Smith*, ed. Nowell C. Smith (Oxford: Clarendon Press, 1953), II 684; ll. 19–20).

5 This quotation is *not* from Charles Lamb, but is again from Sydney Smith, recorded in Lady Holland's memoir of 1855. The original quotation is as follows: "It requires," he used to say "a surgical operation to get a joke well into a Scotch understanding." (*A Memoir of the Reverend Sydney Smith. By his Daughter, Lady Holland. With a Selection of His Letters*, ed. Mrs Austin, new ed. (London: Longmans, Green and Co., 1874), 17). This suggests that one of their luncheon guests may have been a Scotsman.

6 Colonel John Hay (1838–1905), "The Mystery of Gilgal," *The Pike County Ballads*. The line is from a poem about a battle between two men in the frontier U.S.A. regarding who should drink first from a whisky skin in a bar. Colonel Blood and Judge Phinn pull out their knives:

> They carved in a way that all admired,
> Tell Blood drawed iron at last, and fired.
> It took Seth Bludso 'twixt the eyes,
> Which caused him great surprise.

(John Hay, *The Complete Poetical Works of John Hay* (Boston, MA; New York: Houghton Mifflin Company, 1917), 15–16). The mystery in the poem simply pertains to who it was that actually got the whiskey skin.

7 A "nunte" is in fact a sharp, pointed, metal weapon, or Okinawan spear, used in kendo. Stoker appears to have conflated the weapon with the practitioner himself.

Index